D0459162

Come with Me from Lebanon

 Contemporary Issues in the Middle East

Malcolm and Ann, December 1983.

Come with Me from Lebanon

AN AMERICAN FAMILY ODYSSEY

Ann Zwicker Kerr

With a Foreword by Albert Hourani

SYRACUSE UNIVERSITY PRESS

This book is published in recognition of Arpena S. Mesrobian's
contributions to the field of Middle East studies.

All photographs courtesy of the author.

The paper used in this publication meets the minimum requirements of
American National Standard for Information Sciences—Permanence of Paper
for Printed Library Materials, ANSI Z39.48-1984. ∞™

Library of Congress Cataloging-in-Publication Data
Kerr, Ann Zwicker, 1935–
Come with me from Lebanon : an American family odyssey / Ann
Zwicker Kerr ; with a foreword by Albert Hourani.
p.   cm. —(Contemporary issues in the Middle East)
Includes bibliographical references and index.
ISBN 0-8156-0298-7
1. Kerr, Ann Zwicker, 1935–   . 2. Kerr, Malcolm H.   I. Title.
II. Series.
CT275.K45866A3   1994
956.92—dc20   94-9246

Manufactured in the United States of America

*For my parents and my parents-in-law
and for Susie, John, Steve, and Andrew*

Ann Zwicker Kerr, a native of southern California, has spent a total of fifteen years living, studying, and teaching in the Middle East. She was educated at Occidental College, the American University of Beirut, and the American University in Cairo. She is currently at the University of California in Los Angeles where she coordinates the Fulbright Visiting Scholar Enrichment Program for the Los Angeles area. She is also a member of the Board of Trustees of the American University of Beirut and on the Advisory Board of the National Council on U.S.-Arab Relations. Her late husband, Malcolm Kerr, was the president of the American University of Beirut and was assassinated in office in 1984. She is the mother of four adult children.

Come with me from Lebanon, my bride,
come with me from Lebanon.

Song of Solomon 4:8

Contents

Illustrations   xi

Foreword by Albert Hourani   xiii

Preface   xix

Acknowledgments   xxi

PART ONE

An End and a Beginning

1. January 18, 1984   3

PART TWO

The Early Years, 1931–1961

2. Growing Up West and East   23
3. Song of Lebanon   40
4. Meeting Malcolm: From the Regina Bar to the Milk Bar   61
5. Discovering the Middle East   78
6. Spring Comes Early to Lebanon: A Proposal of Marriage   86
7. Return to the United States   101

8. Back to Beirut   108
9. Halcyon Days   121

PART THREE

Between California and the Middle East, 1961–1981

10. Bonds of Closeness Around the World   139
11. Ulyssean Journeys   155
12. Home Fires   166
13. Cairo Sojourn   175

PART FOUR

The AUB Presidency, 1981–1984

14. A Time of Decisions   185
15. Up to the Mountaintops   200
16. Hopes and Fears   219
17. No One Wants to Shell AUB   240
18. The School Year Opens   259
19. Dreams and Goals Still Hoped For   277

Epilogue   299
Bibliographic Essay   305
Index   307

Illustrations

Malcolm and Ann, December 1983   *frontispiece*

1. Ann, Andrew, and John in condolence
   reception line   12
2. In Memory of Malcolm Hooper Kerr, 1931–1984   16
3. After the AUB memorial service   18
4. Kerr family Christmas card from Beirut   29
5. The high school boy's basketball team   34
6. Malcolm and family at Beit-el-Din, Lebanon   35
7. AUB Women's Hostel dining room   44
8. Ann Kerr and roommates at St. Michel Beach   79
9. Malcolm and Ann Kerr's wedding   104
10. Kerr family at the pyramids   142
11. Ann and family with new baby Stephen   144
12. Malcolm with Susie and John   213
13. Kerr family, before inauguration   214
14. Malcolm at investiture ceremony   216
15. Malcolm and Ann at the AUB Track and
    Field Day   288
16. Kerr family at home in Pacific Palisades   301

Foreword

By Albert Hourani

This deeply moving book is the story of a love, or rather of two kinds of love closely intertwined.

In 1954 Ann Zwicker, brought up in southern California and spending a year at the American University of Beirut (AUB), meets Malcolm Kerr, also a student there working on his M.A. They fall in love and marry and live through all the vicissitudes of a happy and productive academic marriage. Graduate study at Johns Hopkins and Harvard is followed by a further period at AUB as instructor in political science, then a year in Oxford, and then an appointment as professor at the University of California at Los Angeles. Four children are born and grow up, a beautiful home is bought at Pacific Palisades, important studies on Middle Eastern politics are published, and Malcolm is promoted and becomes a dean. A successful career sustained by a happy family life seems to reach its climax when Malcolm is chosen to be president of AUB in 1982. Then tragedy strikes: on the morning of 18 January 1984, he is killed by an unknown assailant in his office.

This may seem like a story of success and happiness suddenly cut short by an inexplicable tragedy, but it is more than that. It was not simple ambition or curiosity that led Malcolm and Ann to return to Beirut, but another kind of love and commitment. Malcolm was born and brought up there; his father was a professor in the University and his mother looked after the women students. His early memories were therefore of Lebanon—not only of the

AUB campus but also of Ras Beirut, the city quarter which had grown up around it, and in particular the hillside at Ainab where the Kerrs and four other families had bought land and built summer homes. Perhaps something of the missionary spirit which had created the university lived on in him, together with love of the sights and sounds of Lebanon and its people and the Arabic language which they and he spoke. Ann came to share it all. Faced with the call to be president, there was no way of refusing it: it was his place of challenge, obligation, and fulfillment. Thinking of him making this decision, I am reminded of what Sir Ronald Storrs said when he became Governor of Jerusalem: "There is no promotion after Jerusalem."

But the Beirut of the 1980s was not the same as that of his childhood or their student days. The Lebanon of his early life was ruled by France under a mandate from the League of Nations. The French created the political institutions which provided the framework within which different religious communities could live together and hope to forget a period of conflict in the mid-nineteenth century. The Beirut of the time was a city of some quarter of a million inhabitants; it had been a center of international trade since the early nineteenth century, but the vicissitudes of the franc, with which the local currency was linked, made for economic stagnation. It had also been since that time a center of cultural production; around the American college and the French Université St. Joseph, there had gathered writers and scholars, translating books from English and French into Arabic and putting forward new ideas, which had a resonance far beyond Lebanon in other countries of Arabic speech.

AUB was something of a foreign enclave in a country where French culture was predominant. Ras Beirut, far from the centers of political and financial power, still had the air of a half-rural community; the streets were mostly country lanes, the professors lived in red-tiled houses of one or two storys surrounded by gardens. The university was still an old-fashioned New England college, watched over with care by the families that had created it, but the stirrings of Arab nationalism, directed against the French in Syria and the British in Palestine, could be felt in the student body.

The Lebanon of the 1950s, where Malcolm and Ann met and

lived, was different but not unrecognizable. Beirut had become a city of almost a million people and was one of the focal points of life in the eastern Arab countries. The French Mandate had ended and Lebanon became an independent republic, with close links to the United States as well as Europe. It was a financial center of growing importance, the intermediary between the states of the Gulf region, enriched by the production of oil, and the money-markets of the world. It was a center also of services of many kinds: schools, hospitals, publishing houses, a free press, information for the newspapers of the world, entertainment for tourists and summer residents.

The position of AUB had changed too. The center of gravity of the city had moved towards its English-speaking section. The lanes had become main shopping streets, with hotels, restaurants, and cafés. Apartment blocks were replacing gardens and old houses. AUB had become an international university of moderate size, with an important medical school and facilities for research, and it drew students from the Middle East and beyond.

The political system and the communal understandings on which it was based seemed to have survived several months of breakdown in 1958, with American help and the election of a strong president. Lebanon was in the early stages of a period of prosperity and cultural flowering. It seemed to be one of the success stories of the postwar world, but beneath the surface the foundations were shaky. Rapid economic growth was widening the gap between rich and poor. The capital city was drawing to itself poor migrants from the mountain villages. The creation of the state of Israel in 1948 had brought into the country a mass of destitute refugees and a new generation of Palestinian leaders, and Lebanon was being inexorably drawn into the Arab-Israeli conflict. It had become a center of political activity of every kind: embassies of the Powers, intelligence services, and dissident groups from the surrounding Arab countries pursued their interests and rivalries and enlisted local clients.

By 1982 the scene had changed once more, and in more than one way Beirut was unrecognizable. Internal tensions within a context of international rivalries had led to a breakdown of civil order. Conflicts of various kinds had expressed themselves in communal hostility, and intermittent civil war between rival militias since 1975 had more or less destroyed the authority of the government and the center of the city. Then in 1982 an Israeli invasion, aiming to destroy the political and military presence of the Palestinians in Lebanon, had led to more destruction and polarization of political forces. The temporary presence of American and European forces seemed to offer a new opportunity for the resumption of a more normal life, but it ended when the Americans became involved in the local conflicts. A new and more ominous phase of kidnappings and murders began, with the occupation of much of Beirut by rival militias.

Malcolm arrived in Beirut while Israeli troops still surrounded the city. He knew and understood the politics of Lebanon and its neighbors better almost than anyone. By 1983 he and Ann knew that his life was in danger. They thought of returning to California, but that would have gone against their sense of where they ought to be and what they ought to do. AUB was one of the few institutions that had survived the years of civil war and invasion almost intact, and it must be preserved; besides, Lebanon was still beautiful, full of friends, and the Kerrs' home. So they stayed. The danger grew closer, but they did not quite believe in it. "Somehow we never thought this would happen . . . lots of troubles and problems maybe, but never really this. We were so happy here doing what we were doing . . ."

"It all came to an end today" is Ann's entry in her diary for the fateful day, 18 January 1984. It is good to know that it did not all come to an end for her. She had planned, if the worst happened, to remain for a time in the Middle East, although not in Lebanon, and she did so. Teaching for several years at the American University in Cairo helped her to exorcise the demons of memory and begin a new life. Now, back in California, she has been able to give us this picture of a life tragically cut short, recollected in some tranquillity.

I knew Malcolm and Ann during most of the period about which she writes. I knew Malcolm's parents in Beirut in the late 1930s and have a vague memory of a very polite small boy somewhere in the background. I really came to know them when they spent a year at Oxford in the early 1960s. He was my colleague at the Middle East Centre, and a very good and unusual colleague: well-informed, incisive in judgment, with an unyielding integrity and a subtle mind, always helpful to colleagues and students, amusing, and perhaps amused by some of the local customs. He and Ann lived in a cottage built by John Masefield in Boars Hill, and I have always felt guilty about renting such a cold place for them to live in. After that there were several visits to the University of California, Los Angeles, in particular that in 1979 for the Levi Della Vida Conference which he and I arranged together. My most vivid memory of him, and the last, is of Malcolm's visit to our home in 1983. He was as he had always been, except for a new note of tension, almost of withdrawal. I did not learn until much later that he already knew his life was in danger.

Preface

*T*his book began first as a journal, written in the few months my husband and I had together in Lebanon when he was the president of the American University of Beirut. I wanted to record the cataclysmic events we were living through along with the events of our daily lives, and I vaguely thought that one day Malcolm and I might write a book together about the historic period in the Middle East that we were witnessing. His assassination in January 1984—along with all the other changes—brought an instant change of purpose to that journal.

In the numbness of the months after his death, the journal became tangible evidence of the brief time we had had at the American University of Beirut, fulfilling a long-hoped-for dream. I pored over those pages in a vain effort to hold on to part of what had been torn away.

As the months passed, I began to write in an unburdening of grief, trying to put together the pieces of my shattered life and to retrace the path that had taken us to the American University of Beirut in a time of political uncertainty. The writing grew into a recollection of all our years in the Middle East and our comings and goings to and from California. I wanted to weave together the historical and political events in the region with the growth and development of our family, and I wanted to create a lasting record of two losses—of Malcolm and of Lebanon as it once was.

The process of writing this book has been a healing one over the years since Malcolm's death. I have left it and returned to it at various times between work and travel and time with my family.

It has pulled me up and I have pulled it up, but it was always there to ground me. Now its gestation period is finished, and I am ready to let it go.

My hope is that the book will be useful to other people—to students of the Middle East and to general readers who might be more interested in reading about the area in the context of a personal story than in a textbook account. I would also like it to be a testimony to the enduring strength of the American University of Beirut and to the generations of people from the Middle East and the West who have made it so.

Pacific Palisades, California   *Ann Zwicker Kerr*
1994

Acknowledgments

*I*n every stage of the writing of this book, consultation and advice from colleagues, friends, and family members have been a part of the process. The impulse to unburden myself has meant that I have had to burden them. They probably number in the hundreds, and from each of them I have had a chance to learn and grow.

I would like to thank them all and to mention a few names of people who helped at critical times to keep the book on track. Carl Brandt provided impetus in the early stages of writing. Professor George Irani submitted the manuscript to Syracuse University Press on my behalf where Cynthia Maude-Gembler guided it as an acquisitions editor and provided the author with constant encouragement and advice. Terry Joseph, a family friend and former editor at the UCLA Von Grunebaum Center for Near Eastern Studies, was an invaluable editorial consultant. Sarah McNamer was my Rhodes scholar typist.

The final editing of the book was aided by my daughter, Susan Kerr van de Ven, a loving and stern taskmaster, and by Albert Hourani who helped me as he helped so many students of the Middle East over his long and fruitful life. Albert's critique of the manuscript and the foreword he wrote just two weeks before his death has cast a blessing over this book.

PART ONE

An End and a Beginning

CHAPTER 1

January 18, 1984

Beirut, Lebanon, January 18, 1984. The president of the American University of Beirut, Malcolm Kerr, was killed here today when unidentified gunmen fired two bullets into his head while he was walking toward his office. Soon after, a male caller telephoned the office of Agence France Presse and said the slaying was the work of Islamic Holy War—supposedly a pro-Iranian underground group. A Beirut born American citizen, the 52-year-old Dr. Kerr was trained as a Middle Eastern specialist at Princeton, Johns Hopkins, and Harvard University and pioneered in the study of political relationships among the Arab countries. Fluent in Arabic, Dr. Kerr also took a master's degree at the American University of Beirut, where his father was a professor of chemistry and his mother was the advisor to women students. There he met his wife, the former Ann C. Zwicker, when she was studying as a junior year abroad student from Occidental College in California. (*New York Times,* January 19, 1984)

The two killers must have come right past me as they escaped from College Hall and up the steps to the main gate of the campus. If only I had stopped by Malcolm's office after my 8:00 A.M. English class as I so often did. They shot him from the stairway I always took to avoid the slow elevator. Perhaps they wouldn't have pulled the trigger if there had been a witness. In my fantasies, I imagine that, if only I had been there, I might have been able to surprise them as I was coming up the stairs and knock the gun from their hands.

3

I can't picture the last moment I saw Malcolm. We always exchanged a fleeting kiss and quick good-byes after breakfast, but I'm not exactly sure what happened that morning—maybe because he had an appointment off campus and was in a rush. I want so much to pull him back and just hold on to him. I want to lie close to him and find him beside me when I wake up in the mornings and talk to him about all that has happened.

There is a compelling instinct now to record the events that followed Malcolm's death, as if the telling might somehow help to make order of the chaos unleashed on our family and on the university. There are questions to explore and a desire to unburden myself of this tragedy with the hope of making it more bearable. There is also an impulse to make something tangible out of two losses—Malcolm and Lebanon as it once was, to create a picture in words as a repository for things that no longer exist.

· · ·

It was Wednesday morning, January 18, 1984, a few days before the end of the first semester. I had dismissed the students in my sophomore English class earlier than usual so they could register for second semester. The chimes of College Hall struck nine as I climbed the steps from the campus up to the main gate of the university. A light drizzle started as I stood outside the gate waiting for a friend to pick me up to go shopping for fabrics to redecorate Marquand House, the president's historic residence in the middle of the campus where we lived.

The old gateman, who had probably been in that job since Malcolm's and my student days, tried to coax me into the guardhouse out of the rain. I thanked him but said I preferred to wait outside for my friend. The drizzle was getting a little heavier, so I raised my umbrella. I pulled out my book, *The Moon and Sixpence,* which I was reading to keep ahead of my students.

Five or ten minutes later, the gateman came back, and, with an insistent tug on my arm, pulled me into the guard house. The urgency of the tug rather than any particular expression on his face told me immediately that something terrible had happened. Concern for Malcolm's safety was never far from my thoughts since he had become the president of the university seventeen months earlier.

After the gateman took me to the guardhouse, where a few other guards were gathered, he said to me in Arabic, "Something happened in the president's office." I don't remember the expression on his face or on the faces of the other guards in that small room. I only wanted to pick up the phone and call Malcolm's number, hoping somehow to hear his voice on the other end of the line telling me that everything was all right. But it was Abdul Hamid Hallab, the vice president for external projects and a good friend, who answered. In a choked voice he said, "Malcolm has been shot."

My first flash of thought was that the wound could have been superficial, in a leg or an arm, but there was something in Abdul Hamid's voice on the phone that told me it was more than that.

I ran to College Hall a few yards away and found Abdul Hamid coming down the stairs to meet me. We walked to the second floor together. A few steps in front of the elevator, Malcolm was lying on the floor, face down, his briefcase and umbrella in front of him.

I felt sure he wasn't alive. I saw blood coming from his head, but I couldn't look too closely. It was an instinct; I wanted to know what had happened, but I didn't want to see too much. I could have rushed to him and held him, but I suppose I knew that if I did I would see too closely and be left with a lifelong image even more painful than the one I was seeing. As right as that inclination was, there have been many times since when I've wished I had seized that opportunity to hold him one more time, and on the chance that he could have heard me, to say good-bye. But I felt so sure he wasn't alive, almost as if some predestined plan had been carried out.

It was on this campus, where his parents taught for forty years, that Malcolm was born and raised. It was here during an Ottoman history class on the first floor that we had fallen in love. Three of our four children had been born here—and finally Malcolm had come back as president. Was there some destiny also dictating that his life should end here—and if so, why so prematurely?

A friend and professor in health sciences, Huda Zurayk, who had been waiting to attend a committee meeting with Malcolm pulled me into Abdul Hamid's office. Another close friend came,

Leila Badre, the curator of the university museum. I buried my head in the soft angora collar of her black sweater, not yet to cry but perhaps to hide from all that was going on. How much time passed, I don't know. I don't even know whether or not anyone was attending Malcolm in the hall. I could only be guided by my instincts, but the thought of his lying there unattended is unbearable now.

Sometime later, perhaps after fifteen or twenty minutes, we followed the ambulance on foot to the emergency room of the AUB hospital across from campus. I was aware of a gathering procession as we walked out of College Hall into the damp, pine-scented morning air, toward the Medical Gate, past the banyan tree by the chapel, down under the long row of Aleppo pines beyond Van Dyke Hall where Malcolm's father's chemistry lab used to be. There soldiers had barricaded the gate to prevent anyone from leaving the campus while police searched for the killers. Abdul Hamid persuaded the soldiers to let me through to go to the hospital across the street. I remember holding onto my umbrella and clamping my teeth down on its hard plastic handle as we rode up in the big crowded elevator amid a sea of unfamiliar faces.

In a small room adjacent to the emergency room I waited. A few friends arrived after convincing the guards to let them through the gate. Erica Dodd, who like her husband, had grown up on the campus with Malcolm, came as soon as she heard the news. A nurse came in with a glass of water and a tranquilizer. "Take this," she told me. I took the glass of water and said I didn't want the tranquilizer just then. She thrust a box of them into the pocket of my raincoat.

Someone else came in, the nurse who had brought me Susie, my first child, as a new baby in this same hospital twenty-five years before. We had become reacquainted a few months earlier. When I saw her, at last I cried.

Soon the dean of the medical school came in to tell me what I already knew. Malcolm was gone. It was confirmed by the look on his face before he said a word.

A car took us home—Abdul Hamid and the Dodds and others. I'm not sure exactly who was in the car. Next I had to think about Andrew, our fifteen-year-old son who was in ninth grade. Abdul Hamid sent someone to bring him from school, and

I waited, I can't remember for how long or with whom. Later I learned that Andrew had first heard the news in a shop next door to his school where he was buying something to eat. The owner cried out the news when he heard it on the radio. Andrew ran up through the campus to our house and met Hassan, the house-keeper, who knew I had gone to the hospital. So they had gone there together and then had come home. Finally I saw them walking up the circular driveway. I ran to the door to meet him. We cried together there in the entry hall, unable to say anything for a long time. Finally he shouted, "I want to get those guys who killed Dad."

We went upstairs and lay down on his bed and began to talk, grasping for justification as to why we had come to Beirut in the midst of a civil war, which had been going on for eight years. We talked a long time about how Dad had been doing what he wanted to do. His being the president of the American University had been a long-time goal for both of us and the most obvious use of Malcolm's talents and experience. We believed we were doing something that mattered, something that might make a difference for the United States and the Middle East. How vainly noble those words sound now, uttered during that first shock of disbelief following a sudden tragedy before grief and anger take hold.

Somehow I got through that day. Numbness helped, as well as a certain challenge to rise to the occasion; there was as yet no backlog of suffering to weaken my emotional defenses. The calls that had to be made to our other children kept me going—to John working in Cairo, to Steve at the University of Arizona, and to Susie and her husband Hans studying in Taiwan, to my parents and Malcolm's brother and sisters in the United States. Malcolm and I had spoken to his brother only a few hours earlier that same morning when he phoned to tell us that their mother in New Jersey had suffered a slight stroke.

People began swarming to the house and up to Andrew's room where we were lying on the bed—I still in my raincoat and boots with the phone propped up next to me as I tried to get through to all the family. It was agonizing to have to tell each of them. I forced out the words mechanically, first to prepare them for the bad news, then to blurt out the shocking truth, and then to wait for the horrified reaction.

John would come from Cairo the next afternoon, Susie and

Hans from Taiwan in a few days, and Steve would meet us in Princeton a week later. With the help of family members and friends, it had been arranged that the Kerr family reunion and memorial service would take place there, and then we would all go together to our home in Pacific Palisades, California, for a reunion with my family and a memorial service at the University of California, Los Angeles, where Malcolm had taught for twenty years.

The next few days after Malcolm's death seemed to acquire their own momentum. So many practical decisions needed to be made, the kind of decisions that follow any death and help the bereaved get through those first days, forestalling the deeper grief and loneliness that follow. For us there were additional complications. Malcolm was not only our husband and father; he was a public figure, a new role in our lives that we were only just learning how to absorb. There was the added factor of being in a foreign culture where the rituals that go with the death of a public figure are very different from those in America. Our desire to mourn our loss privately had to give way to public duty.

University officials explained to me the need to have certain public ceremonies. "People expect this, Ann," Samir Thabet, the vice president of the university told me. "It will dishonor Malcolm and AUB if we don't hold the traditional receiving days for people to come and pay their condolences. And we must have a fitting memorial service if security permits. I know it will be difficult for you, but there will be many ministers and government officials who will want to pay their condolences." Samir did not need to convince me for I had no wish to leave Beirut without saying good-bye to the whole community of AUB faculty, students, and staff whom I now regarded as a large extended family.

Our family in the United States urged us to come home immediately for security reasons. Security. What a deceptive word in Lebanon. The assessment of it was always a guessing game we played with ourselves, as did everyone else there. But Malcolm and I were less experienced at it. It was easy to come up with convincing rationalizations. "Living in Beirut is no more dangerous than living in New York City," Malcolm often told friends. And perhaps on a less definable level, we believed we would somehow be protected in doing our jobs that we both wanted so much to do.

The seductive tranquillity of the AUB campus made it easy to believe that everything was still all right. Its beauty contrasted with the ugliness of war-ravaged areas in other parts of the city, and its century-old stone buildings seemed to stand for the forces of good, which the institution had represented since its founding in 1866. The thunderous noise of exploding shells and the evil deeds perpetrated in the guise of religion or some nameless cause were things that happened outside the walls of the campus. In eight years of civil war, there had been no fatalities inside the campus, although the kidnapping and year-long detention of Acting President David Dodge near College Hall in July of 1982 was an ominous reminder that AUB was vulnerable to evil forces.

Inside Marquand House, our presidential residence set amidst gardens with pine and jacaranda trees overlooking the Mediterranean, all our housekeeping needs were taken care of by Hassan and Zeinab, a handsome Sudanese and his ebullient Egyptian wife. In this setting of beauty and comfort, a false sense of security was created which made it difficult to remember that we were living in a country of anarchy where security was always problematic.

Malcolm had had a bodyguard when he first arrived but quickly grew impatient with the encumbrance. "Why should I have to take a bodyguard jogging with me?" he wrote in a letter home shortly after his arrival in Beirut, "particularly since he runs out of breath and quits after the first lap." So he used him less and less, and finally not at all. Just a month before Malcolm's death, the university trustees had voted to instigate a round-the-clock team of military guards who were to begin work shortly. Both of us had been reluctant to accept this loss of privacy.

So what was to be decided now about security? Malcolm was gone. They had got their man. It did not occur to me that anyone would want to harm my children or me. But wanton terrorism at public gatherings was something to consider. We went on playing the crazy game of Lebanese roulette. A two-day condolence reception was planned at the Alumni Club near the university on the assumption that terrorists would not interfere with the hallowed tradition in the Middle East of paying respect to the bereaved of the deceased. Samir said that it would be appreciated if our family could be there during as much of those two days as we could manage.

. . .

John arrived the next day as Andrew and I sat numbly in our large living room, surrounded by perhaps twenty visitors, mostly university friends. We rushed to the door to meet him and then went upstairs to be by ourselves. It was an enormous relief to have him there—my oldest son and so like Malcolm in many ways.

Two days after Malcolm's death, Steve went out and played basketball for the University of Arizona where he had recently started his freshman year on an athletic scholarship. His team dedicated the game to Malcolm, and Steve made his highest score of the season—his tribute to his father who loved sports, both playing and watching. "The only thing in the world I'd rather do than watch Steve play basketball is be AUB president," was Malcolm's comment, so much in character, upon learning that he had been appointed to the job he considered the highest honor he could receive.

As the flow of visitors continued—students, public officials, and friends—I came to appreciate this Middle Eastern custom of the sharing of grief. We were not allowed to be lonely, and it buoyed us to hear the acclaim for Malcolm and all he had accomplished for the university in his short time at AUB. There was comfort and pride in the public attention, while at the same time, it seemed strange to be sharing our incomparable loss with so many people. We were swept up in a series of public ceremonies and interviews with the press, which demanded our response.

Interviews with journalists cast me in a new role, one that Malcolm had formerly filled. Questions were blunt, but I welcomed the chance to say what I thought. "Who do you think is behind your husband's death? What are your feelings toward Lebanon today? What is your message to Lebanon's warring factions?"

I told them I thought that any one of a number of parties could have been responsible for my husband's death. Responsibility could be linked to sinister individuals with personal or political motives or to groups of people with special causes who were threatened by Western culture or American policy in the Middle East. Americans became the focus of their frustration and anger at not being able to control events. Considering the prevailing chaos, we would probably never learn who was responsible for my husband's death. I could not blame an entire country, and basically my feelings for Lebanon had not changed.

As for the warring factions, I could only speak in the context of AUB, a microcosm of Lebanon with every political and religious group represented in its student body. I explained to the reporters that our hope was that, if at this stage of their lives the students learned conciliation and how to get along together, perhaps this spirit would carry on into their adult lives. If AUB and the students here can hold together, perhaps Lebanon can. I told them that Malcolm had spent the last day of his life negotiating with student political leaders about campus politics heading in the direction of this conciliation.

The interview closed with a bit of philosophy which I have tried to hold on to since Malcolm's death. "Basically Malcolm believed that one person can make a difference. And he believed in AUB and all the individual Americans and Arabs who have helped create the standards by which it has functioned. He also loved what he was doing, and so did I. It wasn't just humanitarian motives that brought us here. He wouldn't have come if he hadn't loved his job—and Lebanon."

On the third day after Malcolm's death, John, Andrew, and I were taken in a university car to the Alumni Club nearby where administrators and trustees were already receiving people who wanted to pay their condolences. We joined the reception line at the beginning and listened to the outpouring of sentiments in English or Arabic or French, or a combination of all three. The Arabic language provides a rich variety of phrases to declare for all rites of passage, invoking the name of God, and, in the case of death, saying that it is His will that has caused it to happen and that He will provide for those left behind. It was touching to hear some people try to translate these phrases literally. Some simply poured out their feelings in whatever words came. "Your father was a tragedy," a sweet little man with tears streaming down his cheeks said to John and Andrew. How Malcolm would have chuckled over that linguistic mix-up which he would have added immediately to his repertoire of Arabic English jokes—and how heartbreaking not to be able to go home and tell him about it.

The presiding officer of the Alumni Club introduced a pro-

1. Ann, Andrew, and John in condolence reception line
following Malcolm's death.

cession of portly government high officials, one by one. They
made rather formal statements in Arabic or French and shook our
hands solemnly. Faculty and friends came in large numbers, kissing the three of us on both cheeks or embracing us and then going
to sit quietly in the rows and rows of chairs set up auditorium
style in the large room. A flurry of activity at the entrance drew
my attention to the arrival of the American ambassador, Reginald
Bartholemew, with four bodyguards literally dancing around him.

As Ambassador Bartholemew expressed his condolences, we
both knew that he could just as easily have been the target, if, in
fact the killers were punishing us for our Middle East foreign policy by attacking a symbol of America. But Malcolm, impatient
with bodyguards and working in the openness of a university
campus, even a campus guarded by Lebanese Army soldiers who
checked every person and car that entered, was a more accessible
target than the ambassador.

Perhaps it was Malcolm they specifically wanted rather than

the ambassador. Perhaps by killing him, they thought they could strike an American target far more deeply rooted and historically tied to the Middle East than whatever current political policy the ambassador represented. For 116 years the American University of Beirut had been a meeting place for the best of Western and Middle Eastern culture. What better way for someone who wanted to undermine those cultural ties than to kill the person at the head of that institution? Or perhaps Malcolm was the target of one of several different groups faulting him for beliefs they ascribed to him. It would have been easy to find ideas that he had written in his twenty years as an outspoken professor of Middle Eastern politics. Malcolm wrote about many ideas that could be taken out of context and used to justify individual motives. Or unknown enemies, who abound in Beirut, might seize upon some of the jokes he was trying to learn not to tell in his new role, and find political overtones to use against him.

John and Andrew and I were advised not to go to the airport to meet Susie and Hans. "It would just attract attention," Abdul Hamid said. Besides we were expected to remain at the Alumni Club for the reception of visitors. Meeting them at Marquand House would be more private anyway, and so on the second day of the long condolence reception, we rushed home at lunch time to greet them. The joy of their presence took away a bit of the terrible sorrow that had brought us to this reunion. We stood there, in the entry hall of Marquand House, holding on to one another silently for several minutes.

Having Susie with us made us all feel better. We needed her whimsical sense of humor, and her tremendous gift for expressing her feelings and impelling the rest of us to express ours. After lunch we returned to the Alumni Club where Susie and Hans now extended the Kerr family representation and were initiated into the Middle Eastern way of permitting friends to pay respect to the bereaved.

The next day, Sunday, was the first of many memorial services for Malcolm, but this one at the Anglican church we had been attending was our own, planned by the minister and me informally as part of the regular Sunday morning service. It satisfied our need to have a service just for our family, a time for us to sit close together in the front pew of the small church to sing our favorite hymns, and to listen to the minister talk about Malcolm's life.

The next memorial service that needed to be planned was to take place in the AUB chapel, security conditions permitting. The choir director and organist were to come to the house in the afternoon, after our private church service, to help us select the kind of service we wanted. In the meantime, when the house was empty of callers, Hassan served us a big Lebanese lunch. Afterwards, John and I felt a great urge for exercise. In the spirit of our family, we knew Malcolm would have approved. But what of our Lebanese friends? Risking their censure, we put on over our tennis clothes, new AUB warm-up suits Malcolm and I had been presented a few weeks earlier, and drove to the indoor tennis court in the old gym near the corniche where waves crashed against the sea wall. Malcolm had beaten me soundly just the Sunday before on this court, and he had won a match on it against one of his favorite opponents the night before he was killed.

John and I hit the ball as hard as we could, back and forth, back and forth in an outpouring of pent-up emotions. The rhythmic sound of that ball being hit resounded against the tin roof of the old gym, its walls pockmarked with bullet holes from the last eight years of sporadic fighting between changing combinations of Christians and Muslims.

An hour later we came out into the bright January sun. There were a few joggers making their round of the track as usual, but no one saw us as we hurried into the car to get back to Marquand House before the choir director and organist arrived.

We were fifteen minutes early, but so were our guests. It was mortifying to find them walking up the steps to the front door just as we pulled into the driveway. I muttered to the choir director, a young Lebanese Armenian. "We couldn't do without some exercise," but explanation was useless. He stared at us in utter astonishment.

Amidst the constant visitors pouring into Marquand House and the official condolence calls, there were the other matters to be arranged that go with a death. Again, instinct or perhaps divine guidance directed my decisions. Malcolm's body would be cremated, and we would bury half the ashes on the AUB campus and take half home to California. Susie, Hans, John, Andrew, and I took a walk on the campus to select the place for a memorial. We had no problems deciding where we wanted to place the box of remains.

Under a big banyan tree between College Hall and the chapel, there is an oval garden with a lovely view of the sea. As students, Malcolm and I used to walk by it on our way to class. He told me how he loved to climb that banyan tree as a child and how he had carved his initials in its upper branches.

For a marker stone, we. went to the campus museum and chose a Corinthian capital which was perched against a wall in the garden. All this happened in a very unplanned and spontaneous fashion. I couldn't help laughing a little to myself when I thought of the disparaging comments Malcolm loved to make about archaeological ruins. "The pyramids are nothing but a pile of rocks," he would say when I tried to get him to visit ancient monuments in Egypt. I wondered what sardonic remark he would have made about the Corinthian capital.

AUB and other schools reopened on Monday after a four-day recess in commemoration of Malcolm. It felt natural to meet with my class as scheduled. I had to keep busy, and I wanted very much to talk with the students to whom I had become so attached. At first they were at a loss for words, but as we sat there and talked, they began to feel more at ease and so did I. In a continuing effort to justify what had happened, I tried to explain why Malcolm and I had wanted to come to AUB, about our time there together as students, about why the long history and accomplishments of the institution made it something worth struggling to continue.

Most of them didn't need to be told these things. They had chosen to study at AUB when many of them could afford to go to universities abroad. They came to the campus every day through parts of the city that were unsafe and studied at night by lantern when there was no electricity.

When I think about that week after Malcolm's death, I remember feeling mentally numb but physically comfortable, cushioned by the gathering of the family, by the constant presence and attention of friends, and by the warmth of our home so recently decorated. Hassan and Zeinab took care of all our needs, even sharing with us their two small children who played in the eve-

In Memory Of

MALCOLM HOOPER KERR
1931 – 1984

He lived life abundantly

We are proud that our dad and husband came to A U B

Ann Susan John Stephen and Andrew Kerr

2. In Memory of Malcolm Hooper Kerr, 1931–1984.
Sign made by Susie Kerr.

ning when we four sat in the living room and listened to music on our new stereo, a Christmas gift from Malcolm the month before. Faculty women, from the first day, had organized a rotating shift of helpers to meet callers at the front door and provide hospitality if we were busy. With so many people in the house, Malcolm's chair at the end of the table was seldom empty, forestalling the terrible awareness of his absence, and the children's humor, led by Susie and Hans, helped to temper our sorrow.

I did not want to leave this lovely place where Malcolm and I had just established ourselves for the next stage of our lives, where we were beginning the work we had so long wanted to do. I, as much as he, had accepted the job of AUB president and wife, and I did not want to be cut off from all that we had started together and from the tangible reminders of our new life. We had already taken a major risk and lost. I could not do that again as the single parent of four children, nor could I let Andrew remain in Beirut; as Malcolm's son he too could be a target for someone.

A telex came from our good friend Richard Pedersen, president of the American University in Cairo, offering me a job teaching English. Malcolm and I had spent two happy stints at AUC within recent years, and Andrew had been at home in fifth and sixth grades in Cairo American College, an American primary and secondary school. Going to Cairo would be a way of carrying on something of the life Malcolm and I had embarked upon, and we would be with John who had recently started working there with Catholic Relief Services. We would go to Cairo in time for the opening of second semester, following the memorial services and family gatherings in the United States.

In the strange time sequence that is Beirut, the passing of five days since Malcolm's assassination without any further tragedy was enough reassurance to go ahead with the memorial service. We would carry out our plans and hold it on Wednesday, exactly a week after Malcolm's death. Susie, our family musician, went over the music selection with Mr. Barsoumian, the choir director, and confirmed our choices of Malcolm's favorite music by Beethoven, Bach, and Mozart.

I requested the hymn, "A Mighty Fortress Is Our God," which I vividly remembered singing in the chapel at the memorial service of AUB President Stephen Penrose, who died the year Malcolm and I were students. Penrose was a hero of ours whose qualities and talents I believed Malcolm shared. He stood up for the interests of the Arab world and worked hard to make the U.S. government aware of those interests and of the unique role AUB had to play as a bridge between two cultures. Malcolm's vulnerability in the same job was not his health, but rather his long backlog of political outspokenness and honesty as a highly visible and extensively published professor of Middle Eastern politics caught up in a volatile political situation. Even in those simpler times, the job was tremendously demanding and taxing, so much so that Stephen Penrose died suddenly of a heart attack at the age of forty-nine.

Now, almost thirty years later, there was another memorial service for an AUB president in the chapel, which in the interim had been officially renamed the assembly hall in deference to the presence of the large number of religious groups other than Christian but was still affectionately referred to by old timers as the chapel. Malcolm had been inaugurated in the same historic build-

3. After the American University of Beirut memorial service,
January 1984. *Left to right:* Andrew, John, Ann, Susie, and Hans.

ing only seventeen months earlier, looking rather uncomfortable in
his new academic gown and hood, something he had reluctantly
bought after resisting doing so as a professor. His strong enthusiasm for his new job and his devotion to the university were expressed in his inaugural address in which he challenged the
university community with deep feeling and conviction, "to set
our minds to new beginnings at AUB. . . . Let us pledge ourselves
today to make that effort so that a century from now our descendents will remember that the men and women of AUB in the
1970's and 1980's showed not only the courage to survive eight
years of destruction and turmoil in the country, but the imagination and initiative to bring their university out of the bomb shelter, into the sunlight, and up to the mountaintops of excellence
once again."

Seventeen months was not long enough to achieve the state of
excellence that Malcolm wanted so much to restore. The children
and I sat in the front row of the chapel with our hands clasped
together just a few rows away from where Malcolm and I had sat

in our assigned seats for student chapel services thirty years earlier. Up front, bouquets of white flowers in tall inlaid Damascus vases surrounded the huge old pipe organ. The Ministers of Education posthumously awarded Malcolm Lebanon's highest honor, the Order of the Cedar. I stood up to accept it and went to the podium to give the talk I had prepared, something that I somehow had summoned the power to compose at this unprecedented time.

There was one task left before we could leave the next morning for America. The two boxes containing Malcolm's ashes were ready, and we wanted to take one of them to the oval garden near the chapel and bury it with as little notice as possible. We waited for the late afternoon, when there would be dimmer light and fewer people around, and then walked the short distance from Marquand House to the other side of College Hall next to the chapel—a strange procession, Susie, John, Andrew, Hans, and I with Abdul Hamid and a couple of other close friends as well as our driver Tanios and Hassan, who was carrying a shovel from our garden.

We sat on a nearby ledge under a tree, trying to be inconspicuous, our box beside us, while Hassan dug a hole in the designated spot. I remember feeling surprised that the possession of this box did not strike more defined emotional response. It seemed to have so little to do with the person who was my husband and with the life we had shared for almost thirty years.

When Hassan had finished, the children and I carried our box to the hole, placed it inside, and pushed the loose dirt over it with our hands. Susie pulled out her recorder and played several of the Renaissance tunes that Malcolm loved to hear. If only he could have heard the one in particular whose title always made him laugh, "The King Enjoys His Own Again."

Susie had made a sign to put on top of the Corinthian capital, and we found a glass table top from Marquand House that fit over it to protect it until a permanent inscription was made. We placed it on top of the capital as Susie played. The inscription was derived from the official AUB motto carved over the main gate of the university, "That they shall have life and have it more abundantly."

Susie had written, "He lived life abundantly," and drawn fanciful flowers and birds at the corners in the characteristic decorative style of the cards she had made over the years for all family occasions. She signed it for all of us. "We're proud our husband and father came to AUB, Ann, Susie, John, Stephen, and Andrew."

Proud, yes—but there were so many other adjectives and phrases that went along with the word proud which were not appropriate for the memorial—devastated, shattered, fulfilled for Malcolm that he had accomplished a dream, proud of myself for helping him get there, resentful that it had been pulled out from under us at the moment of attainment and that I was left to start over again, sorrowful that Malcolm would not be able to continue to watch the lives of his magnificent children unfold and, most of all, despairing of facing the rest of my life without him.

Early the next morning just before our departure we made a last visit to this garden to leave some flowers and found that students had been there before us. Single flowers and small bouquets lay on the ground, scattered here and there around the capital. We added ours and stood there a few minutes in the bright January sunshine.

·   ·   ·

Deep red poinsettias lined the pathway back to Marquand House, striking against the wine dark winter sea. Above us, through the pines, my eye caught sight of the windows and balcony of Malcolm's office. How he had loved it there, surrounded by the portraits of the founding fathers of the university, the desk of Daniel Bliss, the first president of AUB, and a few of my watercolors from our early days in Beirut when he was a young professor of political science and I was giving birth to our children.

At the front gate of our house, we found the students from my class waiting to say good-bye. One of them handed me an envelope full of letters which they had just written to express their condolences and appreciation of my being their teacher. I found this gesture among the most moving things that happened during that unforgettable week. They stood and waved good-bye as we were driven out the gate of the beautiful house that Malcolm and I had only just come to think of as our own.

PART TWO

The Early Years
1931–1961

CHAPTER 2

Growing Up West and East

*T*he southern California of my childhood days was far removed
from the Middle East. In the pre-Disneyland, smog-free, un-
crowded times of the late thirties and forties, even the invading armies of World War II seemed distant from the lives of my
younger sister Jane and me. We lived in the security of parental
love in a small world that did not extend much beyond the friends
on our block and the route to and from school, a short distance
from our house in upper middle-class Santa Monica. Only occasionally did we venture away from Santa Monica to downtown Los
Angeles a few miles away, where the highest building was the city
hall, an old Spanish style building of several stories with a high
clock tower which stood out against the grey blue mountains that
ringed the city.

My parents Susan Hawkins and John Zwicker had met and
fallen in love at Dalhousie University in Nova Scotia and moved to
Santa Monica shortly after their marriage in 1931, in the mid-
depression years. They soon decided there was no better place on
earth than this small town, situated on the bay of the Pacific, with
palm tree-lined streets and an eclectic assortment of architecture of
Mediterranean inspiration. My father eventually found a job in a
small business firm with which he remained associated for the next
forty years.

There was still plenty of undeveloped land, and one of our
delights was playing in vacant lots in the high grass that shot up
after the winter rains. But my favorite memories are of endless
play with the kids on our block, of playing "house," as Jane and I

called the make-believe dramas we dreamed up, which must have been inspired by the happy home life our parents provided for us as well as by my inclination toward domesticity.

The Fourth of July was the occasion for a special celebration which my mother organized every year. Waving flags and pounding toy drums, we paraded around the block, dressed in red, white, and blue, of course, and singing patriotic songs. Our red wagons became floats for the day, peopled with teddy bears or small sisters and brothers. Tricycle and bicycle brigades raced along with crepe paper streamers flying. Easter meant a gigantic Easter egg hunt in our backyard, followed by a picnic of tuna sandwiches, Easter eggs, lemonade, beer, and cut out sugar cookies. Aunts and uncles and special family friends were always a part of these gatherings. Without them the occasions would have lost some of their sense of tradition.

A touch of the world beyond entered our lives on December 7, 1941, when the Japanese bombed Pearl Harbor, but even that momentous event did not alter our warm, secure existence very much. With the first news of the invasion, all the kids on the block headed for the bluffs of Palisades Park looking for submarines. We spotted two the first day and four the second. Our contribution to the war effort was to trample the Japanese lilacs that grew wild on the bluffs and in our backyards. I also helped my mother blend the small package of dark yellow food coloring into the white, sallow looking block of margarine she bought every week when butter disappeared from the market. There was a special bond between us in that task which took on an artistry that she brought to the most basic of household routines. Together we kneaded the color into that blob of fat, watching the orangish yellow make streaks in the white and eventually turn from blotch to smooth, soft yellow.

Every wrapping of tin foil that we found was carefully saved to mold into balls which my mother would eventually deliver to the proper place so they could be sent off to factories to melt into other metallic forms that we knew would help protect our country. Hershey bars had the best tin foil wrappings, which gave Jane and me an excuse to ask our parents to let us buy more of this treat that was not often permitted. Even when they gave in, only half a candy bar was allowed. I always wondered what our allotment would have been had we been three children.

My father was the air-raid warden in our area. We never really saw him in action, but the heavy woolen sweater, cap, armband, and whistle on a long chain on his bedroom shelf evoked images of his walking his patrol at night along the beaches, protecting Santa Monica from any Japanese spies who might have come ashore from those submarines we saw.

Like most of the families on our block we had a victory garden where, in a very non-cost-effective production, my father grew vegetables so that we could leave the ones in the grocery store for American soldiers and sailors, wherever they were. I loved helping him water our garden, which was the best one on the block, of course, because everything my father took care of, he tended well.

How innocent those involvements in war were when I was seven and my sister five, compared with the entanglements of the Middle East that would engulf Malcolm's and my life a few decades later.

The closest personal contact we ever had with the war was when a cousin, who was a member of the Coast Guard, came home on leave. Seeing him walk down the sidewalk of our block one day and pointing out to all my friends that he was my cousin must have been one of the proudest moments of my childhood, for the whiteness of his uniform still gleams in my memory.

There was only one occasion when Jane and I actually experienced fright due to the war. We awoke to sirens howling and searchlights piercing the black sky trying to spot what was a suspected Japanese airplane. My father dashed from his bed and donned his heavy sweater, cap, armband, and whistle, and in went my sister and I to the warm place on his side of the bed beside our mother. The sirens continued blaring for what seemed forever in a child's mind. We had seen enough war movies to know that Japanese pilots were likely to be dive-bombing us as they committed kamakazi for the love of their country. The crash never came and we finally went to sleep, comforted somewhat by the knowledge that our father was out protecting us with his armband and his whistle and his good sense and wisdom. The next morning the newspaper reported that all the hullabaloo had been over an unidentified flying object.

The year before the war ended we were evicted from our house because the landlord raised the rent beyond a level my parents were willing to pay. That word *evicted* still has a terrible stinging sound to it, conjuring up images of our being put out on the streets and of Jane and me having to leave our beloved block and our friends forever. Then memories fade—no recollection of moving day or of all the work my parents had to go through to get us to our new house a few streets away and settle us in there. But I remember the final results, the beautiful curtains and slipcovers my mother sewed herself, the red provincial print wallpaper my father hung in Janie's and my bedroom, the long desk they had made for us, and the warm atmosphere they created.

Our room became the new focus of our activities—and our radio. Luckily we liked the same programs. As soon as homework was finished, there was "Tom Mix" and "The Lone Ranger" to look forward to. On Friday nights we were allowed to listen after dinner too. "I Love a Mystery" and "This Is Your FBI" were absolutely petrifying. We were always sure that the current "most wanted criminals" announced on the program that week were peeking through the dark crack between the shade and the side of the window.

August 14, 1945, the day the Japanese surrendered, was a holiday which, from the impressionable age of eleven, I remember only as a time of festivity and hilarity that took hold of everyone's life for several days. No reflective thoughts entered my childish head or penetrated the secure existence of my home and family about the magnitude of change the war had brought to millions of individual lives and to the world. The Middle East was familiar to me only through stories I had learned at Sunday School at the Santa Monica First Presbyterian Church, and I had no inkling of the changes about to occur in that area of the world as the allied powers decided how to find a homeland for the Jews. Their decision was to change the course of history and to play a major role in Malcolm's career and in the life of our family.

Ten thousand miles away in Lebanon, Malcolm spent his early childhood years in ways both similar to, and different from, mine. He too had Canadian Presbyterian roots, a warm and secure family life, and a close community of good friends, but the involvements and interests of our two families were quite different. While my parents had moved west across a continent to find work and make a home during the mid-depression years of the early thirties, his parents Elsa and Stanley Kerr had set out on separate journeys to the Middle East a dozen years earlier. Elsa left her home in Ohio for Istanbul to study Turkish and eventually teach in a mission school. Stanley, prohibited from joining the Army because of an inaccurate diagnosis of heart problems, had spent World War I working in Walter Reed Hospital. Yearning for action and adventure by the end of the war, he traveled from New Jersey to eastern Turkey and Syria to work with the Near East Relief. They met when he was one of the men sent to Aleppo to meet the trains bringing a new group of young women teachers. Their courtship had a dramatic backdrop as my father-in-law conspired to secure food and shelter for the refugees, and my mother-in-law struggled as a new teacher in a new country. They shared a love of adventure and a sense of service and were not afraid of risks or hardships. A year later, in 1921, they were married and soon moved to Lebanon where they ran orphanages for Armenian children.

By that time the American University of Beirut (which had been founded in 1866 as the Syrian Protestant College) had become an integral part of Lebanon and the Middle East. The university had been started by Protestant missionaries at the end of the American Civil War and a twenty-year civil war in Lebanon (then part of Syria) and the Middle East. Missionary spirit was strong in America and Britain at that time, which helped the first president of the university, Daniel Bliss, to convince people to donate money to support a Christian university in Lebanon. The Syrian Protestant College opened in a rented five-room house, with sixteen students and eight faculty members. The College of Arts and Sciences was thus established and soon the Medical School was added. In 1882, English replaced Arabic as the official language of instruction, opening the college to international enrollment.

The Presbyterian affiliation of the college was strong in the early years and sometimes caused controversy. As enrollment expanded, the majority of students came from Muslim, Jewish, and Eastern Christian backgrounds, so it became more difficult to require religious instruction and participation in religious services. The Ottoman government in 1914 passed a law forbidding these practices for all non-Protestants, but Dr. Howard Bliss, who had succeeded his father as president, soon convinced the authorities that Muslim and Jewish students should be permitted to attend an alternate type of meeting dealing with moral education.

With these local pressures, plus diminishing missionary zeal in the West, the trustees of the college decided to concentrate on providing a secular form of education. In 1920, the college was renamed the American University of Beirut, and became known as AUB. In later decades graduate schools of engineering, agriculture, and public health were founded, bringing important training to students from many developing countries. The university prided itself on producing students of high moral quality who were first grounded in the liberal arts and then in their area of specialization.

Stanley and Elsa Kerr were naturally drawn to AUB. The director of the Near East Relief, Bayard Dodge, had been appointed president of the university in 1922, and other friends were teaching there. Dodge's wife, Mary Bliss, was the granddaughter of Daniel Bliss, and daughter of Howard Bliss, the two previous presidents. One of their two sons, David, later became vice-president and then acting president of AUB.

It took only a little encouragement from President Dodge to convince the young Kerrs to come and teach at AUB. With its Protestant roots and educational mission, the institution was a good place for Elsa, the missionary teacher, and Stanley Kerr, the adventuresome, slightly rebellious son of a Presbyterian minister. After several years in the United States for Stanley to complete his Ph.D. in biochemistry, they returned to Beirut and a forty-year teaching career at the university.

While my sister and I had our neighborhood block and our friends in Santa Monica, Malcolm, his older sisters, Marion and Dorothy, and his younger brother Doug, along with the other professors' kids had the entire seventy-two acres of the AUB campus in which to play. Their houses were nestled among the trees and flowers of the campus overlooking the Mediterranean. If they were too young to appreciate the view, they must certainly have relished the terraced hillsides for games of hide-and-go-seek, the AUB swimming beach at the bottom of the campus, and the huge trees to climb. As they grew older, they could enjoy the tennis and basketball courts a few yards from their front door, the large athletic field, and all the activities associated with campus life.

In the summers the professors and their families moved away from the heat and humidity of Beirut to the mountain villages of

Xmas 1937 or 1936

With the best of
Holiday Wishes

Beirut Kerrs

4. Kerr family Christmas card from Beirut, 1936–1937.

Lebanon. The Kerrs and four other families moved to the village of Ainab, an hour's drive away, where they had built simple, local style stone houses with dark green wooden shutters and red-tile roofs in the middle of a pine wood overlooking Beirut and the sea. They piled a summer's worth of clothing, books, games, sports equipment, and food supplies into taxis and made their annual trek, which the generation of teachers and missionaries before them had had to do by horse or donkey, and the next generation would do by private car.

Once settled into this peaceful setting, they rarely budged for the rest of the summer. Each morning, a man came up the mountain from the village on his donkey with the day's order of gro-

ceries, meat, fresh fruits and vegetables, and water from the village
spring. With simple kitchens and no refrigeration, these daily de-
liveries were a necessity. Malcolm and the other children vied for
turns riding the donkey around the hilltop, and they spent many
hours pushing toy cars on the cement roads that their fathers constructed for them in the limestone rock formations under the umbrella pine trees. There were walks through the mountains and
into valleys to favorite swimming places set in rocky gorges where
pink and white cyclamen and an occasional fig tree popped out of
crevices in the rocks. The exquisite view of pine-dotted mountains
in blending shades of blue and purple and of shepherds tending
their sheep or goats on the hillsides gave an illusion of eternal
peace. Even the Turkish gun road, built by the Ottomans and
softened by time, had a historically peaceful quality about it, as if
incursions of battle were a part of the past that would not disturb
the land again. From time to time the hilltop kids hiked up there
to play make-believe war games in old embankments.

Something more than just play war soon entered the lives of
these AUB families. In the late thirties Hitler's army spread out
over Europe and then to Greece and Crete in the Eastern Mediterranean. From there it would be only a short step to occupying
Lebanon, whose French protectorate government was headed by a
Vichy general under the watchful eyes of high-ranking German
officials anxious to ensure support for the Third Reich.

So in the same way that my childhood friends and I watched
for Japanese ships on the shores of the Pacific in 1941, Marion,
Dorothy, Malcolm, and Doug watched for German ships on the
shores of the Mediterranean in 1940. With less than a thousand
miles between them and the enemy, their fears were more justified
than ours in California, where we had the whole Pacific Ocean
separating us from Japan and the American navy to protect us.

Malcolm and his father charted the moves of the advancing
armies on a map of the world. This was partly inspired by their
love of games and their interest in keeping track of what was
going on in the world, but also by the need to make some assessment of potential danger. Being three years older than me and
closer to the real action, Malcolm's impressions of the war were
more realistic than mine. In the late 1930s, the United States had

not yet entered the war, but AUB's clear sympathy with the Allies did not augur well for the university. The administration took all the means it could to guarantee the survival of the university. A document was drawn up to allow the transfer of administration to an Arab committee if it became necessary for President Dodge to leave. Seven hundred students on campus from other parts of the world were given credit for the work they had completed and sent home, and American and European staff were encouraged to leave.

In 1940 the Kerrs joined forces with several other families for a long and circuitous trek south and eastward, and finally home to the United States, where Malcolm had lived before only as an infant when his parents had been on sabbatical. Some months earlier they had made the difficult decision to let Marion, then sixteen, travel with several teenage children of other AUB families to schools and colleges in the United States on the last ship to sail through the Mediterranean before the war started.

Their journey took the families first to Palestine where they spent a month waiting to hear of a ship to board in Egypt to take them eastward to the United States. Nine-year-old Malcolm and eleven-year-old Dorothy had unhappy memories of having to attend an English school in Palestine for a month and disliking its unfamiliar ways. When the families got the news that a ship would meet them in Suez, they traveled together to Egypt. Once there, the Kerrs were prevented from continuing with the others when Malcolm contracted hepatitis. He spent a month in an Italian hospital while the family waited for him in a hotel. Malcolm loved recalling the night he and his father, who was visiting him, stood at his window watching as Italian planes bombed Cairo, hoping that the pilots knew better than to bomb their own hospital.

When Malcolm was well enough to travel, they were able to get another ship, but for security reasons, arrangements had to be made in secret. They were driven to a deserted beach near Suez and in the dark of night ferried out to a ship in the middle of the canal. Once aboard, they discovered they were on the maiden voyage of the *Queen Elizabeth,* which they were sharing with the crew, refugees, and hundreds of German war prisoners. They immediately set sail out into the Red Sea just hours ahead of a major bombing attack which sank every ship in the canal, according to the story Malcolm years later told and retold to his enthralled children. This ship took them to Australia where there was a stop of several weeks, long enough to learn to throw a boomerang, which now hangs in our California house, and to meet their Beirut friends who had arrived ahead of them. Together they boarded a ship which was part of a convoy that would take them through the Pacific by way of Honolulu. They landed in Long Beach, California, in 1941. If only I had known, I would have gone to meet him.

But our meeting was still thirteen years away. I was six years old and Malcolm was nine. The Kerr family went east to New Jersey, which became their home base until the war was over four years later. Princeton has somehow always been a gathering place for AUB families, whether for home leave or college studies or retirement. And there were other Beirut families waiting out the war years there, but apparently not enough to shield Malcolm from the discomforts of culture shock. He remembered with horror being called "the little boy from Syria" at the local public school he attended, and he recalled how different his clothes were from those of his classmates and how uncomfortable that made him feel.

After one year in New Jersey, Malcolm's father and other professors had to return to their jobs at AUB. The Germans had not occupied Lebanon. Rather the British and the Free French Forces, with the help of the American Consul General, were able to force the Vichy general to capitulate. An armistice was signed on July 14, 1941; the general left, and British, Australian, and Free French Forces entered Beirut. For Lebanon, the war had been short-lived.

Since sea routes back to Beirut remained unsafe, Elsa Kerr and the children had to stay behind in Princeton until the end of the war in 1945. There she ran the household with a firm hand and a tight budget, taking over the meager family investments, about which she knew little, and surprising her family with her success. With the money she earned from that and from tutoring students in math, she was able to pay for piano lessons for the children, whose gratitude was not realized until later years.

AUB, as usual throughout its history, barely skipped a beat

during those traumatic times. The administration was careful to stress the university's nonpolitical role and required students to sign a pledge saying they would not participate in political activities. As a foreign institution trying to maintain a neutral position, AUB was able to be a focal point of international relations, providing services through its hospital, sports facilities, dormitories, auditoriums and classrooms. In 1941, the seventy-fifth anniversary of the founding of the university was celebrated. Students continued to come from Lebanon and around the Middle East, and when the first meeting of the United Nations convened in San Francisco in 1948, there were more graduates of AUB among the participants than any other single university, some nineteen in all.

Stanley Kerr and several other bachelor professors spent the war years living on the second floor of Marquand House, the president's residence that would be Malcolm's and my home, for such a fleeting time, forty years later.

Elsa Kerr and the two boys returned to Beirut in 1945, in time for Malcolm, now fourteen, to begin high school at the American Community School and for Doug to go to the elementary section that Malcolm had attended before the war. The two girls stayed in the United States, Marion at Wellesley College and Dorothy at Northfield preparatory school in Massachusetts. Malcolm spent two years there in the comfortable atmosphere of small classes and good friends, just the right environment for the shy boy that he was. Academics had always come easily to him, but there he was a social and athletic success as well. This was all good background for prep school in the United States which many AUB families deemed a necessary transition to university life in America.

Malcolm spent his last two years of high school at Deerfield Academy in Deerfield, Massachusetts, during the days of the venerable headmaster Frank Boydon who, with his wife, had been at the school for many decades. Malcolm had wonderful memories of his days at Deerfield and always liked to say that his time there had made a man of him. His happy recollections seemed only slightly tarnished by the fact that he had to spend almost a whole semester in the infirmary when he came down with debilitating arthritis. He continued his studies from his bed, but his athletic and social life had to lapse for a while. Later he resumed all his former activities, including being a member of the tennis team,

5. The high school boy's basketball team,
American Community School, Beirut,
with Malcolm in back row, center, 1946–1947.

and wasn't bothered with arthritis again until he finished college, when its recurrence actually helped to bring about our meeting.

From Deerfield, Malcolm went to Princeton, along with many other AUB professors' sons. "At Princeton, I finally learned Arabic," he used to say. It was easy in the English-speaking community of AUB in West Beirut to learn no more than a few words of Arabic, as many long-time Western residents there have shamefully admitted. With Malcolm's thoroughness and precision and the excellent teachers he had at Princeton, he did indeed learn Arabic, to the point where he could read weighty texts and give lectures in that language. He majored in international relations and graduated Phi Beta Kappa, which he always said (with characteristic modesty) never would have happened if it hadn't been for his advantage in Arabic. He was also awarded a Rockefeller grant to study at Oxford University.

The summer after his graduation in 1953, Malcolm and a

6. Malcolm with parents and sister Marion
at Beit-el-Din, Lebanon, 1953.

couple of his classmates took jobs washing dishes and waiting on
tables in a hotel at Lake Tahoe, California, again putting us
within a few hundred miles of each other. For some unexplainable
medical reason, or perhaps because of the rigors of being on his
feet eight hours a day, Malcolm again came down with severe
arthritis. The Rockefeller grant had to be relinquished, and he
returned to Lebanon to stay with his parents and to study for a
master's degree in Middle Eastern studies at AUB.

That was in 1953. I was eighteen years old and had just finished my freshman year at Occidental College, the Princeton of
the West, we were told, because it had been founded by some
Presbyterian Princeton graduates. The two institutions shared the
same black and orange colors and the tiger as a mascot, if that was
any proof to the claim, as well as much attention to solid undergraduate training in the liberal arts. But I remember how Malcolm, with a certain East Coast suspicion of things Californian,
raised his eyebrows when I explained the Princeton-California connection to him.

I had gone to Occidental College near Pasadena from Santa

Monica High School, a good public school, where I had been an enthusiastic participant in student affairs and done well academically. Those high school years were so full of fun that I wasn't particularly anxious to leave for college. Occidental was one of several well-established small liberal arts colleges in southern California founded before the turn of the century. Although situated near downtown Los Angeles, the campus was an island of old Spanish-style buildings surrounded by olive and eucalyptus trees. Classes were small, teachers were caring, and the academic atmosphere was challenging. Like most young women of the era, I majored in education in order to obtain a teaching credential and have a means of earning a living after graduation—or support a husband in graduate school. My real love was art and art history, but this preference was not as practical a major as education. I did take a watercolor class in my senior year which led me into a lifelong hobby of painting.

In my freshman year I lived on campus in Erdman Hall next door to a young woman who had just returned from her junior year abroad in Greece. Her travels impressed me, and I began to pay close attention to any information available about junior year abroad programs. Perhaps another reason for my interest in going abroad was the fact that Occidental was a small school of a thousand students, only half as large as Santa Monica High School. By the end of my sophomore year, I was ready to broaden my horizons. A spirit of adventure, more than an academic concern for a certain area of the world, motivated me, but I was also developing new intellectual curiosity and wanted to learn more about the world beyond California. The fascination I felt for India did not win the support of my parents. "Go to Europe," they advised, but that was not exotic enough for me. When the minister of our church and his wife, Earle and Berneita Harvey, came home from a trip to the Middle East extolling the beauty and high academic standards of a Presbyterian-founded university on the Mediterranean shores of Lebanon, we all became interested.

I had to look at a map to find out for sure where Lebanon was, and then I began to make associations—cedar trees, ancient Phoenicia, the biblical towns of Sidon and Tyre, the beauty of Lebanon as described in the Old Testament. The Presbyterian Church had a junior year abroad program, and among the campuses one could choose was the American University of Beirut. Our minister promised to help me learn more about it.

The willingness of my stay-at-home parents to accommodate the wanderlust nature of their daughter was admirable, especially in an era when it was uncommon for young women to travel alone halfway around the world. The Presbyterian sponsorship of the program must have helped, as well as the scholarship money our local church raised to help pay my way. In August 1954, I boarded a propeller plane in Los Angeles for a long, bumpy ride to Boston and a visit with my maternal grandmother before going to New York to meet the other junior year abroad students and take a ship to Beirut. I remember how tightly my mother and I held each other's hand as my father drove us to the airport to see me off. Now with my own children moving out around the world, I can better understand how poignant the departure of their twenty-year-old daughter must have been for them.

The seventeen-day journey to Beirut on a Dutch freighter, the SS *Bantam,* served as a transition from the familiar world I was leaving behind to another world. So different from the twelve-hour jet journey of the present, the leisurely voyage provided a time for mental preparation to live in a new culture.

In addition to the six other junior year abroad students headed for AUB and the Beirut College for Women were eight passengers traveling to the Middle East for various reasons. There were three recent college graduates going out to teach in Lebanon, a young wife going to meet her husband working in Iran, two rather antisocial priests, and a glamorous woman of dubious virtue and uncertain destination. In those suspended days lounging on the deck, we students spent leisurely hours getting to know each other. When we grew tired of comparing new information from our assigned reading for orientation on the Middle East, we indulged in speculation about the activities of the rest of the passengers. We concluded that the two silent priests, who always left the table before dessert was served to resume their continuous pacing of the decks, might be contemplating jumping overboard. The lady of uncertain destination also left the table soon after meals were over, followed undisguisedly by the handsome assistant to the chief engineer for what we presumed was a torrid romance. There were romances of a more innocent nature among us students and teachers, shifting rapidly during those September evenings under star-strewn skies.

I basked in the unaccustomed luxury of shipboard travel and enjoyed the attention of shipbound officers eager for conversation, especially, it seemed, with a young blond from California. At the captain's table the ship's officers told stories of Dutch adventures and gain in Indonesia while Indonesian waiters served us delicious Indonesian meals. Our Dutch hosts also told long stories of the German occupation of Holland in World War II, the particular effects on their families, and the bitterness they felt toward the Germans. There was a notable disparity in these two themes which they were so eager to discuss. In one version, they had been the occupiers; in the other they were the occupied. The subjects of colonialism, war, and occupation were to become familiar ones as I began to learn more about the world of the Arabs and the Middle East.

The first introduction to that world came twelve days after we left New York as we approached the northwest corner of the African continent and prepared to stop in Casablanca on the Atlantic coast of Morocco for a day in port. Before we reached shore, the radios of the crew began picking up the sounds of Arabic music, which blared out in a great cacaphony. As soon as the gangplank was down, dockworkers swarmed onto the decks to unload the cargo from New York. Their loud shouting at each other in the guttural tones of Arabic was another bombardment of unfamiliar noise—and a reminder of how little I knew about the new world I was entering. Between recollections of the Casbah in the film *Casablanca* and Sunday school stories of the tribes of the brothers Isaac and Ishmael, the progenitors of the Jews and the Arabs, there was a large hole in my knowledge of the Arab world.

Once ashore the new cultural contrasts were more appealing. Morocco, which had been colonized by the French for a century, had a flavor of North African Arab with a French overlay. Arab coffeehouses and European-style shops still displayed signs in both French and Arabic or combinations of both. Swathed from head to toe in yards and yards of brightly colored cloth, traditionally garbed women strolled along the streets with only their faces showing, while others wore Western clothing of the latest French fashion. A few men were in Western dress, but most were attired in long flowing galabiya robes in dark browns and blues. Architecture was a mixture of cream-colored Mediterranean buildings, gleaming white-domed North African houses, already with, in 1954, some nondescript cement boxlike structures creeping in. We ate lunch in an outdoor cafe where the waiter spoke to us in a mixture of English, French, and Arabic. "Ahlan wasahlan [welcome], bonjour mesdemoiselles et messieurs. You like some fresh fish today?"

In the mosque across the street, the afternoon call to prayer began. Unlike the unfamiliar music blaring out of the sailors' radios and the loud voices of the dockworkers, this compelling new sound, somewhere between a chant and a song, had a harmonious and timeless quality which pulled me into it and made me want to understand more of the culture it represented.

Casablanca was geographically the westernmost city in an Arabic-speaking world that extended eastward to Iraq and in the Islamic world that spread further east to Indonesia. As I took in all those new sounds and sights, I wasn't aware that I was looking at one of many blends of Arab and Islamic culture. The Arabs had carried the religion of the prophet Muhammad out of the Arabian peninsula after his death in A.D. 630. Within a century it had spread throughout this wide area, and even up into Spain, both imposing itself upon and absorbing the local culture in each new locale. More recent cultural mergings had come about during the past few centuries of French, British, Dutch, and Italian colonial rule.

Now the other junior year abroad students and I were about to become part of further cultural exchange. I had come a long way from Santa Monica, although as I looked more carefully at the architecture around me, I was reminded of the arcaded hallways and domes and arches of Occidental College and many of the Spanish buildings in southern California. Arab styles had influenced architecture in North Africa and Spain and traveled to California via Mexico and the Spanish explorers. Now I was on a voyage in the other direction and already intrigued after these few hours in Casablanca with the confrontation and merging of cultures I had been witnessing. Beirut, still two thousand miles and another five days of sailing away, was closer to the center of the Arab world. I could hardly wait to get there.

CHAPTER 3

Song of Lebanon

*B*eirut shimmered in beguiling colors across the pale blue waters of St. George's Bay as the *Bantam* carried us into the harbor. The coast of Lebanon was a narrow strip of flat land with high mountains rising steeply behind it. In the distance, Mt. Sanneen towered above the other peaks of the Lebanon range, washed to pastel beige and purple in the lingering summer heat. It was already hot and sticky on that early morning of October 5, 1954. Passengers and crew stood on the deck, suddenly becoming disconnected individuals again as the interweaving of the last seventeen days came to an end and we were confronted with new sights, sounds, and smells.

When the gangplank touched the dock, the scene we had witnessed in Casablanca repeated itself. Noise and chaos replaced the tranquility of life at sea. Sweaty dockworkers and government officials swarmed aboard, but this time, we had to deal with them in all the procedures necessary to take up residence in Lebanon. In the midst of the crowds, I saw a man wearing an armband that said AUB on it. It was not difficult for him to spot seven young American students and three young teachers, all looking expectant and eager. He made his way toward us and welcomed us warmly in Arabic and English. "Ahlan wasahlan, ahlan wasahlan," he repeated with gusto. "Welcome to Beirut."

He hustled us from one line to another for passports, visas, and health certificates to be examined before we were allowed to disembark. Then we moved to the even hotter and noisier dock area where hundreds of arriving and departing passengers waited to have their luggage inspected. From just beyond the dockside fence I heard an American voice calling my name and looked up to see a woman smiling and waving. When I stepped over to the fence, she explained that she was Bernice Youtz, an Occidental College graduate whose husband was teaching at AUB. She had heard I was coming to AUB and had come to welcome me. Hers was a comforting voice in the midst of so much confusion.

Entire families sat on cartons containing all their possessions as they waited to board ships which would take them to new countries and new lives. Lebanese have traditionally lived outside the country, often dramatically improving their lot financially and educationally, and then returning to Lebanon later in their lives to build a home with a treasured red tile roof in their native town.

A university car was waiting to take those of us headed for school to our respective hostels at AUB and at Beirut College for Women (today renamed Beirut University College) where two of the young women in our group would be studying. We drove from the port area to the downtown center called Martyr's Square commemorating heroes who had participated in a struggle for independence from the French. The burj (Arabic for tower), as the town center was referred to because of an Ottoman tower that once stood there, was bustling with traffic and commerce. From there we headed out the Beirut tramline street to the western side of the city where the universities were located.

American University of Beirut women were housed in two three-story apartment buildings opposite each other on a small road off Rue Abdul Aziz, a few blocks from the university. Called hostels, these quarters served the same function as dormitories in universities in America. Miss Kurani and Miss Shammas, both maiden aunts of old Lebanese AUB families, were the housemothers, and they were there to welcome us and show us to our rooms.

Five young women were to share the room where I was assigned. Two of my roommates, Naziha Hamza and Roshan Irani, were already there unpacking their suitcases when I arrived. Roshan was small and pretty with long dark hair usually piled on top of her head in a loose bun, and Naziha was taller and plumpish with short dark curly hair and a soft voice. They greeted me in British-accented English with a touch of the Arabic rolled *r*.

Whatever uneasiness I may have felt in anticipation of this meeting vanished with the warmth of their welcome. I was to come to
recognize a more varied social class structure in Arab society than
the predominantly middle class structure of American society.
These classes were determined by birth, by economic status, and
by education, but throughout all levels of society there ran a quality of graciousness, warmth, and hospitality which was uniquely
Arab. Each of my new roommates had an engaging laugh,
Roshan's light and musical, Naziha's soft and deep toned. They
combined the Arab quality of great hospitality and politeness with
the gentleness of the educated families from which they came.

Roshan was a Palestinian refugee, the first of many I was to
meet. Her family was one of many who had left Palestine in the
summer of 1948 after the state of Israel was created when many
Arabs had fled their homes with only the possessions they could
carry. The sad irony in the creation of this new state was that, in
making a much-needed home for the Jewish refugees of World
War II in Palestine, a new group of refugees was created. This
new diaspora sought refuge in different parts of the Arab world,
but the majority went to Lebanon, Jordan, and Syria. The educated and professional elite usually found relatives or friends who
helped them build new lives and careers, while the thousands of
poor became squatters or went to hastily established refugee
camps. In these squalid conditions the resentment of the displaced
Palestinians festered and grew as fast as the birth rate.

Roshan was among the fortunate whose family had had enough
money and education to start a new life in Lebanon. They were
Baha'is from Haifa on the coast of Palestine. As her name, Irani,
indicated, the family had its origins in Iran where the Baha'i religion developed. Lebanon, with its numerous and diverse religious
groups, including many types of Christianity and Islam, was an
appropriate place for them to resettle. Roshan had attended an
English-language secondary school in Lebanon and was now studying at AUB to earn a teaching credential.

Naziha came from an old Muslim family in Lebanon who had
been associated with AUB for several generations. They lived in
Beirut but also had a family home in the village of Bhamdoun in
the mountains above the city. Like Roshan—and most women
students at AUB and Occidental College—she was majoring

in education. She was also interested in art, as I was, and we soon decided that we would like to go on painting expeditions together.

We unpacked our belongings and stored them in the dresser and closets assigned to each of us, saving space for the two roommates who were still to come. I had never shared a room with four people, though my sister and I had always shared a bedroom. It was a large room and had a light and airy feeling from the wide windows opening onto the balcony across the front which over-looked Abdul Aziz Street and directly across to another women's hostel and a small grocery store. Its spare furnishings allowed plenty of space for moving around. There were two beds on one side and three on the other. Roshan and Naziha had taken the two together. I chose the bed opposite Roshan's near the balcony. The steamer trunk containing everything I had brought for the year fit well into the space between my bed and the next one and would serve as a good table as well as storage space.

I pulled out the flowered print bedspread which my mother and I had bought shortly before my departure and threw it over my bed. Its vivid color created a sharp contrast to the university-issue beige cotton spreads of my roommates and made it obvious which corner of the room was inhabited by the new American. I thought briefly of returning it to my trunk, and of using the regulation beige, but I didn't. I liked the colors, and there wasn't much chance of my not being conspicuous. As a Californian of above average height I felt I was towering over Naziha and Roshan. My fair skin and green eyes contrasted with their olive complexions and brown eyes.

Young women from Cyprus, Iraq, and Jordan, as well as other Lebanese, lived in the rooms near ours. The bathroom down the hall that we all used had some unusual plumbing. One of the two toilets was familiar, but the other was a hole in the tile floor with a little foot rest on either side. In an adjacent area was a big water tank with a small oven below and a stack of fuel packets made of crushed olive pits piled beside it. Naziha, noticing my puzzled look, reassured me, "one of these packets lighted twenty minutes ahead of time will provide a good, hot shower."

At lunch time we went to the dining room in the other women's hostel across the street for the first of many disappointing

7. American University of Beirut Women's Hostel dining room, 1955.

meals. In this country of delicious cuisine, it was a shame to eat anything but authentic Lebanese food, but the hostel cooks made the mistake of cooking Europeanized Arabic food or Arabized European food. I never got used to the tough beefsteak cooked in cinnamon, nor to eggs fried to surrealistic shapes in inches of olive oil. "You mustn't judge our food by the hostel meals," Roshan and Naziha assured me. "When you come to our homes, you will have real Lebanese food."

After lunch I set out for the campus down Rue Abdul Aziz, a few blocks from the university, past small shops and walled villas. I turned into Rue Bliss, named after the family of the first and second presidents of AUB, a main street that runs the length of the university and beyond to the end of the Beirut tramline. Approaching the main entrance, I saw a placard above the iron filigree at the top of the gate that was inscribed: American University of Beirut, Founded 1866." I crossed the narrow street and went through the big stone archway of the gate under the lintel where the words were carved: "That they shall have life and have it more abundantly."

It was impossible not to be immediately enraptured with the sight in front of me. I think my ongoing romance with the Middle East took hold that afternoon as I stepped through the gate onto the campus. Before me the Mediterranean sparkled in the afternoon sun as a backdrop to tall cypress trees and pungent Aleppo pines. Benches under the pines overlooked a steep bank of pink and white oleander bushes and blue-violet jacaranda trees to the green athletic field and the rocks of the AUB swimming beach. Everywhere flower beds were ablaze with orange marigolds, blue ageratum, and multicolored petunias, the flowers I loved in my parents' garden at home in Santa Monica.

Immediately opposite the main gate was College Hall, a vine-covered, four-story building with a tower housing a clock that had been striking the hours for eight decades. The rose beige of its stones was the color of the earth of Lebanon and in warm contrast with the greens and blues of the trees and sea beyond.

I entered the building and located the office of Elsa Kerr, the Advisor to Women Students, to learn about classes and activities. Behind a big desk sat a pleasant-looking woman who stood up to greet me when I walked in. Standing up she suddenly gained new proportions. She seemed to be almost six feet tall, a good bit taller than my five feet seven. She explained the registration procedures and asked me about my journey. We carried on a friendly conversation and I felt an easy rapport developing. Apparently she did too, for, as I learned much later, when she went home she advised her son, Malcolm, that he should try to meet the new young woman from California who had just arrived for her junior year.

"This university has a long and rich history," said Mrs. Kerr. She talked a little about Daniel Bliss, the New England missionary who had founded the university in 1866. He had headed the university for almost a half-century and had set a tone for the institution which still existed. I had seen a picture of this imposing man who, with his thick white hair, stern face, and long index finger raised to the sky, resembled a Hebrew prophet. He helped to found the college on the premise that it was for people of any race or religion but that those who came to study would know the religious and educational beliefs of its founders. I asked her about the composition of the student body. It was half Christian and half Muslim, she said, mainly from Lebanon and elsewhere in the Middle East, but there was a sprinkling of students from other countries around the world.

When I left Mrs. Kerr's office, I explored the campus, interested especially in seeing these students she had told me about. With the opening of classes a week away, people were gathering and greeting each other now that the summer holiday was over. My first impressions were of the contrasts between this campus and the college environment at home. In letters to my family, I described the male students lounging on walls and benches who appeared older to me than their counterparts in California. Unlike the fair-complexioned, fuzzy-cheeked youths at Occidental, their beards, though shaven, were very dark, and many young men had mustaches and receding hairlines. Quite a few walked two by two holding hands, which for Arab men, I soon learned, was a normal display of friendship. But for a man and woman to do the same thing would have been considered improper.

There were noticeably fewer female students than male, and for the most part they sat in groups away from the men. Many of the women were dressed to the hilt in spike heels and slim skirts, the Parisian fashion of the day. They had beautiful eyes and hair, usually of dark brown color, though a few had green eyes and lighter hair. They all looked as if they had just left the coiffeur, the same one evidently, for hairdos were very similar. The students were casting as many glances at me as I was at them, and I wondered if they thought me inappropriately dressed in my cotton dress, low-heeled shoes, and natural hair style.

When I returned to the hostel I found that the other two who were to share our room had arrived. Katie Azzam, like Roshan, was a Palestinian Lebanese whose family had been forced to leave Palestine in 1948 and had settled in Beirut. She was fair by Arab standards and very jolly and lively. She was unpacking her things and settling herself next to me. Katie, too, spoke beautiful English. She was from a Greek Orthodox Christian family who had been educated in British schools, first in Palestine and then in Lebanon.

Samia Shammas was an Orthodox Christian from Mosul, a city in northern Iraq, and she looked and sounded different from our other roommates. She was shorter and stockier than most of the Lebanese I had met, and she had a more guttural accent when she spoke English. On one side of her face was a distinguishing scar that came from the bite of a bug peculiar to the area around Baghdad and Mosul.

Samia explained that she had had little English in Iraq and therefore had spent the last year in AUB's special English program in preparation for her freshman year. As we talked she pulled a gallon jar out of her suitcase and opened it. Out came an unfamiliar odor; in the jar were huge, seaweed green, juicy objects. "These are mango pickles," Samia said. "Please take one." I was curious and wanted to please Samia, but I was also leery. I took a small bite, but it was enough to set my mouth on fire for the next ten minutes. That's the object, she explained, as well as being of good assistance to the digestion.

Perhaps sensing my less than enthusiastic response to her pickles, she reached into her suitcase, pulled out another container and opened it, revealing small pieces of what looked like powdery taffy. This, she told the four of us, was manna, which recalled to my mind the biblical manna from heaven. I bit into a piece hesitantly, expecting a sticky, rosewater Turkish delight, but was pleasantly surprised by a subtly sweet delicacy which helped to assuage the fire in my mouth. Samia explained that it was made from a substance that fell from the tamarisk tree on dewy nights. She kept these treats on her shelf so that any time she felt homesick, she just helped herself to a mango pickle or a piece of manna.

The diverse international and religious mix of my roommates intrigued me, and I looked forward to the opportunity to understand these varied backgrounds in the year ahead. I did not yet appreciate the complexities that their different religions brought to the social and political fabric of Beirut. Although there were various sects of Christians and Muslims mixed throughout the city, the east side was principally Christian and the west Muslim. French education and linguistic influence and a Lebanese nationalist spirit predominated in the east while English education and a pan-Arab spirit were more prevalent in the west. In 1954, these two sides of the city seemed to exist together as harmoniously as did my Christian and Muslim roommates. But behind the apparent harmony, Beirut was a city of uncertain identity—Arab or Lebanese, Muslim or Christian, east or west, Levantine or Byzantine? Binding these groups together was the same common denominator of Arabness through native language and culture, which I had observed in Casablanca a week earlier—and which I would later learn gave all Arabic-speaking countries an essential oneness.

Too exhilarated to sleep at the end of that extraordinary first day in Beirut, I sat propped up in bed under a small night light writing to my parents and sister, trying to describe all that had happened that day. It was difficult to convey in words the wonder of all the new sights and sounds and smells, the charm of my roommates, and the distinctive beauty of the AUB campus. But for me, writing was a way of sorting things out and making my family a part of these new experiences. In the past I had always been homesick when I went away from home—to summer camp as a child and when I started college—but in Beirut I was too captivated with all that I was doing and seeing to be homesick.

Sunlight was streaming in the windows, and the noise of loud shouting rose from the street below. I had been awakened from a sound sleep and remembered abruptly that I was in Beirut. It didn't feel like it was time to get up, and, sure enough, the clock only said 7:00; breakfast began at 8:00. I grabbed my robe and ran to the balcony to see what was happening. Men with vegetable carts were shouting what must have been the price and quality of their goods, and women in housecoats were leaning over their balconies, dangling baskets on ropes and shouting out their orders. Those who were yelling most vehemently were apparently haggling over prices. The vendors shouted back more vehemently, and finally some agreement would be reached, the baskets filled and hoisted up into the arms of the waiting housewives. My roommates, obviously accustomed to Beirut noises, were still asleep, but I stood there in the already hot early morning sun, enthralled with the color and novelty of the scene before me.

That morning was occupied with registration for classes, of which several recollections remain—the helpfulness of students and staff in the confusion of the registration process and the strange feeling of being a foreigner. I was conscious of looking different from other people on campus both in my physical appearance and in the way I was dressed, and the only language I knew was English. Everyone around me could also speak good English as well as Arabic and French, and sometimes creative combinations of all at once. By contrast to their beautifully accented English, I wondered if my American accent sounded harsh and if they might have trouble understanding me. I found myself trying to speak more carefully to sound like them.

This condition of foreignness somehow made me feel inadequate, an unfamiliar feeling, but I was conscious, at the same time, of being given privileged treatment. I wasn't sure if the extra courtesies were part of the warm Arab hospitality to newcomers or a certain deference paid to Westerners, especially a suntanned Californian with a big smile who was full of enthusiasm at the prospect of spending the coming year in their city at their American University.

Mrs. Kerr had already helped me map out my courses, a combination of education courses to meet requirements for my major at Occidental and courses on the Middle East. I registered for Philosophy of Education, Psychology of Education, Western and Islamic Philosophy, and Ottoman History. Classes would begin a week later.

Back outside the main gate of the campus on Rue Bliss, antiquated but picturesque red trolley cars jangled by every few minutes, going to and from the downtown area of Beirut. I had noticed them when our taxi had almost plowed into one on our ride from the port to the hostel the day before. I thought that a ride on a trolley might give me a good view of the city, so with a sense of impending adventure, I hopped aboard.

The best place to sightsee was on the small open platform at the back of the trolley where I had a commanding if fleeting view of the passing scene. We swung around one curve after another, barely missing big flashy American cars, donkeys and carts, shoppers, and porters lugging items as large as refrigerators on their backs, most of whom were traveling in the opposite direction because the street was one way for everything but trams.

The people on the crowded street were dressed in a variety of styles. Some men wore ill-fitting Western-style suits; others dressed in the local costume of black billowing trousers, white shirt, and a red-and-white-checked cloth around their heads, which looked much more interesting. Some of the more affluent shopkeepers wore turtle-neck sweaters and sleek, tight pants which I imagined they had imported from Italy. I saw men com-

ing out of banks and fancy shops dressed in elegantly tailored suits
and getting into chauffeur-driven cars. No trolley cars for them.

The passing scene from my perch on the tram platform continued. As counterpoints to all these colorful characters were the
clerics of the many religious orders in Lebanon. Greek Orthodox,
Roman Catholic, and Maronite priests in long white or black robes
peppered the population, adding a note of sobriety to the gaiety of
the streets. Occasionally I saw a small child in miniature priest's
clothing, which I later learned was a means of protecting him
from harm or of showing gratitude for some danger he had been
spared.

Many of the women walking along the street were dressed in
the high fashion that I had seen on the AUB campus, but there
were also more conservatively dressed, perhaps less affluent,
women wearing dowdy black coats or suits covering ample bodies
and a sheer veil which seemed intended to enhance rather than
conceal carefully made-up eyes and lips.

Here and there women wore the distinctive Kurdish costume
of bright cotton print, long-gathered skirt, full bodice, long
sleeves, and a small white headdress. Many carried a baby on their
back, papoose style. They seemed to comprise the scrub woman
contingent for the merchants, for in almost every store we passed,
I saw one of these Kurdish women bent over jack-knife style washing the floor. Those who weren't scrubbing walked jauntily in
groups along the street. Their bouncy gait was quite distinctive
from the slower, heavy pace of the conservative women in black,
or from the self-conscious, slightly shaky gait of the women in
spike heels and tight skirts.

The tram reached the main square of the downtown area, and
there was a great crush to get off. I followed the crowd and wondered which way to go first when a young, jovial-looking Lebanese
man came up and asked me in good English if he could show me
around. "I'm Ramez Azouri," he said and added that he was an
AUB medical student and had guessed that I was one of the new
American junior-year-abroad students. I was torn between this
chance to have a guided tour by a local citizen and being thought
an easy American pick-up in this culture where I knew the relations between men and women to be very formal. Throwing cau-
tion to the wind, I decided on the tour.

The novelty and excitement of what I was seeing in those first days in Lebanon was enchanting and remains in my mind as permanent visual images. They are a reminder of the freshness and innocence of beautiful Beirut in those golden days of the 1950s and 1960s and of the twenty-year-old who was seeing it for the first time. I cherish both the lasting mental pictures and the letters written long ago which are a reminder of a world that no longer exists.

Ramez led me to Bab-Idris, a popular shopping area where several of Beirut's major streets converged. A new attraction there was the ABC Variety Store, which he explained was very popular because Lebanese were used to going to different stores for whatever they needed and now they could do much of their shopping in one place. From Bab-Idris we crossed to Souk al-Franji (literally, foreign market) where many small shops and open stalls were packed closely together. This souk was a flower market full of color, and the air was permeated with the fragrance of jasmine. That led into Souk et-Tawili (long market), a long, narrow street where small wall-to-wall stores with modern facades built over old, domed Turkish buildings overflowed with everything anyone could want to buy in the way of women's clothing or sewing accessories. Souk et-Tawili, though not as long as the literal meaning of its name indicated, ended down by the sea front where we walked out of the narrow street onto a lovely palm-lined avenue, Avenue de Paris.

Slender palm trees stood in front of Mediterranean colonial buildings in rose beige stone with gracefully arched porches and windows. The grandest were the St. George Hotel and the Grand Hotel Bassoul. To the west was St. George's Bay and to the east the port of Beirut, full of gleaming ships whose whiteness was accentuated by the blueness of the sea and the dusky purple of the mountains of Lebanon rising behind the port. More narrow streets led us back to the center of town where we saw the cinemas, the Grand Mosque, small mosques, Armenian churches, Maronite churches, the gold souk with window after window of gold jewelry so bright that it appeared gawdy, and finally the produce souk full of artfully piled masses of brilliantly colored fruits and vegetables. We ended our tour back near the tramway stop where we had started, in a very French patisserie, sipping tea and eating small fancy cakes that looked better than they tasted.

I noticed that many shop and street signs were in French.

When I remarked on this and the stylish French fashions of Beirut, Ramez explained that the Lebanese had been enamored of things French ever since their mandate in Lebanon following World War I and that Beirut had developed a reputation for being the Paris of the Middle East. Even earlier, French culture had become part of Lebanon through the many churches, schools, and universities founded there by the French as far back as the early nineteenth century. The University of St. Joseph was the conveyor of that history and culture in east Beirut as AUB was the bearer of the American missionary and educational mission in the west.

My strongest memories of that tour and of my first days in Beirut are olfactory ones, good and bad. The odor of sun-baked urine emanated from corner walls and combined in my nostrils with smells of perspiration and garlic smothered by rose water. There were more pleasant odors too—roasting Turkish coffee, shish kebab broiling over charcoal, onions cooking in olive oil in preparation for a tasty stew, and the most enticing of all, the scent of jasmine in the warm night air.

Ramez got us onto the tram that led back to the university and escorted me back to the hostel. I hoped my roommates wouldn't see me in the company of a man so soon, for I knew that their culture did not allow the fraternizing of unmarried men and women, and I did not want to offend them. When he said good-bye, he added an invitation for the coming Saturday to go with some friends to the town of Aley, one of the well-known mountain resorts which are popular in the summer.

That night, as my roommates and I got ready for bed, I marveled at their knack of removing their clothes and putting on their nightgowns without ever revealing an inch of bare skin. They asked me about my activities of the day and my impressions of Beirut. When I mentioned having met Ramez, they said they knew him and thought he was very nice and from a good family. I knew that family honor and reputation were highly valued among Arabs and that Ramez had been given a stamp of approval in their comment.

Perhaps I need not have worried about my roommates' attitude toward my recreational activities. I sensed that they might apply a different set of standards for me than they would for themselves because I was a foreigner. I was further convinced of their open-mindedness when, as if to reassure me that I could enjoy social life during my time at AUB, they praised the advisor to women students for lengthening the hostel sign-in hours from 8:00 to 10:00 P.M. on weeknights and from 10:00 P.M. to midnight on Saturdays, all thanks to Mrs. Kerr.

I had accepted an invitation to lunch the next day at the family home of a young Lebanese woman, Shereen Khairallah, who had been a student at Occidental College before me. We had not met, but we had corresponded and she had sent me information on AUB and Beirut. We were now about to meet. Shereen came to the hostel, and we walked to her house down the street from the university. We passed first a small mosque where a few men were saying their noontime prayers, then a café where some less pious looking men were playing trictrac, a board game for two, and drinking small cups of Turkish coffee. Next door to the café a woman was busy beheading a chicken.

Shereen and I entered a small garden through a high iron gate, climbed some stairs past a door marked "Ibrahim Khairallah," up more stairs past a door marked "Yussef Khairallah," and finally up to the third floor to a door marked "Fuad Khairallah." "Those are the homes of my uncles," Shereen told me. "In the Middle East, extended families are very close." A maid came to the door and ushered us into a dark, ornately furnished living room where Shereen's mother and younger sister welcomed us effusively. Mrs. Khairallah looked Lebanese but spoke English with a New York accent. She explained that she had been born in Brooklyn and had met her husband while he was visiting his Lebanese relatives in New York. Their family, like many in Lebanon, had strong ties with the West and were part of both cultures. Two generations of their family had studied and taught at the American University of Beirut where they found a comfortable merging of East and West. Many had then done graduate work in the United States and returned to careers in Lebanon.

We had a sumptuous lunch of chicken and rice smothered in roasted pine nuts and almonds, humus, a dip of mashed chick peas, sesame oil and garlic, and tabbouleh, a salad of chopped parsley, tomatoes, green onions and mint mixed with crushed wheat, olive oil and lemon juice. This was my first real taste of the wonders of Lebanese cuisine and another sampling of the gracious-

ness of Arab hospitality. When it was time to leave they assured
me that I had a standing invitation to lunch whenever I was free.

That delicious meal was more than an introduction to the delights of Lebanese cuisine. The next morning when I tried to raise
my head from the pillow, it wouldn't budge. My insides ached. I
realized I had come down with the ailment common to newcomers
to the Middle East, familiarly known as tourist tummy or the
Lebanese leaps. My roommates and our house mothers hovered
over me feeding me yogurt and dry toast; by noon I thought I
would live. That was the most serious case of dysentery I had that
year. An immunity seemed to build up so that succeeding cases
were lighter.

Another open invitation for meals came from the families of
the Presbyterian missionaries working in Beirut schools and technical training programs. The American Board of Foreign Missions
had been sending missionaries, teachers, doctors, and students to
the Middle East since 1819. In coming to AUB, my fellow junior
year abroad students (known as JYAs) and I had joined the long
tradition of American educational and cultural exchange in the
Middle East, of which the Khairallahs, Kerrs, and countless families like them were a part. I had noticed the names of some of the
early missionaries and educators on the buildings of the campus,
Bliss Hall, Fiske Hall, and Van Dyke Hall. Like the Presbyterian
Church program that sponsored us, the founding fathers of AUB
had had a religious impetus behind their mission. Although the
major concern was less with proselytizing than with education and
medical care, there had always been some ardent souls eager to
make conversions for Protestant Christianity. After 1915 when
student protests and an Ottoman government education law
caused the college to end mandatory religious instruction, a required assembly was instituted which concentrated on moral con-
duct. This institution was still in place in the fifties, and my
roommates and fellow JYA students attended regularly three times
a week.

One day shortly before classes began, Ani Davanian, the
cousin of an Armenian friend from California, stopped at the hostel to welcome me to Beirut. After we got acquainted she asked
me if I would consider teaching English in a Catholic school
for Armenian children in the downtown section of the city. It

sounded like it might be interesting, and the thought of some extra money was also appealing. So Mrs. Davanian took me in her car to visit the school, a harrowing drive through the burj, the center of town where all trams, taxis, and private cars converged at high speed, and then through a maze of alleys past old walled villas. We came to a stop in front of a high wall of cream-colored stucco with orange trees peeking over the top. This was the Immaculate Conception School For Girls, almost indistinguishable from the other walled villas around it with hints of lush gardens inside, visible through open gates or cascades of bougainvillea streaming over the walls. There was no clue in the vitality and clamor of the burj or in the quiet stability of this old residential quarter that a war would rage here twenty years hence, leaving it a no-man's-land of deserted, burned-out buildings.

Hanging beside a heavy wooden door was a long rope. My friend yanked on it a few times, which caused a loud clanging that brought several nuns and several girls in blue uniforms to the door. A particularly ethereal looking nun was a cousin of Mrs. Davanian. She escorted us to a dark, high-ceilinged room decorated with potted palms and pictures of Jesus. Chairs and sofas ringed the room with small tables at frequent intervals. We sat down to await the arrival of the Mother Superior, joined by the other nuns and girls who had opened the door. Within minutes of our arrival small cups of sweet, muddy coffee were brought to Mrs. Davanian and me in the typical Middle Eastern gesture of welcome. I had a hard time swallowing the unfamiliar drink, which I later learned to savor.

When the Mother Superior entered everyone jumped to attention and several students rushed to pull up a chair for her. Sister Suzanne, with the ethereal face, and Mrs. Davanian led the discussion in a combination of Armenian and French. Arrangements were made for my teaching schedule, or so I learned once Mrs. Davanian translated everything into English for me. With business matters completed, the Mother Superior and Sister Suzanne escorted me into the classroom of my prospective students. There at hard wooden desks sat twenty or so plumpish, blue-uniformed Armenian girls in their early teens. They jumped to attention and then, almost in unison, a sigh of disbelief came forth as if they had never seen an American before, at least not in their school. Shy

smiles broke out on their faces as their attention was diverted from
the commanding presence of the Mother Superior to me, a foreigner only six or seven years older than they. "Good–Af–ter–
noon," they all chimed out. "Most of the girls know only a few
words of English," Mrs. Davanian explained. "The sisters would
like you to teach a class of beginning English to girls of thirteen
and fourteen and another slightly more advanced class to girls of
sixteen and seventeen." I explained that I would be taking classes
every day at AUB until 2:00 P.M. but would like to teach at their
school after that. My salary would be three Lebanese pounds per
class, about a dollar in 1954.

The next day I began what was to become a routine, four
afternoons a week for the entire school year. At 2:00, after my
classes at AUB were over, I took the tram from the university
down through the burj, got off two stops beyond, and then
walked through the maze of narrow streets, hoping to end up in
the right one. I found the door, pulled the rope, and waited for
Sister Suzanne to come. After hearty "Bon Jours," we began com-
municating vigorously in smiles, nods, and sign language as she
escorted me to my class.

When we entered, the plump, smiling girls all clambered to
their feet and said haltingly, "Good–Af–ter–noon." This was the
advanced class and I had visions of introducing them to great literature, so I was understandably disappointed when I instructed
them to open their books to page one and got only blank looks in
response. I wondered if their lack of interest could be blamed on
the dullness of the books. So I put the textbooks aside and decided
to talk to them informally and find out what their interests were.

I started by telling them what I was doing in Beirut and got
nothing but more blank looks. Perhaps my American accent was
unfamiliar, or perhaps I spoke too fast. I plunged in again. "My
home is in California." "Cal–ee–forn–ya," several girls chirped.
"You go to Hol–lee–wood?" they questioned. I tried to explain to
them that Hollywood was just a few miles from where I lived.
They must have gotten the point, for they all piped up, "You
know Mar–leen Mon–ro?" "You know Dor–eese Day?" "You look
like Dor–eese Day."

We used up a good ten minutes exchanging tidbits of information while the girls betrayed their vast knowledge of movies
and movie stars. I was congratulating myself on the excellent

classroom atmosphere of balanced discipline and free expression when Sister Suzanne stood up and left the room.

The instant the door closed, all hell broke loose. Everyone started talking at once in Armenian. They jumped up and down, racing from seat to seat. I implored them to please be quiet but could not be heard above the uproar. Anyway, even if they had not been so noisy, they probably would not have understood me because I now knew that their English was limited to the subject of movies and movie stars.

When Sister Suzanne glided back into the room everyone jumped to attention. The stern tones of her reprimands brought the students to order. She turned the class back to me and remained in the corner of the room while I struggled to redeem my reputation during the remaining class time. The second hour with the "intermediate" group was much the same story but the students were even less advanced in English. I felt more and more dejected.

Assuming that my services would be terminated, I left the class when the bell clanged, wondering how "you're fired" sounded in Armenian. My morale was somewhat boosted by the crowds of girls that swarmed around me asking more questions about Cal—ee—forn—ya and Hol—lee—wood. Sister Suzanne smiled and thanked me profusely and said something in French that sounded like it might mean see you tomorrow.

So the next day I returned, hoping I still had a job. The fanfare of the day before greeted my arrival. This time when Sister Suzanne left the class, the rise in noise volume was not so noticeable. The girls must have been given a good lecture by the Mother Superior. With the small age difference between us and my American informality and lack of experience in disciplining teenagers, order never reigned in my classes as it did in those of the nuns. If it had, the students probably never would have learned much English.

As the year progressed, we became good friends and the students learned to talk about something other than movie stars. I realized that I loved teaching for the exchange and communication it made possible and for the opportunity to see how differently individual minds worked. Our constant conversation meant access for me into their world as much as it opened mine to them.

I heard many stories from my students of the flight from the

Turks of their parents and grandparents during the Armenian massacres in the earlier part of the century and of their resettling in other places in the Middle East. Similar accounts were later told to me by Malcolm's father who had lived through some of these events in Turkey at the end of World War I, when he had worked with the Near East Relief. My students seemed to have been raised on tales of atrocities to the Armenians which went back more than fifty years.

Since leaving California I had heard a lot about the feeling of bitterness of one national group for another. The Dutch officers on the freighter to Beirut had poured out their stories of German offenses in World War II. My roommates Roshan and Katie had told me about their families losing their homes and property when they fled from Israel in 1948. And now I was learning about another historical animosity between the Armenians and the Turks. I was both struck and saddened by the way these national resentments were perpetuated and passed on within families from one generation to the next.

The last days before classes began at AUB were busy with the usual school preparations. We bought textbooks, the same American textbooks used in United States universities; we had physical exams, got library cards, and tried to find out something about our professors and the classes we would be taking.

We Presbyterian junior year abroad students were part of a larger group of perhaps thirty Americans studying at AUB, some graduate students, some Americans living in the area, and a few other junior year abroad students from different programs. Mrs. Kerr invited the fifteen or so new American girls at AUB to her house for a little advising and preparation for the year ahead. She lived in a Mediterranean-style house at one corner of the campus in a wooded canyon with a view of the sea through the trees. As we approached down a hill and across a bridge over a small creek to get there, I wondered what Mrs. Kerr was doing with such a big house. One of the young women explained that she had a husband and four children. Professor Kerr was a biochemistry professor in the medical school but only one of the two sons was living at home while studying at AUB.

We sat in the garden sipping tea while the maid passed us cookies. Mrs. Kerr pointed out some of the cultural differences we would be encountering, some of which I had already glimpsed in my roommates and my new friend Ramez. In a caring manner she told us that American girls had a reputation among Lebanese for being casual with men and that we should be careful not to be taken advantage of. We were also admonished not to cling together in small groups of Americans, and to study hard.

Unconcerned about being taken advantage of, I went with Ramez to the mountains as planned on Saturday. Our taxi driver took us at high speed around hairpin curves, evidently trying to prove the Lebanese claim that the mountains were only a twenty-minute drive from the sea. Regardless of proximity, they were the most beautiful mountains I'd ever seen, steep rising and craggy. We drove through villages dotted with houses with red tile roofs and clumps of pine woods.

Beirut looked even more beautiful as we got further away from it. Distance and sun made it sparkle white against the blue Mediterranean, contrasted on the outskirts of the city by patches of rust-colored sand spotted with the deep green tops of umbrella pines. Beyond this narrow coastal plain, the mountains rose up steeply in shadowy beiges and blues that changed to pink as the sun set. We drove up and up, past villagers doing their late afternoon chores, shepherds caring for their sheep, and donkeys bobbing along laden with passengers or produce, stopping occasionally for a rusty hee-haw.

When we reached Aley, the pastoral scene changed abruptly. We had arrived at a small Beirut. There were high apartment buildings with small stores tucked between them, street vendors, tourists, expensive cars and luxurious hotels. After strolling a while we found La Piscine, the restaurant that was our destination, perched on a mountaintop overlooking the coastline of Lebanon and surrounded by pools and gardens. The diners gave evidence of what Ramez had told me: that Lebanon was the vacation spot for people from all over the Middle East and that for them this was indeed a small Paris.

Kuwaiti and Saudi shaykhs sat regally in their long robes puffing on their nargilehs (water pipes), basking in the coolness of the Lebanese mountains after the torrid summer heat of their own countries. Beirut socialites sipped their drinks at their tables and nibbled on a meza, a sort of Lebanese hors d'oeuvres consisting of up to twenty different delicacies, each served in a small dish, including tiny birds fried whole that had a suggestion of boney bacon, and pickled sheep's testicles and intestines. My taste ran more to the salted almonds and juicy black Lebanese olives or to the humus and tabbouleh and baba ghanouj, the latter a dip of charcoal-broiled eggplant mashed with sesame oil, garlic and lemon juice.

For me it was not just the Frenchness nor the Arabness nor the Armenianness that made Lebanon so appealing, but rather the collage of them all in a cultural and linguistic blend of charm and style and color. I was happily unaware of the precariousness of the political and religious underpinnings of this collage and of the tragedy the instability portended.

Along with the appeal of the blend of cultures was the physical beauty of the country in its variety of seascapes and mountain vistas, added to the genuine warmth and hospitality of the people who lived there. In the few weeks since my arrival, I had become completely smitten with this lovely place.

CHAPTER 4

Meeting Malcolm

From the Regina Bar to the Milk Bar

As classes got underway, Mrs. Kerr's fears for threats to the virtuous reputation of young American women proved to be needless, at least in my case. I was caught up in a whirl of international dating. During the first two weeks of school, I went out with two Lebanese men, a Palestinian, and a Greek, men I had met in my classes or through introductions in my quickly widening circle of new friends.

One evening, however, when I was with my Greek friend at the Regina Bar, a popular dive in Beirut's glamorous nightclub district down near St. George's Bay, I was perhaps beginning to feel nostalgic for things American. Across the small, jam-packed room, I noticed a couple of blue cord summer jackets. In the eyes of a young college woman from California, these jackets represented East Coast Ivy League America, a realm of ultimate culture and sophistication. Inside the jackets were two men who, either because of the smoke-filled room or because of my recent preoccupation with non-Americans, looked virtually the same: tall, slim, clean-cut, boyish features, light brown hair. Whether through homesickness, the appeal of the Ivy League, or newly discovered chauvinism, I felt a certain interest.

The next weekend there was a Sunday afternoon tea dance at the hostel. I was dancing with someone when one of the cord jackets cut in. This time it was easier to see who was inside. Filling it out in a rather skinny fashion was a tall, nice-looking man. "I'm Malcolm Kerr," he said in an accent that sounded as if it might be British. I'd heard his last name before, but I'd never met anyone named Malcolm. How could he be Mrs. Kerr's son if he were British, I wondered.

"I'm working on an M.A. in Middle Eastern Studies," he said, "and spending two years in Beirut with my family." Well, he may have been an intellectual, but he wasn't a very good dancer, and I was glad when he suggested refreshments. My suspicions about his Ivy Leagueness were confirmed when we began to discuss where we had come from. He had graduated from Princeton before coming to AUB, which explained the cord jacket, an unfamiliar commodity not only in Beirut but also in California, as were clipped accents, the name Malcolm, and Americans who could speak Arabic. I didn't quite know what to make of all this, but I felt an undeniable attraction and hoped we would meet again.

Two weeks passed without my seeing Malcolm anywhere on campus. Then one day he came hobbling into my Ottoman history class on crutches. Professor Zeine's exuberant stories in expressive, slightly accented English of the escapades of the Turks and the administering of their Middle Eastern empire were lost on me that day. I was consumed with curiosity for an explanation of the crutches and the long absence, but for all I knew he wouldn't even remember me.

Finally the class ended and I lingered in my seat hoping to be intercepted. Out of the corner of my eye I saw Malcolm coming toward me with a shy smile of recognition. "Have you been skiing?" I asked him. "I just had a bout of arthritis," he explained. "It's something I've had before; it comes and goes." Then he added, "Would you like to go to the Milk Bar?" There's nothing I'd rather do, I thought to myself, but I just said, "Sure."

The Milk Bar was the campus snack shop on the second floor of the student union building, a short walk from College Hall and a popular hangout for students and faculty. We chose a table by the window looking out through the tops of pine and cypress trees to the Mediterranean. A young waiter with a big smile came up to take our order. That same smile on an increasingly older face was to greet us each time we went back to Beirut over the next decades, though in time he graduated from the Milk Bar to the faculty dining room. He obviously knew Malcolm for he started talking to him in Arabic. Then he disappeared and soon returned with two tall glasses of frothy, freshly squeezed orange juice. "How did you learn to speak Arabic so well?" I asked Malcolm. "I should speak it a lot better than I do since I was born here, but I didn't learn much till I went to college in the States." He went on to say that his family had had Armenian maids when he was growing up in Lebanon and that everyone around AUB spoke English, so he had had too little opportunity to speak Arabic. I detected a certain modesty in this explanation, perhaps combined with high standards of expectation for performance difficult to fathom for one who was proud to have recently learned to say *marhaba* (hello) and *masalama* (good-bye).

What a nice nose he has, I thought to myself, as I observed the smooth line of his profile when he turned his head toward the view through the trees outside. There was a suggestion of an upward turn at the end, just the kind of nose I had always wanted, instead of the aquiline variety I had inherited from my maternal grandmother.

"What made you want to come to AUB?" he asked, his head tilted slightly to one side, suggesting gentle curiosity. Unable to feign a burning intellectual interest in the Middle East, I admitted I had come out of a sense of adventure. Then I told Malcolm about the geographical compromise that had come about between my wish to go to India and my parents' preference for Europe. "If the minister of our church hadn't come home from a trip to the Middle East and raved about the AUB campus, I might never have come here."

"Are you glad you chose AUB?" Malcolm asked in that slightly British accent that was so appealing. Indeed I was, and I tried to explain the fascination I had felt from the day I arrived with all the new sights and sounds and smells of this intriguing country. "It sounds like you've seen more of it than I have," he remarked, "at least lately since I've been tied down with this arthritis."

When I asked Malcolm about his arthritis he talked about it in an offhand way, almost as if the subject bored him and he was anxious to get on to something else. That was, in fact, the way he treated this ailment all his life. It was a nuisance that bothered him sometimes and not others; when it was bothering him he accommodated it—took aspirin or cut out tennis and other physical activities.

Our orange juice glasses were empty and I thought that maybe he wanted to leave, but then he suggested that we have some Turkish coffee. I had tried this sweet, muddy beverage a few weeks earlier at Shereen's house and hadn't liked it very much, but it made a good reason to stay longer.

We compared notes on the classes we were taking, and Malcolm told me that he was doing a Master's thesis on the civil wars in Lebanon between 1840 and 1860. "It's an old story," he explained summarily, in response to my query as to what they were about, "one big tribal family fighting against another, usually Christians, Druze, and Muslims. These rivalries have been going on in this country for centuries." I sensed a reluctance in him to talk further about his work, and I was disappointed because I wanted to know more.

It is difficult to recreate now just what specific words or glances or gestures occurred during that first extended conversation or to give any explanation for the mutual attraction we felt. There was certainly an element of admiration on my part for Malcolm's linguistic and academic accomplishments, along with liking the shape of his nose, the slight shyness of his smile, and the unfolding discovery of his irreverent sense of humor. For Malcolm's part, perhaps he too was attracted to what was different about me than what he was used to, a Californian unhampered by eastern or Middle Eastern reserve.

·   ·   ·

It is difficult, too, to recreate these two young people who grew and changed over the next thirty years incorporating those youthful selves into layers of experience and maturing that made us quite different people by 1984. From the Regina Bar and the Milk Bar, our friendship moved fast. The day after that first meeting in class, Malcolm came into the Ottoman history class and sat down beside me and those seats became ours for the semester. After class, visits to the Milk Bar grew into a daily occurrence with long conversations over orange juice and Turkish coffee.

A few days after that initial encounter in Professor Zeine's Ottoman history class, Malcolm asked me if I would like to go to a concert at West Hall and have dinner at his parents' house first. I said yes, of course. It was quite different being at the Kerrs' house that second visit than when I had gone there for tea as a new junior year abroad student. All of Mrs. Kerr's friendliness and Dr. Kerr's jokes allayed my self-consciousness only a little. I remember just nibbling at the delicious, home-cooked American dinner, partly from the nervousness of infatuation and partly to make my appetite appear more delicate than it really was.

At West Hall that night, a well-known Lebanese pianist, Diana Takiedeen, played Mozart and Bach to a full house against the challenge of a less than perfect piano and poor acoustics. The music was beautiful anyway and became all the more so when Malcolm slipped his hand over mine. I soon forgot any other romantic interests that might have been brewing, thereby closing my brief period of international mingling with the opposite sex.

Before long Malcolm and I found that we had an even greater common interest in the movies than in Ottoman history. He was anxious to show me that the cinema in Beirut added a dimension of adventure beyond that in America.

One Friday night we took a tram downtown to the burj where every other building seemed to be a movie theater showing the latest American films. Huge signs covering the whole side of a theater advertised each movie, portraying the actors in dramatically charged scenes. "I'll bet you never knew Doris Day was an Arab, did you?" Malcolm asked me as we looked at the wall coverings. Painted by a local artist, she did have a surprisingly Middle Eastern look about her.

Student tickets at the movies were half-price, which brought the cost down to practically nothing. This was going to be a big movie year, I could see. Malcolm confirmed what I had gleaned from my Armenian students, that any year seemed to be a big movie year for Beirut students. He told me about a poll (taken by the AUB newspaper questioning how many times a week students went to the movies) which reported that the majority of students fit into the five or six times a week category. A slightly smaller number attended more than seven times a week. "Maybe we can top that," Malcolm suggested in a challenging tone.

The theater inside looked pretty much like an American one with customers crowded around the popcorn machine and candy counter. We sat in the balcony, apparently the only proper place for women, judging from the looks of things below where there wasn't one in sight. The few women around us were students or foreigners. At that time Middle Eastern women in lower socio-economic groups usually stayed at home when their husbands went out to public places, preferring family visits or staying at home with their children.

Loud music blared out while advertisements in phosphorescent colors on a black background flashed on the screen. Some ads were in Arabic, some in English, some in French, but most were in an amusing linguistic and cultural combination of the three. An Arab woman told us in French why we should buy Tide, and an American woman in dubbed-in Arabic told us the importance of Johnson's Baby Powder. When the previews of coming attractions came on, Malcolm was enthusiastic about all of them. "Let's go next week to see that Henry Fonda film," he announced with anticipation. "Maybe there'll be a double feature with the Alfred Hitchcock mystery." Malcolm's taste in movies was varied and uncritical, unlike his taste in music which was limited to early classical and an occasional opera. But it could be argued that movies of the fifties were the classical era of cinema, with actors who were truly stars and themes that were romantic and idealistic. We of that generation were surely influenced by those themes.

The ads and the music competed for about twenty minutes until finally the lights came on and we had louder music but no ads. Flashing signs on the screen announcing NO SMOKING were soon obliterated by a smokey haze that grew denser and denser. Looking around for a neon exit sign, I realized that the only way out was the entrance we had come through earlier.

Lights dimmed and the newsreel came on showing one round of Arab officials after another shaking hands or kissing each other on both cheeks at some function promoting Arab unity. "What do you suppose they're really thinking about each other behind all that glad-handing?" Malcolm conjectured as we munched on our popcorn. The newsreel was whetting his appetite for the subject he loved most, the complexities of inter-Arab politics.

The movie we saw had been filmed on location in California. Seeing familiar scenes from home was somewhat startling, but the real shock came when it was over and we walked back out into the bustle of the Arab world. It was a busy time of day in a popular neighborhood. All manner of people waited to pounce on the out-coming crowd. Beggars cried to us that God would be pleased if we gave them some money, while Chiclet boys pushed boxes of chewing gum in our hands demanding money whether we wanted to buy them or not. A variety of salesmen tried to sell us sticky Arab pastries or combs or collar tabs. Malcolm guided me out to the street where a bumper-to-bumper line of taxis awaited us, each of whose drivers commanded that we should ride in his taxi. Choosing the least vociferous, we drove back to Ras Beirut and the tranquility of the AUB campus.

In the Kerrs' kitchen we opened a can of Campbell's soup and made sandwiches for another throwback into a more familiar cul-ture. "Ham or cheese or both," Malcolm asked, as he pulled some American packaged food out of the refrigerator. The smell of the vegetable soup heating and the atmosphere of that American kitchen brought welcome familiarity after the recent bombard-ment of new sights and sounds. But the contrast was invigorating and the accessibility of both the novel and familiar cultures at the same time tickled my sense of adventure. It also added to the appeal to be falling in love with someone who was part of both worlds.

Malcolm's parents conveniently disappeared upstairs, and we sat on the living room couch, sipping the warm soup and eating our sandwiches, lingering long after the food had been consumed. Mrs. Kerr had said nothing about amorous advances from Ameri-can men, particularly her own son on her own couch. So every-thing was all right.

With so many new things to see and do it was hard to concen-trate much on schoolwork, but going to the library served the dual purpose of convincing me that I was studying and providing a convenient place to meet Malcolm. The library had recently been built in back of College Hall with a large terrace in between. The new building of plain white concrete did not fit well with the beautiful old rosy stone campus buildings which had been built seventy-five years earlier, and the slab of concrete in front did not enhance it. Several small palm trees were planted across the ter-race. Over the years each time Malcolm and I returned to Beirut those trees had grown taller, and when he occupied the president's office on the third floor of College Hall, the tops of those palm trees were visible outside his windows.

I would enter the library reading room and sit at one of the long tables beneath the big statue of Daniel Bliss, trying to concentrate on my work but looking up occasionally to see if Malcolm had come into the reading room. When he arrived, the charade would cease as we went outside and headed for one of the campus benches beneath pines overlooking the sea where the fragrance of hot sun on pine needles mingled with sea breezes. Malcolm always kept his eyes peeled for the sooty black-shelled snoubar pine nuts which fell from the trees, a habit he learned in childhood which soon I, and later our children, adopted. In the rocky land of Lebanon there was always a stone close at hand for cracking open the hard shell so that we could pick out the delicious nut inside.

"The nicest place in Lebanon is our summer house in the mountains," Malcolm told me as we sat on a campus bench one day looking out at the Mediterranean. "How can it be nicer than this?" I asked. There was a cool breeze coming from the sea and the air smelled fresh. "It's not that it's any more beautiful, it's just different. You'll have to see for yourself."

The next weekend, a Sunday in late November, we drove with his parents to their house in the village of Ainab for a picnic. The route was familiar to me from my earlier trip to the restaurant in Aley with Ramez, but this time we turned off before reaching the town and drove south along a winding mountain road amidst the huge pines and red tile-roofed houses, all the while looking down the steep drop to the coastal plain and the sea sparkling beyond. The fall season in Lebanon reminded me of California when cooler air brought clearer views but the sun remained strong and warming.

The first village of any size we passed through was Souk El Gharb, literally, western market in Arabic. True to its name, stalls of bright colored fruits and vegetables lined the streets, interspersed with small grocery stores where merchants packed their floor to ceiling shelves with every possible supply village people might need. Shopkeepers were bundled up in heavy pullovers or long woolen caftan robes to protect themselves from "the change of seasons" which I have observed people around the Mediterranean refer to as the cause of any ailment that befalls them in spring or fall.

"Take three kilos," the handsome, ruddy-cheeked man with bright brown eyes said to us as we surveyed the huge, red apples he and his two young sons were artistically piling up in broad baskets at the front of their shop. The morning sun accentuated the redness of the apples as well as the ruddiness of the cheeks of these handsome mountain people. We settled on two kilos to add to our picnic and went on our way.

The road continued from Souk El Gharb on to the next village of Shimlan, a smaller and even more beautiful village of stone houses and gardens linked by narrow alleys and steep stairsteps, all overlooking a vast expanse of blue. "Look up there in the mountains above the road," Malcolm's father told me. "That's the British Arabic language training school. They're often accused of being a spy training center—maybe they are," he added with the same irreverent chuckle I often heard from Malcolm.

"There's my favorite restaurant," Malcolm said, pointing down a small road where built right on top of a rocky cliff was an old stone house with a long terrace covered with grapevines. Still too early for lunch, only a few male customers sat at a couple of the tables sipping Turkish coffee or puffing away at their water pipes and playing trictrac. By a round walled pool under a huge tree in the entry courtyard sat the women of the family, pounding ground lamb in stone basins to make into the famous Lebanese kibbeh and chopping parsley, mint, tomatoes, and onions to make tabbouleh. Too bad we couldn't wait for lunch.

From the restaurant, which was on the outskirts of Shimlan, we drove through pine woods and then right into the village of Ainab, less picturesque and less prosperous than its neighbor but bestowed with the same magnificent view. Observing church steeples as well as mosques in the village, I asked Malcolm how these people got along together. "There are a lot of mixed Christian and Muslim villages here in the Shouf region," he told me. "They've been coexisting for a long time, though occasionally they have problems. The Christians are better off financially than the Muslims." Malcolm explained that more than half of the Christians in Lebanon were Maronites, a sect named after their patron saint, Maron of Antioch, who is thought to have introduced Christianity to the area in the fourth century. There was also a sizable group of Greek Orthodox and other Eastern Orthodox groups, as well as

Roman Catholics and Protestants. The largest concentration of Maronites lived north of Beirut in the central part of the country.

As we drove through the village, church bells were chiming and the midday call to prayer was ringing out of mosques, all in a medley of sounds that seemed strange but beautiful to me. We turned off the main road and headed up through Ainab until we came to the end of the village. The spring after which the village was named had one of its outlets there and nearby was a cluster of stone houses completely shaded from the sun by huge mulberry trees. Although we seemed to have come to a dead end, there beyond the spring was something resembling a road, but it looked almost impassable. A small, hand-painted signpost in English and Arabic said "Private Road."

"It always seems as if we're not going to make it up this road, but we always do," Malcolm's mother assured me as we bounced along the road. The four of us were thrown back and forth from one side of the car to the other, but each bend going up the road brought a view of distant mountains and valleys, a different vantage of soft colors at every turn.

The road leveled out at the top of the mountain, and we drove into a pine grove and stopped right beside a tennis court. A village tennis court it certainly was with pine tree roots pushing up through the surface here and there and piles of pine needles blown into the corners. Dr. Kerr proudly explained that he and four other AUB professors who shared the hilltop had built this court themselves some thirty years earlier.

The five AUB families who bought the land in the early thirties had divided it into half-acre parcels, leaving the center for the tennis court. Each built their own local style house under umbrella pines which produced the delicious snoubar Malcolm had described to me. The entire hilltop was carpeted with layers of pine needles which gave the Ainab air a distinctive fragrance. "Hunting for snoubars in these pine needles was like a perpetual Easter egg hunt," Malcolm reminisced nostalgically.

Up the hill visible from the tennis court through the trees were two stone houses similar to the ones we had seen in the villages below, but with a certain American flavor to them. They were simply constructed with one or two stories, red tile roofs and Mediterranean-style wooden shutters. Unlike the houses in the village, these all had uniformly painted dark-green shutters, and the hilly land around them was left completely natural. "Our house is down on the other side of the hilltop where no one can see us," Malcolm's mother said in a manner revealing a preference for the Kerr site.

We unloaded the car and carried our picnic paraphernalia over the west side of the hilltop down a long path under umbrella pines to the Kerrs' house. Amidst the pines were two wooden cabins, in addition to the main house, which Malcolm referred to as sleeping shacks where he and his brother and sisters slept. "Under here is our water supply," he explained as we walked across a large flat cement terrace supported by a stone retaining wall along the canyon side. "Rain water collects on the roof and runs down that pipe into the cistern," he said, pointing to the corner of the roof.

A double arch in stone led to a small entry porch and big wooden door of the house. Dr. Kerr unlocked the door and pushed it open. We stepped from the brilliant sun into the cool, musty air, entrapped there since the house had been shuttered up at the end of the summer. The faint smell of dank ashes emanated from the fireplace that took up half of one wall of the small living room. Two hallways extended from the living room, one leading to the kitchen and bathroom, the other to the master bedroom.

Mrs. Kerr threw open the shutters on the living room windows in a gesture that I had seen among Beirut housewives in apartment buildings near the campus at the end of the afternoon when the sun sank and it was time to let in cool air. In the kitchen, Malcolm and his father primed the pump which brought water up from the cistern to a single spigot above a small sink. Beside it was a two-burner primus for heating water and cooking. Coleman lanterns were lined up on a shelf above. "You can see why we bring our maid up with us in the summers," Dr. Kerr told me. "If we didn't we wouldn't have much time to play tennis."

After lunch, Malcolm took me on a tour of the hilltop to show me favorite places from his childhood. There were no boundary markers between the five properties. One flowed into the other with their separate houses nestled into different parts of the hilltop, each with a different stunning view of distant mountains and valleys, and from the northwestern side, the Mediterranean and the city of Beirut far in the distance. "The families who didn't want to see Beirut in the summer chose the side of the hilltop away from the city when they were dividing up the land in the early thirties to begin building," Malcolm explained. Each house had an open space under the pines with table and chairs set up for outdoor eating and another area in the woods designated as the tea place where families would have afternoon tea and read or talk.

"After tea time everyone gathered here by the tennis court," Malcolm said as we reached the center of the hilltop with its funny bumpy court and makeshift chicken wire fence. Stone slabs had been piled in a semicircle by one side of the court with a large bonfire pit in the center for special evening barbecues and singing. Malcolm always knew every word to campfire songs, the result, he claimed, of years of Ainab barbecues and songfests.

Malcolm's greatest nostalgia was for the intricate network of miniature car roads built into the limestone rocks near his house by the resident fathers. He had spent long summer hours pushing toy cars around those roads just as our own children would do some years later.

In a small ravine at the edge of their property Malcolm showed me his father's vineyard, the only one on the hilltop, and the variety of grafting of different sorts of grapes and fruit trees which was one of the many hobbies of this versatile professor of biochemistry. From there we followed a trail that led into the woods to an old manzanita tree, the favorite climbing tree of the hilltop children. It was easily recognizable by its large size and slippery red bark which had caused the children to call it "the slippery tree." The rusty redness of its bark and the low fat trunk with branches spreading out to form a large place to sit made it stand out against the slender pines and chaparral around it. Its location high up in a canyon giving access to a view of the Mediterranean far in the distance added to its appeal. We sat there for a long time while Malcolm reminisced about the antics of the hilltop children.

Another of their favorite places, but far more mysterious, was the Druze khalwa, or temple, further up the trail. It was a holy place, looking now like a crumbling haunted house, where the elders of the local Druze families met to perform the secret rites of their religion, rites that went back to the twelfth century in Egypt when the Druze sect broke away from traditional Islam. We had passed some of these old village shaykhs on the way up to Ainab, striking looking with their flowing white beards, craggy faces, red tarboosh hats, and billowing black pants. Even now the old khalwa seemed rather forbidding. It was easy to understand why Malcolm and his young friends had found it scary.

On the other side of the mountain we emerged from the woods and came to an old Turkish gun road running along the crest overlooking a huge valley and beyond to the shadowy blues and purples of the Anti-Lebanon range. We were standing on the western or coastal side of the pair of mountain ranges, called the Lebanon and the Anti-Lebanon, that ran the three-hundred-mile length of the country from its northern to southern border. The name Lebanon came from an ancient Aramaic word for white, aptly named for its many snow-capped peaks in winter, including Mt. Hermon in the south and Mt. Sanneen which provided a striking view from the AUB campus.

The breathtaking beauty of these ancient hills and valleys brought to mind passages from the *Song of Solomon* evoking the glory of biblical Lebanon. "Come with me from Lebanon my bride, come with me from Lebanon. . . . Your lips distil nectar, my bride; honey and milk are under your tongue; the scent of your garments is like the scent of Lebanon. . . . Your shoots are an orchard of pomegranates with all the choicest fruits . . . a garden fountain, a well of living water and flowing streams from Lebanon . . ."

Malcolm described the story of the old gun roads with relish. I observed that his enthusiasm for talking about Middle Eastern history in this context was much keener than it had been at the Milk Bar when I asked him to tell me about his Master's thesis or to review our notes from Professor Zeine's class. As if reliving the impressionable days of his childhood when he and his friends had played mock war games on these gun roads, he described how Ottoman soldiers had trekked and pulled their artillery, stopping to set it up in the strategically placed gun embankments he took me into—now overgrown with grass and red anemones mingled with goat droppings. In their innocent games, those American children had no inkling that some decades later a real war of such complications would rage in these mountains that their own countrymen would be shelling the local inhabitants, striking even the Ainab hilltop houses and the old tennis court.

Alongside the gun road further on, we came to some large flat boulders shaded by tall pines, clearly another of Malcolm's favorite spots. He led me down to the edge of the boulders where there was a steep drop to a village perhaps a hundered feet below. "That's Baysoor, the poor neighbor of Ainab. It's mainly Muslim and not very prosperous, like most Muslim villages." From our bird's perch vantage it was hard to judge its economic status, but Baysoor did not have much of the classic nineteenth-century style architecture of Shimlan and Ainab, whose fine arcaded stone buildings with balconies and arched windows gave these towns such character. It did have, however, a rich assortment of village noises that wafted right up to where we were sitting—babies crying, donkeys braying, snatches of conversation caught by the wind, and the muezzin calling the faithful to mid-afternoon prayer. We sat there for a long time, listening to those sounds and gazing at the distant mountains, feeling very close to each other and to the land of Lebanon.

Malcolm pointed out snowcapped Mt. Hermon far to the south and told me about how he and some friends had climbed it as young boys, camped at the peak, and the next day raced back down to see who could make it the fastest. In the mountains to the north were dark green splotches barely discernible in the far distance. Malcolm explained that these were among the few remaining cedars of Lebanon that covered much of the country in biblical times. On the nearer mountains were terraced farmlands with orchards of almond trees, waiting for early spring to be the first of the flowering trees to blossom. Far down at the bottom of the valley was a narrow river wending its way to the sea. "That's Damour," Malcolm pointed out. "We used to take a trail down there to go swimming." He described the steep canyon where high rock walls formed a big pool and the water was deep enough for diving into the cold water.

By the time we got back to the Kerr house, we had circled the whole mountain. Malcolm's enthusiasm for all he was showing me had made him forget his arthritic feet, but now he was tired and we collapsed in the big wicker chaise longues beneath the pine trees. This introduction to the Ainab hilltop, the Kerr house, and visits to childhood haunts had given me a taste of Malcolm's love for his adoptive country and served also to enhance my growing affection for this land.

We drove back down to Beirut in the late afternoon, watching the mountains become rose-colored as the sun lowered over the Mediterranean leaving a brilliant glow in its path across the sea to the horizon.

That evening in the hostel, I described the unspoiled beauty of Ainab to my roommates, and then I wrote about it in my Sunday evening letter home to my parents. I wanted for them to come and see the beauty of this new country I had discovered, but I knew the travel expense would be prohibitive when they had to worry about sending two daughters through college. But I prevailed upon my sister Jane, now a high school senior who had an afternoon job working in a dentist's office and did frequent baby-sitting, to save her money to come and visit at the end of the school year. From then on in our letters back and forth, we talked about making this idea a reality.

Christmas is a well-celebrated holiday in Lebanon and by early December in the hostel we were busy planning our Christmas party. Muslim students joined Christians for this event, for they had no scruples against the celebration of the birthday of Jesus, who was considered one of the prophets of their own religion. In any case, the party would be a decidedly secular event. Names were drawn for gift exchanging and decisions made about whom to invite and what to serve. Naturally, we would have tabbouleh and humus and some Christmas cakes from a favorite patisserie.

I invited Malcolm, even though I knew that his mother would be coming anyway as the guest of honor and that he might come with her as he had to the tea dance at the beginning of the semester. Most of the hostel girls did not invite a male guest, but we issued a general invitation to the men's dormitory for anyone who was interested to join us.

As I walked up the stairs of the hostel to my room on the day of the party, an unfamiliar sweet burning odor filled the air. I opened the door and found half the young women from our floor busily rubbing their arms and legs and faces with what looked like taffy. "What are you doing?" I asked. Salma, a good friend from the room down the hall, explained that they were removing the hair from their bodies. "We boil sugar and water and lemon juice until it becomes very sticky and then roll it over our skin. It pulls the hair right off." "Doesn't it hurt?" I asked. "Yes," she replied, "but we don't have to do it very often." On a little burner where Salma had often made coffee for us was a bubbling pot of syrup, dripping over the edges and burning, thus causing the strange odor.

Salma's roommate, Souad, was manipulating a long twisted string held taut between her teeth and her toes. "I prefer this method," she explained, pulling the strings up and down her legs very rhythmically. "Why don't you try it?" Souad asked me. So I did, but with complete and utter failure. I could not even hold the string tight between my toes and my teeth. And I was not interested in enduring the pain nor the stickiness of the caramel sugar method.

That night we were allowed extra olive pit fuel packets for the hot water heaters to accommodate the necessary bathing and primping. All the excitement and conversation of the hours before the party changed dramatically to embarrassed silence when the hostel women descended to the living room to greet their guests. I spotted Malcolm and his mother at one side of the room, and we exchanged smiles. "Ahlan wa sahlan," one of the more gregarious girls called out in welcome. And then with the wonderful device of the twenty or so different ways of saying hello in Arabic, the ice was broken. The Lebanese are so friendly and sociable that even in that relatively new and unfamiliar situation for most of the students, the party was soon in full swing.

My roommates and I made our way toward Malcolm and his mother. "Ahlan wa sahlan," they chimed out. Malcolm charmed my roommates by speaking Arabic to them. "You speak it better than we do," they insisted. "And you have a real Beirut accent." Indeed, he did speak it well, but this compliment was standard. The hostel maids said the same thing to me when I said to them, "Marhaba, keef halik?" (Hello, how are you?)

Gifts were exchanged and the tabbouleh and humus and cakes were devoured just about as soon as they were put on the table. Helping themselves to food was one thing these students were not shy about.

A little later, Malcolm and I slipped out and went to the Regina Bar in the St. George nightclub district where I had first set eyes on him three months earlier. We sat drinking beer and eating salted almonds for quite a while, reluctant for the evening to end. For my Christmas vacation I had accepted an invitation from one of my classmates, Widad Irani, to go home with her to Bethlehem for the holidays. From there I would go to Cairo and meet other AUB friends for a trip by train to Luxor. I was to leave for Jordan the next day, and it was with a few pangs that I said goodnight and good-bye, exhilarated to be going off on such an adventure but sad to leave just as romance was blossoming.

It is easy to look back on those exciting days, so like a movie of the fifties, and wonder what would have happened if I had chosen to go to India for my junior year abroad instead of Lebanon or if Malcolm had indeed gone off to study at Oxford. But being a product of that generation and all those movies, I suspect that our meeting on the shores of Lebanon was the way things were meant to be.

CHAPTER 5

Discovering the Middle East

*A*fter two weeks in the arid climes of Jerusalem and Egypt, flying back to Lebanon was especially beautiful. In my absence snow had covered the mountains. The air was clear and below us on the ground everything was blue and white, sea and snow, with patches of red sand and green umbrella pines. The buildings sparkled and looked deceptively white from the sky.

"Hamdillah as salaami," Roshan, Naziha, Katie, and Samia chimed out, as I lugged my suitcase, heavy with souvenirs I had bought during our travels, over to my corner of the room. It was obvious that they were praising God for my safe return, judging by the customary attributions to Allah on such occasions. "How are you? Tell us about your trip. You look a little tired," they chorused. "Did you like Bethlehem? How was Egypt?" they wanted to know. What a nice welcome. I was glad to be home.

I tried to tell them as much as I could about my trip while I unpacked—the hospitality of Widad's family, the sandy hills of Bethlehem dotted with olive trees and grazing sheep, my strange shocked reaction to the gaudiness of the holy places and the number of different religious groups who shared them and who often competed aggressively for dominance of them.

Katie and Roshan were full of questions about Jerusalem, a city they had known as children in Palestine. I told them about visiting Arab Jerusalem, now under Jordanian control, and the medieval beauty of the old city surrounded by the imposing stone wall built by the Ottoman sultan, Suleiman the Magnificent. "All that must be the same," they conjectured, "but what about the

8. Ann Kerr and roommates at St. Michel Beach, 1955.
Left to right: Katie Azzam, Samia Shammas, Naziha Knio,
Ann Kerr, and Roshan Irani.

other side?" They were referring to the fact that the city had been divided since the Arab-Israeli War of 1948 when their families had been forced to leave. And they knew that I, as a foreigner, would not be allowed to cross into Israeli territory and return to an Arab country on the same passport.

I described how I had looked across the barbed wire and burned-out buildings of no-man's-land into Israeli Jerusalem. Widad's relatives who lived in the Israeli sector stood in line for many hours at the Mandelbaum Gate to cross this no-man's-land for a once-a-year, Christmas Day visit to their family in Arab Jerusalem. A good part of their short visit was spent in telling about the daily problems and humiliation of living under military control. It was sad to think of this jewel-like city so fraught with rancor and divisiveness.

"What about Cairo?" my roommates asked. "How does it compare to Beirut?" I told them how big and spread out it seemed by comparison and how strange it was to see traffic lights and big department stores. I described the hospitality of the relatives of our classmate, Widad Saba, whom we had stayed with, and the sightseeing excursions they had taken us on around Cairo. The gardens of the Cairo zoo were full of exotic flowering plants and trees that were as unusual as the collection of animals from all over Africa. From the center of Cairo we had taken a street car through several miles of agricultural land, brilliant green with new winter wheat, out to the Giza pyramids on the edge of the desert. The memory of Cairo in the new year of 1955, then a city of a few million people, seems like a tranquil illusion compared to the teeming, overpopulated city it has become with buildings encroaching onto the land surrounding the pyramids.

The most memorable part of the trip was the third class train ride along the Nile and a three-day stay in Luxor, seeing changeless Egyptian village life and ancient pharonic temples. My roommates were quite envious that I had been to this sister Arab country which they had never seen. At least they had a few souvenirs which I had brought them from the Khan el Khalili bazaar of Cairo.

As I was unpacking Malcolm phoned to welcome me home and to invite me to an afternoon movie. I was so glad to hear his voice. It seemed that much more than two weeks had passed since our last evening at the Regina; I had almost forgotten his slightly clipped accent and the deep tone of his voice. As soon as I finished unpacking I walked down to the tramline on Rue Bliss to meet him. Always prompt, he was waiting for me with a big smile, looking tall and slim and reassuringly American. The tram came immediately so we climbed on, swinging back and forth on the rickety old vehicle, raising our voices to be heard above the din. Malcolm asked me if I'd like to see *On the Waterfront* with Marlon Brando at the Roxy. I told him I'd seen it in Cairo, in fact on New Year's Eve, but since I had slept through most of it after the Luxor trip and the night train rides, I didn't mind at all seeing it again. So we got off at the top of the burj and headed for Cinema Roxy where a bigger than life Marlon Brando stared down at us through Arabized eyes from the outside wall of the theater.

It was still light when we came out. Again that shock came of walking back into a foreign culture after having been so totally immersed in my own for the two hours or so that the movie lasted. The contrast between Beirut and Cairo struck me as well. Cairo then was a cosmopolitan world capital, only two years into the postmonarch Nasser era, not yet overcrowded, and still sporting much of the architectural grandeur and wide avenues of its British Empire days. Beirut, though cosmopolitan in its own way with an eclectic willingness to adopt the latest American and French styles and change them any time for a newer one, was still a fairly small city with narrow streets and a certain feeling of intimacy.

After the movie, we went to Uncle Sam's hamburger shop across the street from AUB, and I philosophized about these contrasts to Malcolm. He had not been to Cairo since the Kerr family's departure from Lebanon to escape the Germans in 1940, and the subject of cultural contrasts did not seem to capture his imagination as much as it did mine. I remember thinking smugly that I was learning a lot more about the Middle East than Malcolm and my roommates who had all been born and raised there. We finished the dry hamburgers seasoned with cinnamon and drank our cokes, agreeing that we preferred the good Lebanese food of Faisal's Restaurant down the street.

"Hope you're free tomorrow night," Malcolm said as we bade each other goodnight. "I've been invited to a dinner dance at the St. George Hotel by an oil company executive who's buying up a lot of tickets to support some worthy cause." The St. George Hotel was the classiest place in town, and I thought it would be wonderful to go there. I went home and looked for the one long formal dress I had brought, a white chiffon, over-one-shoulder creation which had inspired my date at an Occidental College fraternity party to call me "Blithe Spirit." Hoping that in this Mediterranean setting the over-one-shoulder style would create more the aura of a Greek goddess, I pulled it out of my trunk and ironed it.

The next day I decided to have my hair cut before the big evening. Roshan told me of a good hairdresser and gave me directions for getting there. The name of the place was "William's Fairy Saloon," one of the many Beirut shop names created with interesting adaptations of English and French language. William must have been used to American customers for he said to me in English, "Sit down. Only five minutes." I already knew that in the Middle East, five minutes usually meant half an hour, but I resigned myself and sat down.

The shop was small and full of plump, bourgeois-looking

ladies. Most of them were sitting with towels around their shoulders to protect their black dresses, with hair sticking straight up in the air owing to the thick purplish black dye that had been applied to the roots. They sipped coffee and jabbered away with each other and with one another and with William, undaunted by the dye dripping down their foreheads. I realized now why I had seen hardly a gray hair since I arrived in Lebanon.

"Marhaba," called a woman of the same model as the others who poked her head in the doorway. "Marhaba, ahlan, tfaddali," hello, welcome, come in, called those inside. She did not come in but just stood in the doorway chatting for half an hour or so. Two other women walked past her and came in. One sat down and joined in the conversation. The other sat in a chair in the corner, closed her eyes, and went to sleep for twenty minutes or so, then woke up and left. Several women loaded with bags of vegetables and fruits came in, had a cup of coffee, gossiped awhile, and then went on their way. It seemed that the beauty salon was a social institution for these Arab women, tantamount to the institution of the coffeehouse for Arab men.

That evening I put on my finery to the approving comments of my roommates. I was especially appreciative of their approval, knowing that going out on dates with men was off limits for them. While I was at the St. George, they would be studying and perhaps taking a break to read the *True Confession* and *Real Love* magazines I had noticed on their bedside tables.

Malcolm, looking very handsome in the tuxedo he had worn for formal occasions at Princeton, picked me up in a taxi, and we drove down to the corniche below AUB to the penthouse apartment of our host, Mr. McPhearson, where we were to have cocktails before going to the hotel. A servant ushered us into a large living room which opened out to an even larger terrace looking out to the sea, harbor, and mountains. There seemed to be more servants than guests circulating through the crowd with drinks and silver trays of delicious tidbits to munch on. The guests were mostly Americans from the embassy or oil companies or private businesses.

Our host hired limousines for all of us for the ride down to the St. George Hotel. We were a small caravan of Americans riding in style through the Muslim quarter of Ain Mreisseh, past beautiful old houses with red-tiled roofs, a few new multilevel buildings, and the shanties of the poor so often tucked into Beirut neighborhoods, rich or poor. The huge American cars preferred by the Lebanese, but so inappropriate for their narrow streets, were driven less by steering wheel than by horn. When they inevitably got caught in gridlocked traffic, the horns blared louder than ever and beggars seized the moment to approach the car and thrust a maimed or filthy bandaged hand through the car window, pleading for money in the name of Allah.

It was not only the Americans who personified the "haves" in Beirut. Rich Arabs from the Gulf, not yet as much drawn to Europe, swarmed to Beirut in those days, often bringing with them whole entourages of wives, children, and servants. One well-known Saudi prince in Aley even had his herd of camels camped outside his summer villa. And there were many extremely wealthy Lebanese, as well, to provide a spectacle of conspicuous consumption for their less fortunate countrymen. From within that lushly upholstered limousine looking out on the world, it was hard not to feel self-conscious and acutely aware of the imbalance of wealth in Lebanon.

Not so from within the St. George Hotel, where there was nothing but tasteful opulence upon which to feast our eyes. Built on a spur of land jutting out into the bay of the same name, the hotel was situated on one of the best pieces of real estate in Beirut outside the AUB campus. A vast terrace overlooked the St. George yacht club and swimming dock where guests sat gazing out at the lights of the ships in the harbor and far off villages in the mountains.

We were directed toward the ballroom of the hotel where immediately glasses of champagne were offered to us and later a filet mignon dinner served. The business and embassy people asked Malcolm and me about AUB, and we inquired about business and the embassy. When the music started, I thought I noticed Malcolm grimace, but he soon suggested that we dance. I did not know if the pained expression came more from his recent arthritic pains or from the fact that he didn't care much for dancing. In any case, we both liked the fact that the dancing lessened the distance between us, and the arthritis made a good excuse for his plodding fox trot.

One day I had a note from Mrs. Kerr asking me if I would

like a job tutoring a Lebanese professor's wife in English. This seemed like a good way to get to know a Lebanese family well and a means of earning additional income. I could tutor a few hours a week in the morning, between classes at AUB and before I went off to teach at the Armenian school in the afternoon. So I made an appointment to meet Professor Abdulmonim Talhouk, and he took me to his home a few blocks from the AUB campus to meet his wife. The building had no elevator so we walked up six flights of stairs to their apartment where Mrs. Talhouk and their four daughters were waiting for us with big smiles. The entire family was so charming that I took the job on the spot. We agreed that I would come two mornings a week for an hour and a half.

Mrs. Talhouk already knew a little English, so with the help of an old English grammar book she had had since her school days and an instant liking for each other, we began twice weekly lessons which usually ended up in discussions about her family or Lebanon or the United States or whatever we felt like.

We always sat in the less formal of two adjoining salons or sitting rooms, one crowded with velvet upholstered chairs, the other, more formal with ornately carved wooden furniture upholstered in brocade. The circular arrangement of chairs around the entire room, one touching the other, as I had seen in all the homes I had visited, accommodated the large number of relatives that gathered in each other's homes in the late afternoon and evening. Both rooms had oriental carpets on the floor and dozens of paintings and photographs of handsome Talhouk faces on the walls.

Halfway through the lesson, their maid, a small girl of about twelve, brought me a glass of lemonade or a cup of Turkish coffee. And by the end of the hour, the Talhouk daughters began arriving home for lunch, all in blue school uniforms. Leila and Souad were twelve and ten, Leila with brown eyes and dark hair like her father and Souad with green eyes and fair hair like her mother. A younger pair of six and four were almost duplicates of the older pair, Amal dark like Leila and her father, Afaf fair like Souad and her mother. The older sisters knew English quite well from school and loved to come in and translate more complicated ideas that their mother's and my linguistic efforts could not handle.

Malcolm explained that the Talhouk family was one of the oldest and most historically important in Lebanon and played a major role in the subject of the thesis he was writing about civil wars in Lebanon between 1840 and 1860. They were Druzes, a key religious group in the assortment that made up this small country, and Professor Talhouk was a Druze shaykh. He was surely a far cry from my Hollywood-inspired image of the shaykh of Araby in flowing robes charging across the desert on a white stallion. Shaykh Talhouk was an outstanding entomologist who had various insects named after him and was a very popular professor at AUB. Since Talhouks usually married Talhouks, as was customary among Druzes, Mr. and Mrs. Talhouk were second cousins. The family seat was in the village of Aley. On weekends and in the summers the family gathered there and Shaykh Talhouk tended to his duties as a leader of the Druze community.

Looking back to that first year of knowing Malcolm, I do not remember his being overwhelmed with the work required of someone working on his master's thesis and studying Arabic. In fact, I was hardly aware that he was working very hard on both projects, so adventurous and amorous and full of fun were our times together. If he were here now for me to ask how he made it all look so effortless, I can imagine him shrugging and making some self-deprecating remark, sincerely meaning that it didn't require a lot of effort for him to write a thesis that was later published as a book and to improve his Arabic to a high level of proficiency. That shrug would also reflect a touch of reluctance or even boredom at the idea of having to discuss his academic work.

Just as our meetings in the library did not usually lead to much studying, neither did my visits to him at his house to ostensibly review our Ottoman history notes and prepare for exams. Perhaps his superior knowledge of the subject was off-putting to me or my inferior knowledge off-putting to him. Or perhaps we just found better things to do. As I remember, his attempts to teach me to play chess, sitting on that same couch where we had tried to study Ottoman history, also failed!

CHAPTER 6

Spring Comes Early to Lebanon

A Proposal of Marriage

*I*n mid-February 1955, after a mid-semester break in Damascus with a classmate and her family, my second semester classes got underway. I was also back teaching in the Armenian school four afternoons a week and meeting with Mrs. Talhouk for English lessons. Some of the courses were the second half of classes I had been taking; others were new. Particularly interesting were Philosophy of Education with Professor Habib Kurani and a comparative Western and Middle Eastern philosophy course with Professor Majid Fakhry. I was required to take a course in statistics, which I think I ultimately passed only thanks to the special help and kindness of the teacher, Professor Korf.

Malcolm was bringing his Master's thesis on the civil wars in Lebanon between 1840 and 1860 to a conclusion. We were no longer taking Ottoman history together, but the time was long past when we needed that class as an excuse for a daily meeting.

While St. Patrick's Day on March 17 was not on AUB's long list of Muslim and Christian holidays to celebrate, it will always be on mine as the day Malcolm proposed marriage. We were reclining on the living room couch in his parents' house in the increasingly well-worn middle section, not making any of our old pretenses of trying to study Ottoman history or Malcolm vainly attempting to teach me to play chess. His parents were out and the mood was mellow. In a few simple words he asked me to marry him. Although the suggestion did not come as a complete surprise, I remember marveling at how decisive Malcolm was. How could he be sure, when we had known each other only five months, that he really wanted to marry me? Always more prone to pondering and to detail than Malcolm, and with a certain shyness, I hemmed and hawed and gave an elated but indefinite reply.

I wrote to my parents to tell them that this young man I had been describing in my letters over the past five months had proposed marriage. I recounted all the admirable qualities that attracted me to him—his special brand of humor, his nice family, his intelligence, his integrity, and the easy rapport and fun we had together. The thought occurred to me that it might be difficult for parents to feel happy about their first child finding the man she wanted to marry halfway around the world—a man they didn't know and a place they had never seen—but I was too much in love to dwell on those thoughts for long.

They wrote back to me in a noncommittal but accepting way, most probably mindful of the fact that their romance had begun in similar fashion when my mother left Missouri to study at Dalhousie University in Nova Scotia and soon met her husband-to-be.

The question of marriage had now been raised, and it was just a matter of time before Malcolm and I both felt ready for the positive answer that was inevitable. There were four months left in the school year before I would leave to go back to my family in California and my senior year at Occidental, and Malcolm would have to decide on what he was going to do after completing his M.A. at AUB. These months were filled with more of the same adventures and discoveries as my first months in the Middle East, but with the added feeling of responsibility for decisions that must soon be made.

Spring comes early to Lebanon as it does to southern California. Malcolm and I took advantage of some of the university-sponsored Sunday bus trips to sites of interest around the country with other students and faculty members to see the country in its spring glory. With each trip new varieties of fruit trees and wild flowers were coming into bloom, first almond blossoms and pale pink cyclamen, then apricot and peach blossoms and bright red anemonies. One Sunday we joined a trip going to Lebanon's richest historical site, the ancient holy city of Baalbek, situated in the northern portion of the Beka'a Valley between the Lebanon and

Anti-Lebanon mountain ranges. As we traveled up over the high Lebanon range on the Damascus Road and then down into the Beka'a Valley, spring seemed particularly beautiful. Wild flowers poked out of bright green grass and tender new leaves sprouted from the poplar trees which lined the sides of the road and marked the boundaries of fields where wheat, alfalfa, corn, and, in hidden corners, opium poppies grew. In the town of Chtoura, we turned off the Damascus Road and drove north up the valley to Zahle, a town famous for its excellent restaurants beside rushing streams where melting snows gush down from the mountains. After a lunch of meza and charcoal-broiled chicken with garlic sauce, we continued on our way to the modern town of Baalbek and to the ancient temple site of the same name adjacent to it.

The majestic columns of the Temple of Jupiter were visible from a long distance, striking against the backdrop of the snow-tipped Lebanon mountains to the west. A short distance before the entrance to the temple, a massive slab of stone lay near the side of the road which our guide explained was Egyptian granite brought to Lebanon by ship to exchange for cedar wood for use in the construction of Egyptian temples. Inside the large temple complex, we wandered through the Temple of Diana and the Temple of Bacchus and across the huge plaza in between where a few years later we would go hear the New York Philharmonic Orchestra play in the Baalbek Summer Festival. Along with the magnificence of the architecture and the huge scale of the holy city, I was impressed by the archaeological layers of civilization revealing worship sites going back to the dawn of history—ancient Assyrian, Egyptian, Phoenician, Greek, Roman, Byzantine, and Arab. This beautiful area of Lebanon would suffer one of its saddest historical periods twenty years later when it became embroiled in civil war, a place split by its own Christian-Muslim population, infiltrated by Iranian Shiites, "protected" by Syrian soldiers and attacked by Israeli fighter planes targeting the Soviet military equipment of the Syrian "protectors." In the anarchy of civil war the drug trade grew, and Baalbek became an area of captivity for western hostages. Such tragedy was impossible to imagine on that fresh spring day as Malcolm and I sat on an exquisitely carved Greek cornice gazing at the tranquil Beka'a Valley spreading out before us.

On another trip, we traveled south on the coast road to Sidon, a two-hour drive from Beirut, past stretches of long, white deserted beaches and multicolored stripes of sea ranging from pale aqua close to shore to deep blue further out. The narrow coastal strip of fertile farmland before the steep rise of mountains was full of banana orchards, orange and mango groves, and palm trees. We passed through the town of Damour where the Damour River flows into the sea. Brilliant colored fruits and vegetables were artfully arranged in stalls along the road, tempting passers-by. Varieties of pots, made from the red clay of the river valley, were also for sale. The scent of orange blossoms from the groves stretching up into the valley permeated the air.

Layered with history like Baalbek, the town of Sidon was once an important Phoenician naval stronghold, along with Tyre thirty miles or so further south. The land of Tyre and Sidon was a familiar biblical reference to me. As we drove along the shore, I looked for scenes implanted in my mind from Sunday School days. They were not hard to find. Leathery old fishermen in loose-fitting cotton shirts and pants cast their nets from boats while others sat on shore in groups of two or three mending large clumps of nets. Donkeys clomped along the narrow streets of the town laden with straw baskets containing clay pots or firewood or sacks of flour.

Jutting out into the harbor on a spur of rocks was a picturesque crusader castle which I had seen beautifully rendered in a painting by the nineteenth century Scottish artist, David Roberts. The sea lapped up around it and the few small boats anchored there.

We stopped to visit Gerard Institute, a secondary school founded by American missionaries, and were shown around the beautiful campus which looked like a small version of AUB with old stone buildings and gardens full of orange trees and flowers. One of the teachers at the school invited us to visit her home in the village of Mieh Mieh in the hills behind the school. As we trudged up a steep path behind Gerard Institute, heavy rain began to pour down, turning the path into a river. It was impossible to keep dry. Villagers peeked out of their houses urging us to come in out of the rain, but we trudged on to the home of the teacher. An extended family of about ten people of different generations were gathered in the small main room of the two-room whitewashed house, seated in chairs covered with bright cotton print which encircled the room, one touching the other.

Our hosts insisted that they dry our clothes and brought us Damascus brocade dressing gowns to change into while our clothes dried over a floor heater in the center of the room. As I held the lovely brocade fabric, it occurred to me that Lebanese people, even in the simplest homes, tended to put their money into fine clothes before other budgetary items. We were ushered separately into the smaller room of the house to change. It appeared that all the members of the family slept in this one room where sleeping mats were neatly bundled and stored in corners. There was also a small kitchen with a tiny sink and drain board and a two burner stove which ran on tanked gas. It was hard to believe that elaborate Lebanese meals for a large family were prepared every day in this kitchen. One or two cupboards contained plates, glasses, and a few pots and pans. Light came in through one small window. There was no refrigerator, nor was one needed because women shopped daily.

From this kitchen, an array of refreshments was served to us over the next hour, a round of Turkish coffee followed by lemonade, then chocolates and sticky sweet Arab pastries and finally "some fruits," as our hosts referred in English to a tray of apples, oranges, and bananas. There was also mountain bread with labani (yogurt with the liquid drained off), honey, and dried figs. Even without great economic resources, Lebanese hospitality was bountiful.

Bowls of bizr were passed, a collection of pumpkin, sunflower and watermelon seeds which had been dried and salted. The object was to eat the juicy tidbit inside without swallowing the outer seed. I had noticed my roommates' facility for doing this in a continuous process carried out so discreetly that one would hardly know anything was going on. A handful of bizr is swept into the mouth and stored on one side. The tongue then gently guides a seed into cracking position. Teeth come together with just the right kind of pressure to split the seed but not splinter it. Next the tongue deftly removes the inner tidbit and simultaneously transfers the shell to a storage place on the other side of the mouth. The center seed is then eaten and enjoyed.

The hospitality of these people we had never met before was

overwhelmingly warm and genuine. Malcolm spoke Arabic with the older members of the family who knew little English, and I spoke with the children in the carefully enunciated English I had learned to use with my students in the Armenian School. Like my students, they knew some English from school, reinforced by American movies. The oldest brother in the family was a student at AUB and spoke good English.

When our clothes were dry, we surrendered the soft brocade dressing gowns to our hosts and prepared to make our way back down the hill to meet the AUB bus. The warmth and richness of the welcome from this simple family has remained vividly in my mind, and come back again and again during the fifteen years of civil war when the village of Mich Mich was in the center of vicious fighting between shifting factions of Palestinians, Lebanese Christians and Muslims, and Israelis. Were those kind and generous people victims or participants in the fighting, or had they fled and become refugees in a foreign land? As Malcolm and I walked down the mountain after the rainstorm, the sky was a painting of billowy clouds with slants of late afternoon sunlight shining through, turning the Mediterranean into a multitude of blues.

AUB had a spring break in the week between Palm Sunday and Easter. I spent the first few days of it on a driving tour into Northern Syria with family friends from California who drove up from Tel Aviv where they were posted at the U.S. Embassy. Only people with diplomatic passports could drive through the Israel-Lebanon border which, since the Arab-Israeli War of 1948 and the establishment of the state of Israel, had been an enemy line on Lebanon's southern border. The name Israel was rarely uttered in Beirut. I had heard people at AUB refer to it as "Disneyland" or "Dixie."

Lebanon's northern border with Syria was much quieter than its eastern border on the main Beirut-Damascus thoroughfare which I had visited two months earlier with my classmate from Damascus. Our destination was a crusader castle some twenty miles north of the border, the Krak des Chevaliers. One of more than a dozen such castles along the eastern coast of the Mediterranean, the Krak was the largest and best-preserved of them all. It was occupied for over two centuries by generations of Europeans who came for a variety of reasons under the banner of Christianity with the goal of claiming the Holy Land for the West. Seeing the solid grandeur of the castle constructed with features of Byzantine, Arab, and European fortifications gave a revealing impression of the dramatic encounter between East and West caused by the Crusades. The Christians living in the Lebanon mountains had welcomed the Crusaders as allies. We saw evidence of the mingling of East and West in the blond children who lived in the village at the foot of the castle. Some of them followed us around as we made our way through the vast fortress and out onto its windswept ramparts with views of distant hills sweeping eastward to the Syrian desert.

The day after I returned, Malcolm and I decided to go swimming at Pigeon Rock, a massive formation making a natural bridge just off the cliffs of West Beirut. From the termination point of the tramline near the lighthouse at the end of Ras Beirut where a protrusion of high land juts into the sea, we turned eastward toward the outskirts of town. I remember the rhythmic tapping of stone masons shaping stones for apartment buildings that were beginning to replace the old gardened villas that had prevailed in Malcolm's childhood years. Beirut's growing population meant that the city had to expand into the sandy land to the east toward the airport. The bluffs further out near Pigeon Rock, as yet undeveloped, were covered with new green grass and yellow coreopsis.

We walked along the beach and then up over a grassy promontory where sheep were grazing and a farmer tilled a small field. From the end of the promontory we looked down on our destination, a cove of sparkling water and a pristine beach of white sand. A few yards from the shore was the majestic rock formation that was one of Beirut's landmarks. The little cove was all ours as the nearest people seemed to be the farmers' children playing up the hill with their donkey. We spread out our beach towels and lay close together in the sun until it got so warm we had to go in the water. The sea was an aqua blue of such intensity that we felt that we were trespassing against nature to be swimming there—or that we were entering some unreal world not usually known to humans. That feeling continued as we swam out into the grotto under Pigeon Rock and listened to our voices bounce back and forth from one wall to the other with eerie resonance.

Later we climbed up the hill to a café above Pigeon Rock and ordered beer and peanuts. Sipping our beer, and gazing out at the expanse of vivid aqua, glistening below us in the afternoon sun, gave a feeling of timelessness that made it seem as if we could stay right there and be just as we were then forever. But we had only a few more months before this magical year would end, and though we had committed ourselves to each other, each of us had to go ahead with our separate pursuits as well. For Malcolm there was a possibility of a job in Saudi Arabia with the Arab American Oil Company (ARAMCO) the next year. He had applied to the U.S. State Department to join the foreign service and to several graduate schools in the United States for a Ph.D. in international relations. We were both hoping for the latter as the way for us to best be in close touch while I was back at Occidental finishing my senior year. As the sun sank in the sky we walked back through the fields to Ras Beirut feeling the glow of that extraordinary day but mindful of considerable concerns about our future.

A few days later in that vacation week I suggested to my roommates that we spend a day at the beach together, as Malcolm and I had done, but I got a negative reply. "We don't swim till the end of May," said Roshan. The weather seemed like midsummer to me, but I had noticed that most people were still wearing winter clothes and remarked on it. Katie laughed at my puzzlement. "It's just the custom here. People are afraid of becoming sick if the weather is warm one day and cold the next, so they wait to swim and wear summer clothes until May when summer has definitely set in." Roshan confirmed this, adding "I got pneumonia last year from swimming in April."

Since they had put a damper on my beach suggestion, I asked if anyone had any other ideas. "Many of my clothes need sewing," Samia said in hesitant English. "Mine do, too," said Katie. "Why don't we sit on the balcony and do our mending?" Everyone agreed to this idea, although Naziha said she would prefer to do watercolors instead of mending. Samia brought out her jar of mango pickles and her box of manna and a bag of bizr, and we spent the morning gossiping, munching, sewing, and painting. Several friends from neighboring rooms joined us. One was a glamorous Iraqi from Baghdad, Amal Rassam, who lived in the room opposite ours. She had just won the annual spring contest for Miss AUB which she seemed to take with great aplomb. Like Samia,

Amal had the scar on her cheek from the bite of an insect peculiar to Iraq, but it only seemed to add to the appeal of her dusky beauty.

Another friend who joined us that day was Salma Jayoussi, a tall fair-skinned, rather queenly looking person from Amman, Jordan, whom I had become friends with during the past semester. She had told me much about her conservative family to whom she was very close. They were Palestinians who had moved to Jordan in 1948 after being forced to leave their hometown when the state of Israel was established. Like many educated Palestinians, they had become prominent citizens in Jordan, contributing to the growth and development of that country.

Salma's father was a cabinet minister and apparently as authoritative and respected within his family as he was in the government. He had married his cousin, Salma's mother, and they had had three daughters. Presumably because there were no sons, he married a second wife, a custom no longer much practiced but condoned in order to produce a male heir. In many families the traditional desire to have a male heir still held at that time and continues to do so in some parts of the Arab world today. From this match a daughter was born and finally a son. But when the little boy was only a year old, he died of a rare disease.

As she sat telling me about her life at home in Amman, wearing a blue skirt and blouse and looking much like other AUB students, I wondered how she could manage the double life she led. With her family, she dressed in black with mandatory long sleeves and could only leave her home veiled and properly accompanied, and never at night. Such behavior and dress were not the norm of her community at that time but required of her by her father because of his conservatism. He must have known that at AUB she was free to wear what she wanted and to come and go as she pleased.

"I begged and begged my father to let me come to AUB," Salma told me. "Finally he consented," she continued. "If I can get my B.A. in English and go home and teach, I will have everything I could hope for." "Wouldn't you like to be married someday?" I asked her. "I can never marry," Salma replied, "because the male cousins in the family are already married or engaged and my father will only allow us to marry cousins. This is the way families are kept close."

Such dedication to educational and family ideals was admirable, but it was hard for me to fathom how those could be ranked higher in importance than marriage. As a college girl of the fifties, I knew my time schedule. I would be married after I graduated from college, which naturally meant that I should become engaged by the end of my junior year. It was lucky that Malcolm had come along to make everything go according to plan.

My friends spoke in Arabic peppered with a little English and French, but switched occasionally to English for me. Our talk that day was mostly of ourselves, our studies, and the sewing and painting we were doing at the time, but occasionally conversation turned to politics. I sensed that my friends' interest in politics was strong and more developed than mine but that most of them were not involved in political activist groups. I was still a novice to the world of Arab politics and would not have understood much had they switched to English, but I began to learn more in the next few weeks.

Along with warmer weather and the Miss AUB contest, spring brought a resurgence of the always present, diverse political energies of AUB students. Campus political demonstrations were almost as predictable as the red anemonies that sprouted up on the terraced bluffs above the athletic field. That spring the impetus for demonstrations came when Lebanese President Camile Chamoun joined several other pro-Western Middle Eastern countries in signing the Baghdad Pact with England. The United States did not initially join it but took part in much of its work. The pact was an economic and defense agreement of the early Cold War period which declared that military assistance would be given if Iraq were threatened or if it asked for help. Arab nationalists believed that this pact, signed by Pakistan, Iraq, Iran, Turkey, and England for the purpose of regional defense, was contrary to the objectives of Arab unity.

Many students, mostly Muslim but some Christian as well, were attracted by the appeal of Arab unity, an idea that had begun stirring in the early part of the century in reaction to Ottoman and then European colonial rule. By the mid-fifties the notion of Arab unity was finding its voice after World War II and the Arab-Israeli War of 1948 which created the Palestinian diaspora. President Abdel Nasser in Egypt was a magnetic spokesman for the ideas of Arab nationalism which were discussed widely in the open intellectual atmosphere of the AUB campus. Some Christian students, particularly Maronites, saw Arab unity as a threat to their historic stronghold in Lebanon, already isolated in a sea of Muslims.

Small groups of students took up positions near West Hall under pine and cypress trees planted by founding fathers of the university fifty years earlier. They gave speeches and chanted their causes in loud voices, attracting more students to join them. As a member of the "silent generation" of the 1950s and as a relatively nonpolitical person anyway, I found that behavior all very new and rather frightening. I had little appreciation of the significance of this demonstration as a microcosm of a complex and explosive problem that plagued Lebanon and the Middle East. I could only liken the enthusiasm of the AUB students for this cause to that of Occidental students who got a little out of hand for an October football rally against a fierce cross-town rival.

The spring air was as conducive to romance as it was to riots. Malcolm and I spent our free moments every day sitting on our favorite campus bench looking out over pink oleander bushes and budding jacaranda trees to the sea beyond. Soft breezes blew and we became quite unaware of time until the chimes of the College Hall clock tower reminded us it was time for a class or work in the library. We never wanted to be far from each other, and so we walked off together to wherever it was we had to go with plans to meet as soon as we could. It became clearer and clearer that we would like to spend the rest of our lives together and never have to be apart.

Malcolm learned that he had received a sizable scholarship from Johns Hopkins School of Advanced International Studies in Washington, D.C. That was a long way from California, but at least he would be able to come for Christmas, and we would be married the next summer after I graduated from college. All that remained was to buy a ring and to formally announce our engagement.

Buying our engagement ring was a memorable adventure one day in May. Malcolm's father, with all his experience working with Armenians in Turkey, was in very good standing with the Armenian community of Beirut, many of whom were in the jewelry business. "Let me take you to one of my friends to look for a ring," he suggested one evening when I was having dinner with the Kerrs. The next weekend, we took the tram down to the burj and headed from the big main square into the narrow maze of streets that was Beirut's old bazaar. The gold souk was in the first streets just off the burj. One shopwindow after another was ablaze with gold necklaces, gold earrings, gold bracelets and gold rings, dazzling in their density. Malcolm's father led us down an alley and up some rickety stairs to the shop of his friends. The sight of their American friend from the old days in Turkey brought forth a rush of greetings in Armenian and Turkish, to which Dr. Kerr responded with impressive fluency. And then in a combination of English, Turkish, and Arabic he announced that Malcolm and I were planning to be married and that we would like to buy an engagement ring. Another rush of effusive greetings poured forth in an assortment of languages, and then we were asked what kind of ring I would like. I tried to describe my grandmother's diamond ring in a tiffany setting and told them I wanted one like it. They had trouble understanding what I was talking about, and found a pencil and some paper so that I could draw a picture of what I had in mind. Then from the bowels of a little box safe resting on a dusty table, they pulled the diamonds out one by one to display on the counter. The stones all looked about the same, some a little bigger, some a little smaller. "We'd like to see the less expensive ones," Malcolm said, setting the tone for thrift that would guide the economic policy of our marriage. "Here is a good one, but it is a little broken," one of the Armenian jewelers suggested. "It is only six hundred pounds." In U.S. money that was two hundred dollars, which sounded better but was still a small fortune to us. The other diamonds were much more expensive, and since we were unable to see the flaw in the "broken" one, we settled on it. Turkish coffee was served all around, and we sat listening to tales of the days when Malcolm's father was helping Armenians escape from the Turks.

With the ring ordered Malcolm and I felt officially engaged, and we hastened to send my parents a telex to confirm the news about which I had been telling them in my weekly letters. As a parent now of children in the marrying stages of their lives, I can empathize with how my mother and father must have felt about their twenty-year-old daughter deciding to marry a stranger from a faraway land. They knew little of him, or his family, or his country.

Not to be outdone by her sister as an adventurer, my young

sister Jane, just graduated from high school, was soon to arrive in Beirut. After much planning in our letters throughout the year, she was convinced to spend all her earnings from after-school jobs to come and see how I had spent my year and then to go through Europe together. She would also be the family emissary to help celebrate Malcolm's and my engagement. Again our parents were supporting another daughter in her wanderlust. At seventeen, she was the only female traveling on a Dutch freighter from New York to Beirut.

On an early June morning, Malcolm and I went to meet Jane on the same dock where I had debarked nine months earlier. I wondered how our sisterly closeness would be affected by all the changes that had taken place in those nine months. It was easy to spot her fair head in the crowd of mostly dark ones coming across the dock. When she saw us, the relief of reaching her destination and completing that seventeen-day journey by herself brought a rush of tears to her eyes, and in turn to mine as I hugged my sister who represented the family I had been away from for so long. I was feeling a bit divided between my new attachments and my old, wanting these two special people and my two worlds to come together.

The adaptability of this young woman who could earn her fare, plan so unique a journey, and even learn some Arabic during the voyage was not about to end when she got off the ship. Jane moved into the hostel with my roommates and me and accommodated herself readily to the tours of Lebanon that Malcolm and I had been planning for her.

We took her to visit the cedars of Bisharri, starting out at sunrise and driving by taxi up the coast with a stop at the ancient Phoenician city of Byblos, then to Tripoli and its old Crusader castle. From there we went inland up into the high mountains back to the craggy Khadisha Gorge on top of which the red-roofed villages of Hasroon and Bisharri were perched. In Bisharri, we stopped at the museum home of Khalil Jibran, the famous Lebanese poet and author of *The Prophet,* and came to understand the inspiration behind his work. From his house we looked across the valley to Hasroon and down the deep purple and burnt umber colors of the gorge, laced with green clover on stair-step terraces. Above us towered the still snow-tipped Lebanon mountains, dark green patches on the mountainside revealing some of the few remaining cedar trees which had survived the greed of men for the durable wood and of goats for the tender shoots of young trees. We went up into one of the small forests to eat the picnic we had brought, sitting in the filtered light coming down through the filigree branches of those lovely trees.

On another day we took Jane south to Tyre to a long deserted beach that stretched all the way to the Israeli border. But the beach was not deserted for long. We were soon surrounded by small and not so small boys who moved with us almost in unison wherever we went—into the water and out of the water—like a moving magnetic field.

But what I most wanted Jane to see and appreciate was the AUB campus and my life and friends there. We spent hours with my roommates, one day going with them to Naziha's weekend house in Souk el Gharb where we were to have a picnic in the mountains nearby. Astonished when two family cars picked the six of us up to chauffeur us to a favorite picnic spot a five-minute walk away, Jane and I were even more surprised when we found the picnic already laid out for us on a linen tablecloth, delivered a few minutes earlier by the family servant. This was not the kind of rustic picnic we were used to in California.

When we weren't sightseeing, we could stretch out in the sun at the swimming place at the bottom of the campus. Though there was no sand in sight, this favorite warm-weather retreat for students was familiarly known as the AUB beach. There we could watch the sea splash up over the rocky shoreline or gaze at the exquisite view of bay and mountains. In winter storms, I had seen waves crash over these rocks and up onto the corniche road separating the AUB athletic field from the "beach."

In the evenings we took Jane to the movies or to visit friends. At the end of her two-week visit Malcolm and I celebrated our engagement at a party arranged by Mrs. Kerr. I remember little of it now, mainly the pastel-colored lanterns strung amongst the pine trees in the beautiful garden of the Kerr house and dozens of the Kerrs' friends, few of whom I can now recall, milling about in the garden. There was a big cake with our names on it, which Malcolm and I must have cut as we received the congratulations of family friends and fellow students.

Memories of the end of the evening stand out as vividly as any of the entire year when I had to say good-bye to my roommates and close friends from the hostel. Malcolm and Jane and I were to board a ship for Europe the next day en route ultimately back to the United States. I would not see these friends from the hostel again for a long time, and it was very hard to say good-bye. Jane, too, was affected by this parting, having had a microcosmic experience of my longer one at AUB. Our farewells were tearful but interjected with promises to write and meet again not too far into the future.

The next day, in mid-June of 1955, we boarded the SS *Iskandarun,* a Turkish passenger liner, to set sail for Naples, Jane and I in deck class for $27.31 apiece and Malcolm only a little higher up the scale of nonluxury in class 4 B. My former advisor to women students, now future mother-in-law, and the popular professor of biochemistry, now my future father-in-law, waved good-bye to us fondly from the dock. I knew, as we sailed away, that a part of me would always belong to the Middle East, but with Malcolm there, I was carrying some of that world with me.

CHAPTER 7

Return to the United States

Vivid recollections of that carefree summer of 1955 remain—
watching flames shooting out of Mt. Etna on a warm June
night as we sat on the deck of the SS *Iskanderun* and sailed through
the Straits of Messina toward Naples. Jane, Malcolm, and I were a
congenial threesome as we viewed the splendors of Italy together
and savored the delicious cuisine at the cheapest restaurants we
could find. We feasted our eyes on dramatic Alpine scenes on a
train ride from Venice to Munich and then on to Bad Reichenhall
where Malcolm was to spend a month studying German in preparation for his Ph.D. language requirement. Jane and I spent that
month traveling and visiting friends in Holland and a childhood
friend, Kirsten Bjerknes, in Norway, and then met Malcolm again
for a few romantic days before departing on separate ships for Canada. My parents responded with disapproval later when we informed them of the daring deed of the three of us having shared a
room together in Paris. They and our maternal aunt and uncle
were to meet Jane and me in Quebec where our ship docked, and
then we would have a reunion with our Canadian family. Malcolm
would join us at that gathering in Ottawa.

I remember the sight of my parents looking youthful and
handsome with my mother's older sister and her husband, Olive
and Ralph Wetmore, next to them waving to us at the dock, and
finally the joy of being reunited. It did not take long, however,
for our parents to find that Jane and I had become so caught up in
all our travels that we were having a hard time returning to the
bosom of the family. "The girls are certainly feeling their oats,"

101

my father remarked to my mother as we drove toward Ottawa. In later years they were more specific in recounting our behavior. "You were quite obnoxious at that stage," my mother reminded me at a moment when I was complaining to her of the unpleasant behavior of my children on occasion when they came home from college for a visit in a state of self-absorption.

Recollections of Malcolm's arrival in Ottawa and his first meeting with my family are surprisingly vague. I think of that occasion now from a parent's viewpoint, trying to imagine how my parents felt when they met their future son-in-law for the first time, a rather skinny stranger from a faraway land. But I was not thinking of how they felt. I was elated to be with him again. The commitment to our future marriage had been made, and I assumed that they would support it as they had supported other decisions I had made.

Malcolm drove south with us across the border into the United States and went on to Washington on his own to begin his Ph.D. studies at the Johns Hopkins School of Advanced International Studies while the Zwicker family drove west to California where Jane began her freshman year at Stanford and I returned to Occidental for my senior year. Malcolm would come for Christmas and then for the summer for my graduation and our August wedding. The prospect of that year's wait was a gloomy one, but it was good for Malcolm to launch his Ph.D. studies and for me to have that time with my family. I also knew that I had to finish college before marrying, and Malcolm did not try to persuade me otherwise.

We got to know each other on a new level that year through correspondence which deepened our relationship. I remember running to my mailbox in the Student Union Building at Occidental to look for his letters which came several times a week. I grew to love Malcolm even more through those letters which brought out more of his reflective capacities than he revealed in person. And there was always his wondrous wit, as vivid in writing as in person. Sadly none of those letters remain. We discarded them for some reason, perhaps in the prudishness of our generation not wanting our progeny to read the passages of amorous longing for each other. Those must be the only letters ever discarded in our family of avid letter writers and savers.

That summer of 1956, along with our personal milestone events, brought another Middle Eastern crisis of international import, the Suez War which erupted when Egyptian president Gamal Abdul Nasser took over the Suez Canal Company from Britain and France after being refused money to build the Aswan Dam by U.S. Secretary of State John Foster Dulles. Subsequently, Nasser got the money to build the dam from the Soviet Union. Israel, with French and British approval, successfully invaded Egypt to protect their interests in the Canal. This drew the attention of the United States and the Soviet Union whose own interests were threatened. There were fears of atomic war and international financial collapse. Ultimately, world disapproval and United Nations action, supported by the United States, brought Israeli, French, and British withdrawal and the clearing of the canal for passage.

In June, Malcolm's and my long period of separation ended, and we were too caught up in my graduation celebrations and plans for our wedding to think much about problems in the Middle East. We were married on August 18 in the Santa Monica Presbyterian Church, in a candlelight ceremony. The memory remains as a misty vision of the white silk of my wedding gown and the bridesmaids' dresses accented by pink roses and echoes of music of Bach and Mozart which Malcolm had chosen. We had little inkling then of how much that new love and commitment would grow and deepen, although, had we been able to see beyond our years, the example of our parents' excellent marriages might have given us some hints. At the wedding reception in our garden I downed glass after glass of champagne punch, the only liquid available while standing in the reception line, to quench my dry mouth after the nervousness of the wedding ceremony. My parents had created a wonderland with candle lanterns and baskets of pink and white geraniums, which seemed all the more dream-like after so much champagne punch. Guests strolled under our old rose arbor laden with pink roses to the walnut, lemon, and avocado trees in the back garden.

Malcolm, never one to enjoy standing around talking in groups, whisked me away with undue haste almost as soon as the last hand was shaken, to go off on our honeymoon at a beachside inn up the coast. The old green Chevrolet we had bought a month earlier had been festooned with streamers, tin cans, and

9. Malcolm and Ann Kerr's wedding, August 18, 1956.

old shoes by Malcolm's brother Doug, the best man, my sister Jane, the maid of honor, and by her new friend, Tim Sanders, whom we had recruited as an usher to complement the large number of bridesmaids.

With streamers flying we made our way up Pacific Coast Highway to the Pierpont Inn in Ventura, where we stayed in a small cottage perched in dunes under windswept cypress trees. We were alone with the sound of the waves and the wind blowing through the branches above.

A few days later we returned to pack our wedding gifts into the back of our Chevrolet, bid farewell to my family, and set off across the country for Cambridge, Massachusetts, where we were to live for the next two years. I remember the poignant feeling in parting from my parents and sister that our family unit of four was now permanently changed.

After completing his year's residence at Johns Hopkins School of International Studies, Malcolm wanted to write his Ph.D. dissertation at Harvard University with Sir Hamilton Gibb, a renowned scholar in Middle Eastern studies. He had decided at the end of the previous academic year that the Harvard Middle Eastern program was a better place to pursue the subject of his dissertation on the political and legal theories of Muhammad Abduh and Rashid Rida, two early twentieth-century intellectuals in Egypt. I was delighted at the prospect of having a chance to discover the Ivy League firsthand and to be near New England relatives. My uncle, Ralph Wetmore, was a professor of botany at Harvard, and he and my Aunt Olive, the eldest of my mother's three sisters, provided a family base in Cambridge in a beautiful old house a few blocks from our apartment. Aunt Olive had found the apartment for us at the corner of Ware and Harvard streets in a handsome brick building a few blocks from Harvard Square. For eighty dollars a month, we had an apartment with a fireplace, handsome molded wood work, and a view looking out on the steeple and gardens of the New England Telephone Company next door.

Aunt Olive had also made inquiries about teaching jobs for me. She drove me around to various schools, and within a day or two I found a job teaching at Warren Junior High School in West Newton, a half-hour drive from Cambridge. I was grateful for my B.A. in education from Occidental and the California teaching credential I had earned which transferred easily to Massachusetts. I was to earn $3,500 a year, $1,000 less than my male counterparts in the Newton school system, but that money, along with a similar amount Malcolm had that year from a Rockefeller grant, made it possible for us to live comfortably in 1956.

Our married life started out in the mid-fifties in much the way prescribed for a modern liberated marriage. As I drove off to work through the autumn leaves of New England, Malcolm washed the breakfast dishes before starting his work. He used to love to tell friends about the remarks of the announcer on the radio program he listened to as he finished the kitchen chores, "Well ladies, now that you've got hubby off to work and finished the dishes, it's time to sit down and have another cup of coffee." At that point, he would settle down to read the political and legal theories of Muhammad Abduh and his disciple Rashid Rida.

As we discovered that Harvard Square offered almost as many

movie theaters as Beirut, we eagerly resumed our old habits. By
the end of the day, Malcolm was tired of thinking about Islamic
reform, and I was tired of students and American history; movies
were the ideal antidote. There were old classics to be seen at the
Brattle Theater and current films at the Harvard Theater. Malcolm
occasionally helped me grade my students' papers so that we could
get to the movies on time. The square had even more bookstores
than movie theaters. While shopping in the afternoon after teaching, tempting displays in the windows lured me inside to browse.
The intellectual atmosphere of Harvard was stimulating, especially
when one could attend lectures by the authors of the books that
were for sale in the bookstores. Seeds of intellectual curiosity
planted at Occidental and AUB started to grow. I began to read
authors I would not have read before, Paul Tillich and Reinhold
Niebuhr who lectured at the university or spoke in the Harvard
chapel services Malcolm and I attended on Sunday mornings. Exis-
tentialism was the in-vogue topic with Albert Camus and Fran-
coise Sagan, the young writers everyone was talking about.

For Malcolm, the great intellectual satisfaction of that year was
studying with Sir Hamilton Gibb, who was one of the most wide-
ranging and competent scholars on the Middle East of this century. Sir Hamilton was a quiet, modest man with a profound
knowledge of all aspects of Middle Eastern history, politics, language, and culture. He and his wife had recently come to Harvard
from Oxford and seemed to enjoy their new life in America, mixing easily at student-faculty social gatherings.

There were many diversions during those two years, lectures
at the Harvard Middle Eastern Center, concerts and plays in Boston, and picnics on the banks of the Charles River a few blocks
from our apartment. There, on Sundays, we ate our sandwiches
and read our books. I remember my sense of excitement one spring
afternoon when I was reading Paul Tillich's *The Courage to Be,* and
he and his wife strolled by. On those weekend picnics, Malcolm
and I also took up the new game of Frisbee, which soon became
popular across America. A natural talent for throwing that brightly
colored plastic disk kept us from losing too many of them in the
river. Our addiction to Frisbee was affirmed in those two years,
and it became our sport. Henceforth, we never traveled anyplace
without one. Later our children learned to throw a Frisbee almost

as soon as they learned to throw a ball, and I found that that flat disk which fit easily into a suitcase could double as a palette for my watercolors.

During the summer of 1957 between our two years at Harvard, my sister Jane married Tim Sanders, a bright Stanford student of physics. I went home to California for a month to be with my family and celebrate the wedding. Malcolm had to go to a conference in Washington and to spend some time back at SAIS, so we were separated for a month, the longest separation of our marriage until he went ahead of me to Beirut to assume the AUB presidency in 1982.

Studying the Middle East was not the same as living there; Malcolm and I both felt nostalgic for Lebanon, and as we thought about job possibilities for Malcolm for the year after the completion of his graduate work, AUB was at the top of our list. When news came that his job application to teach in the political science department had been accepted, we were overjoyed. A few weeks later we had more news to celebrate, this time completely unanticipated. I was pregnant with our first child who would be born in November shortly after our arrival in Beirut.

By the spring of 1958, Malcolm had completed his thesis and was ready to defend it. He passed with flying colors and in June we drove to Baltimore to the main campus of Johns Hopkins University to attend his graduation ceremonies. Never having been there before, we had to ask directions to find the campus. Milton Eisenhower was the president of Johns Hopkins at the time, and his brother President Dwight Eisenhower was the graduation speaker.

After packing up our few belongings in Cambridge to send off to Beirut, we went to California to be with my parents for the summer. Our good-byes to them in August were difficult, for we were to be in Beirut for three years and trips back and forth for them or for us were unlikely. This was to be the first of many trips Malcolm and I, and soon our children, were to make back and forth between California and the Middle East.

CHAPTER 8

Back to Beirut

R evolution in Iraq," "King Faisal and Prime Minister Nuri al-
Said Assassinated," "Americans Killed in Baghdad," "US Marines Land in Lebanon" read the headlines during the summer of
1958. The momentum for Arab unity symbolized by Gamal Abdul Nasser combined with rivalries between Christian and Muslim
sects in Lebanon to spark a brief civil war that summer. At the
same time in Baghdad the problems of a pro-British Iraqi regime
in an increasingly anti-Western Arab world erupted in violence.
The Hashemite king, a first cousin of Jordan's King Hussein, was
killed along with the Prime Minister, Nuri al-Said, and a group of
Army officers seized power. In an effort to stabilize the region, the
United States sent troops to Lebanon and Britain sent troops to
Jordan. They remained for only a short time. Lebanon's Christian-
dominated government, formerly headed by President Camile
Chamoun, continued in power but in a very different form under a
new president, Fuad Shihab, using the slogan, "No victors, no
vanquished," but the fragility of the sectarian balance between
Christians and Muslims was underscored and revealed the potential
for future civil war. A backdrop to these regional eruptions was
the Cold War and the American attempts to keep the Middle East
free of communism by building alliances with pro-Western Arab
countries.

Any doubts we had about returning to Lebanon were forgotten
when we read that Lebanese "Chiclet boys" and street vendors met
the 5,000 or so U.S. Marines delivered by the Sixth Fleet to Beirut beaches, and sold them chewing gum and Coca-Cola at highly

108

inflated prices. This meant business as usual and with 500 percent profits. The tourist shop business boomed on Marine payday. The economy survived in spite of the crisis—or because of it—and not an angry bullet was fired.

We landed in mid-September two months after the Marines had come and gone and two months before our baby was due. As we taxied along the tramline toward the university, I asked Malcolm if he didn't think Beirut looked a little disorderly. And wasn't the traffic worse? As we were trying to decide if our expectations were too high because we had just been traveling in neat and tidy Switzerland with Malcolm's parents, our driver, his fist jammed to the horn, pulled out into the left side of the street and went barreling past a bumper-to-bumper line of cars until he inevitably came face to face with a car coming toward us head on. The approaching driver made a pretense of planning not to stop and then came screeching to a halt two inches away. Our driver leaned his head out the window and started lambasting him for not stopping sooner. Naturally the other driver cursed out ours for driving on the wrong side of the street against the traffic. Then both drivers got out of their cars and started shaking their fists at each other, cursing louder and louder. A very un-Lebanese looking policeman in a spic-and-span white uniform and plumed helmet came striding toward us blowing a whistle. We later learned that he was part of a group of Italian policemen who had been brought over as part of a plan to solve traffic problems. While this handsome specimen of authority blew and blew on his whistle, the two taxi drivers yelled louder and louder. Meanwhile other drivers started solving this problem with brazen Lebanese know-how. They merely drove up over the curb onto the sidewalk and bypassed the traffic jam. When the road was finally clear, our driver got back in the taxi and took us on our way, leaving the beplumed Italian standing there blowing his whistle. The similarity now occurs to me of this incident to other displays of futile international efforts to curb the Lebanese.

As we drove into the city that September afternoon in 1958, we were aware of the recurring pattern in Lebanon of rival religious groups competing for power and the intrusion of Western powers to aid the side where their vested interests lay. The city was still under curfew, our taxi driver told us, and shooting could still be heard at night in some areas. When we reached the AUB campus we were shocked to see U.S. tanks at the main gates, left behind after the Marine landing to protect American citizens and interests. There were also American warships in the harbor visible from the campus.

From the medical gate, I looked up Rue Abdul Aziz, the street where I had walked daily between the hostel and the university. At first I wasn't sure it was the same street. Eight- and ten-story office and apartment buildings had replaced some of the small shops and villas. There were fewer gardens and more big American cars on the street than before. These were the tangible bits of evidence for the changes in my perception of the old neighborhood Malcolm and I had known so well. But three years of life in oversized, superclean America, and three years of idealizing our memories of Beirut were the less tangible explanations for my disorientation.

We drove up Abdul Aziz through an unseasonable thunderstorm to Malcolm's parents' home in one of the new high buildings. Their beautiful campus house had been torn down to accommodate new women's dorms. What a lot of changes in only three years! The Kerrs had arrived home in Beirut from our European trip a week earlier. It was comforting to have parents there to welcome us and help us settle in. When the storm subsided, we went and had a look at our home for the coming year in the faculty apartment building on Abdel Aziz Street a few steps from the university. It was spacious and clean and looked very luxurious to us, particularly after the small apartment in Cambridge where we had spent the last two years. The university also provided furniture, simple but distinctively designed in local wood, wicker, and leather. There was a wide balcony across one side which looked down on the AUB alumni club and tennis courts. While Malcolm's parents and I were still discovering what we could see from the balcony, Malcolm's voice called excitedly from inside, "Come see the baby's room." Baby's room—I thought for an instant as I heard the elation in his voice. What an intrusion on our privacy! Until that moment it hadn't occurred to me that no longer would I get to have Malcolm's attentions all to myself.

During the next weeks the nesting instinct set in and I became absorbed in turning that small plain bedroom into the kind of baby's room I had always dreamed of. Malcolm, in separate endeavors, stayed up many nights until midnight preparing lectures in political science and international relations for his first year of teaching. Even if there had been time to go to the movies, we would not have been able to because of nightly dawn to dusk curfews that continued in the wake of the recent political disturbances, locally referred to as "the events." This was not the Beirut life that Malcolm and I had felt nostalgic for over the past three years. The sound of distant guns at night and in the early mornings in September and October of 1958 indicated that the "events" were not completely over. When General Fuad Shihab was inaugurated as president after the forced retreat of President Chamoun's government, a counterrevolution erupted. This was initiated by the right-wing Christian party who called a general strike that closed down most of Beirut. Curfews were lengthened which left only a few hours a day to go out to buy food.

As it turned out, the most severe battle in our part of town was waged between housewives to see who could clear the shelves the fastest during the brief shopping periods each day. But the sound of distant gunfire continued, and, in a ceaseless search for explanations, rumors flew as to what was really happening. The absence of usually abundant fresh fruits and vegetables told us that roads into the city were blocked. But food shortages or not, Beirut hostesses continued to prepare delicious meals and invite friends who lived nearby. Outside on the streets the garbage piled up and mail and newspapers remained undelivered, but there was plenty of free time and no shortage of liquor. Curfews were a time to get to know your neighbors better.

As a pregnant lady of leisure I was happy to have a lot of social life and to meet some new friends. The halo I felt I wore by virtue of carrying within me a member of the next generation did not go unappreciated in the Middle East, where motherhood is venerated. I was surprised, however, as I observed the certainty with which the sex of my child was identified. "Look at how pointed her stomach is; surely Ann will have a boy," one well wishing woman stated emphatically. And with just as much certainty, another woman challenged, "But look at the circles under her eyes. It's going to be a girl."

During that fall there were times when more serious war

seemed to be a real possibility, but the precarious and peculiarly Lebanese religious/political balance was eventually restored, and danger passed for the time being. The counterrevolution produced a compromise cabinet without having to recognize victors. By the end of October, curfews ceased and none too soon for us, as our daughter Susie wanted to be born.

It almost happened at a tennis match. The first signs of her imminent arrival had already occurred, but I wanted to keep calm and go watch Malcolm play in the first postcurfew tennis tournament. In those pre-Lamaze days we had not thought of making elaborate preparations for joint birthgiving, and I figured that when the time was right I would go to the hospital around the corner from our apartment and let the doctors take over. Unfamiliar with just what the right time should feel like, I sat with Malcolm, watching the match before his, holding his hand tightly, and pressing my feet firmly against the low cement wall in front of us. As it began to feel that the cement wall might break from the pressure I was putting on it, I told Malcolm I thought it was time. I would go to the hospital, and he could come as soon as his match was over.

I wish he were here now to ask him if he remembered who won the tennis match or if he even finished the match. In any case, it was a quick victory for someone because Malcolm arrived in time to hear Susie's first cries, and perhaps some of mine too, from the hall outside the delivery room—all of which were uttered within about an hour of my arrival at the hospital.

She was a tiny little thing, five-and-a-half pounds, and looked like a rosebud to her adoring parents, albeit a rosebud with funny dark hair sticking up all over her head. I remember the immediate postbirth elation, thinking that I had produced this lovely little creature who would not only be my child but also a best friend for the rest of my life. Then within a day or two came the mysterious postpartum letdown when tears flowed without any understandable stimulus and without any focus.

"Maleesh, tani mara fee sabe," the Kerr family barber said to Malcolm on his first visit there after Susie's birth. "Never mind, next time you'll have a boy." And in an attempt to further reduce the disappointment of one of his favorite clients having produced a female first child, the barber added in Arabic, "and besides, she will help her mother."

Although this prophecy was eventually to be fulfilled, it would take a few years. It was a discouraging prospect to come home from the hospital and face mountains of diapers without a washing machine. Malcolm's mother came to our rescue and found a woman to work for us who had been employed by AUB families for many years. Najeebe, a strong, handsome woman of around forty-five with high cheekbones, luminous dark eyes and gray streaked black hair pulled back in a bun, became not only our laundry woman and babysitter but also a granny-like figure for Susie, and later for our other children. We developed great respect and fondness for Najeebe and got to know her well. Her house was on the next street from ours, a lean-to, corrugated metal shack of the sort common in Beirut that hover against large modern buildings which house the upper and middle classes. Through geographical proximity and our close relationship with Najeebe, Malcolm and I had an increasingly keen awareness of the living circumstances of the poorer segment of the Lebanese population.

This strong and dignified woman was a widow with two stepchildren and three of her own whom she had raised by working as a housekeeper. They were grown up now except for a fourteen-year-old boy who worked after school as an apprentice in a patisserie, learning how to make fancy cakes. One son was a taxi driver, another a shoemaker. They earned their own money, and yet like many a mother in Lebanon, Najeebe spoiled her sons and probably passed on some of her hard-earned wages to them if they asked for money. It would have been economically difficult and socially uncustomary for these working men in their twenties to set up housekeeping outside their mother's home. Even if their income had been sufficient to support themselves, they would have been inept at housekeeping, accustomed as they were to having their mother and sister serve them. By the time they were thirty-five or forty, perhaps they would have earned and saved enough money to marry and set up their own households. They would have to find a suitable girl in her twenties who was a distant relative or family friend of the same religion.

The child who caused Najeebe the most anguish was her daughter, Adeebe, who had married a taxi driver of weak character by the name of Ilyas. Immediately after their marriage, they moved into two-room quarters with his ill-tempered mother and various other members of his family. Adeebe had the same natural dignity as her mother, but she seemed less indestructible. Najeebe's concerns for her daughter bore evidence in the fact that poor Adeebe's life seemed to move from one trauma to another.

One morning Najeebe arrived an hour late for work, completely distraught and spilling out the story of how Adeebe's husband's taxi had been demolished in an accident. Najeebe knew no English, so I was learning Arabic fast, but not fast enough to pick up all the details. "Itnashr alf lira," (12,000 pounds) she kept repeating woefully. This was evidently the payment that Ilyas owed on his taxi. I wanted to ask if he had insurance, but I didn't know how to say insurance in Arabic. Anyway, from her melancholy, I judged that they were quite destitute.

Eager to help, I asked Adeebe to come and sew for me. At the end of each workday, I gave her a ten pound note to help her feed her family. It never occurred to me that when she got home, her husband or mother-in-law might force her to hand over her earnings and unilaterally decide how it should be spent.

Somehow the family weathered that crisis and later went on to others, equally unfortunate. If my private poverty program didn't do too much good financially, there were other benefits. Adeebe and I became good friends on those sewing days. She had learned some English working for her previous employer and in school, so we spoke in a mixture of English and Arabic and the natural nonlinguistic communication of friends. We had an easy rapport that was unhindered by different cultural or social or economic backgrounds. And we had in common the fact that we were young women of the same age and each had a new baby daughter.

Our complaints about the world, however, were different. While Adeebe's troubles stemmed from poverty and a rough and thoughtless husband, my occasional gripes came from the restrictions of being a housewife rather than having the freedom to pursue an exciting career. The fact that I had a loving husband, friendly in-laws, a beautiful baby, and a pleasant woman to help with housework only made me feel more remorseful for such dissatisfactions. My image, formed in the fifties, of an idyllic marriage and family of four children did not allow for mixing in a career until the children were older. This was a concern Adeebe and I did not have in common. She had not had the privilege of a college education and travel halfway around the world nor the resulting inclination to put such experience to use. She would have settled happily for a little more kindness from her husband and her mother-in-law and the certainty of knowing there would always be enough money for the next meal.

There were antidotes to my "housewifeitis" and feelings of being cooped up in our apartment. While Susie was at home having her morning nap and Najeebe was helping to prepare our next meal, I audited courses at AUB and stopped for visits with Malcolm in his office. As a first year professor, he was very busy learning how to teach international relations and introductory political science, but if I caught him at the right time, he liked to be interrupted. In the afternoons I took Susie for outings in her new Italian baby carriage over the bumpy sidewalks of Ras Beirut. Hula hoops and television had come to Lebanon, though the latter was still too expensive for most people to have their own sets. When we passed a congregation of people standing in front of a shop window, it usually meant they were watching a television set tuned to the latest Egyptian produced soap opera or an old American western. Lebanese children and teenagers, as adept at picking up the latest trends from the West as their parents, moved in rhythmic motion to support the hula hoops that whirled around their hips. Most of the shopkeepers along these streets were the same ones I had gotten to know three years earlier walking to and from the university. If they weren't engrossed in business, they stood near the doors of their shops ready to socialize with acquaintances who walked by. Susie and I became a daily object of attraction for these shopkeepers whose attentions seemed complimentary and harmless as long as I had my baby with me. Several became friends who have remained so over the years.

When we reached the campus we found a host of other mothers who had also brought their babies to this haven of green away from the city. We mothers and children were an added ingredient to the varied complexion of the campus where, amidst Lebanese and other Arab students, Ethiopian women strolled to their classes cloaked in filmy white gowns, and Indians and Nepalese were draped in saris in a range of exquisite colors. Pakistani girls wore full trousers with long jackets. And there was even a handful of Far Easterners, Japanese and Chinese, something we had not seen three years earlier. Another new sight, it seemed to

Malcolm and me, was an occasional Arab couple sitting on our bench overlooking the sea, well apart from each other but obviously together and romantically inclined.

Students were as concerned as ever with the Arab-Israeli problem, and the university continued to be an open forum for discussing this issue. Malcolm, as one who had grown up in the Arab world and as a political scientist, felt intricately involved with the question of justice for the Palestinians and constantly drawn to this issue. At the same time he grew impatient when the Arab-Israeli question dominated discussion in his class to the extent that it was difficult to discuss anything else. He would come home and complain of this or that student who had "once again managed to turn an analysis of a political theory being studied into a diatribe on the Palestinian problem." With more fairmindedness than patience, and with a conviction that the core of AUB's existence was the open expression of ideas, Malcolm tried to give his students free rein while attempting at the same time to help them see the tremendous complexities that lay behind the Arab-Israeli problem. Malcolm was always impatient with devil theories or polemics on both sides, which ignored these complexities. He saw the Arab-Israeli problem as a real tragedy, with rights and wrongs on both sides and tremendous potential danger. He spoke his mind in academic and popular debate as he emphasized the necessity of viewing this as a two-sided issue; Arabs needed to confront the de facto existence of Israel, and Israelis needed to recognize the Palestinian loss of a homeland. A one-sided victory was unworkable. In audiences where the thinking prevailed that if "you're not with us, you're against us," Malcolm's open expression of principles sometimes brought him enemies, but he was incapable of not saying what he thought.

The principles that Malcolm believed should be applied to finding a solution to peace in the Middle East were stated by the Security Council in Resolution 242 after the Arab-Israeli war in June of 1967. The main tenets are Arab recognition of the state of Israel, the return of Arab territories occupied in 1967, and a solution to the refugee problem.

In the first pages of the introduction to the book, *The Elusive Peace in the Middle East,* which Malcolm edited and completed at

UCLA in 1975, he wrote of the complexities underlying the process of finding a solution to the Arab-Israeli problem (1975, 1, 3).

> The best way to begin a book about peace in the Middle East is to acknowledge that it is not a promising subject. Everything in the historical record must encourage the most pervasive pessimism. While it is good to favor peace, comforting to suppose that peace is what the mass of ordinary people in the world desire, and tempting to ascribe the persistence of conflict to needless fears and misunderstandings, in the Middle East it is too late for such simplemindedness. Clearly we are contending with fundamental difficulties so that peace has been at best an intermediate objective for some and indeed a negative value for others. At key moments prolongation of the conflict has always been a tolerable price to pay, if it was a price at all, for the pursuit of other interests. This holds true not only for Israelis and Arabs but for the leading members of the United Nations, notably the United States.
>
> Not only Arabs and Israelis have widely differing visions of the conflict between them, but outsiders too: statesmen, journalists, academics, men in the street. The disparaties among statesmen's perspectives add to the difficulties of negotiation, and ultimately the same must be said about men in the street—different men in different streets, conditioned in part by what their own political leaders and newspapers tell them.

We often had Malcolm's students to our house for tea, which provided an opportunity to see them in a different light than in the classroom. There was little evidence of their strong political ideas or of their loquaciousness. During the first half hour of their visit, Malcolm would try to break the ice with informal conversation, with jokes, with tales of Beirut and AUB in his childhood. But in this unaccustomed social situation with their professor, these young people felt awkward. On one occasion I began to wonder if it would have been kinder not to invite them, but then Susie woke up from her nap. We brought her out and the change was magical. Soon all the students were talking at once vying for Susie's attention. The ice was broken, and from speaking of children and families we moved easily on to other subjects.

As we were getting into the swing of our new life as parents and professor and wife, Lebanon was returning to the free and easy place we remembered. It was still the country where you could brag about skiing in the morning, swimming in the afternoon and going to nightclubs in the evening. Although we never managed to do all these things in one day, we enjoyed them all at different times.

On an early spring Sunday we left Susie off at her grandparents' and joined our former AUB classmate, Chris Nagorski and her husband, for a day of skiing at the Bisharri cedars. As we got close to our destination we became choked in bumper-to-bumper traffic. In front of us, blocking out any view of what was ahead, was a huge bus full of students singing and yelling. Behind us was the chauffeur-driven, black limousine of the American ambassador. The small American flag atop the hood flapped in the mountain breezes, and the ambassador sat regally in the back seat with his constant companion, an oversized black poodle, at his side. When the crowds reached their destination, there would be a natural separation. The haute societe of Lebanon and high placed foreigners would go to their chalets or the finer rooms of the ski lodge. The bus loads of students and service taxis full of village people out for perhaps a once in a lifetime view of this sporting scene would have to rough it, gathering around an outdoor fire where tables and chairs were set up and the ubiquitous Coca-Cola was for sale.

We inched along and finally found ourselves in a large parking area where it looked like half of Lebanon must have parked their cars. In front of us was a white mountainside dotted with humanity on skis. It struck me how incongruous this scene of Arabs on skis was with the popular Western image of Arabs riding across the desert on camels. More incongruous to us were two men standing at the edge of the parking lot talking loudly to their friends, one of them holding in one hand a gun and with the other hand fingering his prayer beads.

The length of time we spent standing in line for the ski tow was far longer than the length of time I spent on skis. Knowing neither how to ski nor how to start learning, I went to the top of the mountain with Malcolm who knew only a little more than I did but was fearless. It looked terribly steep and no place for beginners, but we started down. Predictably, I was soon sprawled on the mountainside with my legs going agonizingly in the wrong direction. Malcolm was already far down the mountain and oblivious to my predicament. With good Lebanese efficiency, I was soon picked up by someone on a sled with a big red cross on it and whisked at frightening speed down to a chair by the outdoor fire. From my resting place I watched Malcolm, still unaware of my fate, ski cautiously but steadfastly down the mountain with a look of great pleasure and satisfaction on his face. Near the bottom of the hill the ambassador was sensibly taking lessons, starting slowly on a low slope. Behind him his giant poodle was sloshing about in the snow.

An easier form of recreation and more to my liking was picnicking on the wonderful Beirut beaches. We had the use of a friend's cabin at St. Michel beach on the outskirts of the city on the way to the airport. Once or twice a week when Malcolm had a light course load, we put Susie and a picnic lunch in the car and drove out for a leisurely lunch hour. In winter and spring we and the fishermen had the beach pretty much to ourselves. We lay on the beach on those brilliant clear days watching the gulls perched on the gnarled rock formations in the bay, waiting to pounce on fish entrails cast into the sea by the fishermen. The only interruption of this nautical tranquillity was a new, very loud kind of airplane. The first jets flying in low over the city to Beirut Airport made the gulls flurry and the faces of the fishermen turn upward in awe. But this interruption was mild by comparison with the devastation that would envelop them twenty years hence, turning St. Michel beach into an overcrowded refugee camp of makeshift houses and misery.

Beirut's social pace became a routine part of our existence, though we tried to be selective. There were lunch parties, cocktail parties, dinner parties, and an occasional very splendid affair like the party we went to one evening given by the well-known Lebanese historian from Princeton, Philip Hitti, in honor of the visiting AUB trustees. The party was held in the home of Professor Hitti's brother, a wealthy Beirut doctor.

Police patrolled the street in front of the doctor's palatial home when we drove up. Once inside we saw why. Most of the officials of the government were there, as well as ambassadors and company executives. The house was filled with museum-like collections of Arab and Western antiques and books and artifacts. Rooms were done in different styles alternating among Arab, French, and Turkish, each authentic in its representation.

After the party some friends took us to one of Beirut's many night clubs, a dimly lighted place called the Casbah. The people in Beirut night clubs always looked different to me than any other gathering of people in Lebanon. Unlike the hardy, ruddy-cheeked mountain people or the highly energized Beirut merchants, night club people sat in overjeweled, overindulged ennui, almost as if they were permanent properties of the place.

As the end of the school year drew to a close, we had to start looking for another place to live, for faculty apartments were available to newcomers for only one year to help them settle into life in Beirut with ease. It was a perplexing prospect at first, but we eventually tracked down a beautiful place to live which we immediately dubbed our "penthouse." It was a rustic rooftop apartment on Rue Sadat a few blocks from the university, a lovely spot overlooking the red-tiled rooftops of the AUB campus and the Mediterranean and Mt. Sanneen beyond. There were two bedrooms, kitchen, entry hall, and good-sized living room with a fireplace and windows on three sides looking out on expansive views. Before the summer holiday began we moved our few possessions in; it would be our home for the next two years.

Ahead of us lay the pleasure of a summer in Ainab with Malcolm's parents and a trip to Cyprus by ourselves while Susie had some time alone with her Kerr grandparents. I don't remember talking about it then, but we must have gone off on our trip at the end of that school year with a certain sense of accomplishment that we had personally made the transition to different roles in a different Beirut than we had known in our students days.

CHAPTER 9

Halcyon Days

*T*hose next two years from the fall of 1959 to the summer of 1961 in our "penthouse" apartment, with our cabin at St. Michel Beach, a ten-minute drive away, and summers and occasional weekends in Ainab were always halcyon days in Malcolm's mind. While the height of my Beirut nostalgia lingers with that first carefree year as a student when I was falling in love with Malcolm and the Middle East, it seems to me that his nostalgia focused on the period from 1959 to 1961 when he was a young professor and new father and when we were living idyllically overlooking the university that he had loved since childhood. He occasionally talked about those times as being among the best of our lives.

Summers in the hilltop above Ainab meant a stream of days reading on a sunny pine needle–strewn porch or sitting at the tennis court, visiting with our neighbors while awaiting our turn to play. Good Lebanese food was spread before us in our outdoor dining area by the maid Malcolm's parents had hired from the village. She and the boy who brought up our groceries on his donkey were our principal contacts with the village of Ainab. Once a month or so Abu Ali and Um Ali, an octogenerian Druze shaykh and his wife from the neighboring village of Baysoor paid us a visit.

Abu Ali was a colorful sight with his white turbaned headdress and long white beard, red tunic jacket, and baggy bottomed black pants. He was as tall and lean as his wife was short and plump. Um Ali carefully kept the white cloth around her head pulled across her face below her eyes in the traditional custom of many village women, of covering their faces in front of men who were not members of their family. We learned little of their personalities. After the first round of inquiries about members of respective families, there was stony silence, broken only by the passing of cookies and lemonade, for which they had a remarkable capacity to consume enormous amounts. Finally they would proceed to the next house, having paid their obligatory respects and satisfied their curiosity that the Americans on the hilltop were spending their summer vacationing in the same way they had in previous summers over the past twenty-five years.

While Um Ali and other village women still covered their faces in front of strangers, veiling was no longer common in Beirut and other Middle Eastern cities by the 1950s. The custom of veiling, which predates Islam, has always varied among different social classes and regions and changes in reaction to political and historical trends. It is basically a Muslim practice, but Christian women in the Middle East also consider modesty important in their dress, for that is the atmosphere surrounding them. A few women began to shed the veil after World War I and others gradually followed. In Turkey, Kemal Ataturk banned the veil in the 1920s as part of his efforts to modernize his country after the end of the Ottoman Empire. Veiling became common again, particularly among urban women, in the 1970s and 1980s as Islamic fundamentalism replaced Arab nationalism as the popular wave of thinking.

During our Ainab summers we were sometimes joined on weekends by friends from Beirut who came to sample our brand of village life. So pleasant and peaceful was that life that only rarely did we ourselves feel the urge to venture away. An occasional picnic to the Damour River in the valley to the east of us for swimming and a visit to a picturesque potterer by an old Turkish bridge was the main change from the rhythm of Ainab days. Once or twice a summer there was also an expedition to the music festival at Baalbek with a stop for dinner in Zahle in one of the restaurants situated by the stream that coursed down the mountainside through the town. Malcolm and I were never sure which was the real incentive for this two-hour journey, the New York Philharmonic playing in the middle of the illuminated Temple of Bacchus or the grilled chicken with garlic sauce and the Lebanese meza in the colorful Zahle restaurants.

In our Beirut rooftop apartment we had only to open our eyes in the morning and look out our bedroom window to see which shade of blue the sea would be that day. We could forecast the weather ahead of anyone. If the clouds were coming from the southwest, there was bound to be rain, and with the rain there would be spectacular rainbows arching from one horizon line to the other which our 360-degree view allowed us to watch unhindered.

Along with weather watching, we liked to "boat watch." We learned the schedules of all the ships so that soon we could tell which day it was by which ships were coming in. A huge lighthouse dominated the westernmost point of Beirut not far from the campus to keep those ships from crashing onto the rocky shore. As we turned out our light the first night in our "penthouse," we discovered that the lighthouse lined up directly with our bedroom window. It helped to close the shutter of the window tightly on that side of the room, but still the rhythmical play of lights shining through the cracks onto the bedroom wall left an indelible impression.

While Malcolm taught the usual overloaded schedule of a young professor and Susie occupied herself in her playpen, I set to work transforming our rooftop terrace into a garden. I was terribly ambitious for this garden and started off with a magnolia tree which Malcolm helped me lug up the five flights of stairs to our apartment. From the disparaging comments I got from him on the effort and expense involved in the acquisition of my magnolia tree, I decided to carry up the rest of the garden covertly by myself. Up came a rose bush, three eugenia bushes, margeurites, geraniums, asparagus fern, a small pine tree and a climbing jasmine. Then came all the pots to put them in. I dragged up pails of earth from the garden below, painted the pots, filled them with earth, and planted my great collection of growing things. Finally, after days of labor, it was just the way I wanted it. When Malcolm came home I took him out to show him my handiwork. His comment, very much in character, was, "Say, this is nice. Where'd we get all the flowers?"

Lingering over lunch under our magnolia tree, which helped

to hide the blackened chimney protruding up from the apartment below, became so pleasant a habit that I almost regretted having agreed to teach at the American mission school for Arab girls three afternoons a week. The school was formerly called American School for Girls and then changed to Beirut Evangelical School with the nationalizing of the Protestant mission. Under both names, it was one of Beirut's good English-speaking high schools for several decades. Teaching there would be a chance for me to get to know Arab girls and teachers on a day-to-day basis, and it would help to dispel the frustration I felt with being a stay-at-home housewife.

Miss Elsa Farr, the dedicated German-American principal, divided her time between directing the school, playing the church organ, and being a part of the missionary community of Beirut. I had gone to see her to inquire if she could use a very part-time teacher. She decided I would be the ideal teacher for the rejects class. "This is the group of students," she explained to me, "who have flunked out of one or two and sometimes three other schools in Beirut because they can't learn English. We take them in and try to get them to learn." She continued, "This sounds like a place where you might be able to help us."

I was to teach them English in the guise of European history. If the lure of history was meant to sweeten the pill, the originators of this plan were unrealistic. The unwillingness of these students to study made for a difficult teaching situation, and I was going to be hard put to add any new knowledge to their heads. As at the Armenian school, my biggest advantage was being a young female American and as such an object of great curiosity.

Malcolm and I were increasingly asked to participate in extra-curricular activities at AUB, which I welcomed as a chance to be more a part of the university. Malcolm was less enthusiastic than I but willing to do his part. I was delighted when students from the School of Agriculture asked us to be chaperones for a Sunday trip to the AUB farm.

The School of Agriculture was founded in 1953, as a place where students from all over the Middle East and Africa could study both theoretical and practical aspects of agriculture. Its model farm in the Beka'a Valley, an hour and a half's drive from Beirut on the road to Baalbek, survived the civil war, and so did its courageous dean of the early eighties, Tom Sutherland, who was kidnapped and kept in captivity for more than six years before he was finally released.

The few agriculture professors and their families who lived on the farm in the late fifties were rather isolated and liked to host visiting groups of students and show them the work of the farm. The bumpy bus ride over the mountains to the Beka'a on a crisp fall day reminded us of the bus trips we had taken as students a few years earlier. We had tours of chicken and egg production, of cows and milking, of agricultural mechanization and crop experimentation. These projects were run by an international mix of students who talked with enthusiasm about their plans for going back to their own countries to implement the new methods they were learning at the AUB farm. Later they served us a bountiful meal of farm-grown foods.

Since returning to Lebanon, I had seen my former AUB roommates separately but never together. After several attempts, we found a date when they were all free to come to lunch. Of the original five, only Samia was missing, for she had become a teacher in a girls school in Mosul, Iraq. They arrived bearing gifts for Susie, who instantly became the center of attention. Within a few minutes, the four-and-a-half years that had elapsed since we parted in the Kerrs' garden at Malcolm's and my engagement party dissolved, and we were all very much at home together, catching up on what had happened to us in the four-and-a-half years since we had lived in the Women's Hostel.

Roshan and Naziha had also become teachers, Roshan in a school in the mountains above Beirut, Naziha in a Beirut high school. Of the five of us Katie was the only nonteacher. She had found a good secretarial job with a Beirut business firm. These friends were part of a small minority of women in the Middle East at that time who finished college and continued on to a job afterward. Most went into teaching, as did most young women in America of that era. In later years Naziha was to become a well-known artist and Roshan the director of a private secondary school in the Gulf. Of the five, I was the only one who had married, though within a few years everyone except Samia married. We were all around twenty-five at that time. In the years since, we have managed to stay in touch sporadically, in spite of interruptions by wars and preoccupation with work and families.

A semiannual event in Beirut of great portent to merchants

and to American housewives like me was the arrival of the Sixth Fleet. Only a year and a half after the Marine landing of 1958, the U.S. Navy was still visiting in the capacity of a protective force. For the merchants it meant an infusion of dollars into the economy, and for the housewives it meant baking, dancing, and listening to sailors talk endlessly about home. The embassy wives were responsible for organizing the American community into a great entertainment force for the double purpose of giving the troops a good time and keeping them out of trouble. The latter was a big order in a time when Arab nationalist feeling ran high. Many Lebanese looked with disfavor at their country playing host to the American navy. But fortunately for those sailors the government was officially pro-Western and welcomed them to what must have been one of their most pleasant ports of call in the Mediterranean, especially when there was no imminent prospect of fighting.

Malcolm's mother had almost lost her job as Dean of Women on a previous visit of the Sixth Fleet when an innocent gesture on her part backfired. She made an announcement that any women students who would like to go were invited to the canteen sponsored by Americans living in Beirut to dance and talk to the sailors. This was soon picked up by a newspaper that was not particularly friendly to AUB to begin with. Big headlines read something like, "AUB Madam Procures Unsuspecting Women Students for American Sailors." Mrs. Kerr began receiving anonymous phone calls and stony glances from some of her friends. The newspapers stepped up their campaign against her, demanding that she resign from her job as Dean of Women. Although this stung, she was patient, and being long familiar with the ways of the Middle East, wisely said nothing in response. The AUB administration gave her its firm backing and finally the situation blew over, but American sailors met very few Lebanese girls that year.

The arrival of the fleet was a spectacular sight from our rooftop. We watched the ships turn from small specks on the horizon at 7:00 A.M. to a collection of massive ships sitting practically in our front yard by mid-morning. My activities for the next three days were cut out for me. I was to bake cakes and cookies that day, have two sailors to dinner the next night, and be at the canteen with Malcolm to entertain the troops the third night. It was that third night that was the memorable one—spending an evening with a thousand enlisted men. "They look so young and so innocent," I observed to Malcolm, "far too young to understand the complications of war." We were to feel the same reaction twenty-five years later when another generation of American marines came to Beirut and the AUB campus.

Malcolm and I had long wanted to spend a weekend by ourselves at the village of Bisharri in the remote Maronite heartland of the central mountains of Lebanon. We had been there as students to explore the cedar trees of that region and on our ill-fated skiing trip during our first winter back in Beirut. We left Susie in the care of her grandparents one weekend just before Easter and drove into the splendid craggy mountains inland from Tripoli where snow-capped peaks dropped abruptly into the gray-blue depths of the Kadisha Gorge. Clusters of small houses perched on vertical slopes gave the impression that their inhabitants would roll down once they stepped outside their front doors. The ruggedness of the scenery was softened by the countless rows and rows of agricultural terraces which generations of farmers have cultivated over the centuries.

At the top of the gorge, below the largest remaining grove of cedar trees that inspire Lebanon's flag and logo are the twin villages of Hasroon and Bisharri. Hasroon came into view first, a remarkable array of red-tiled roofs and church steeples, and beyond it, on the other side of the gorge, Bisharri. It was always something of a disappointment, after that first stunning view of sunlit red roofs against magnificent mountains with their green patches of cedar trees, to drive into Hasroon and find touches of dirt and shabbiness. Bisharri was more spread out and less picturesque from a distance, but cleaner and tidier within. It was dominated by a huge church which that week was decorated with palm branches in celebration of Easter.

This lovely village is the port of entry for viewing the historic cedars and for skiing, and it is also the home of Khalil Jibran and the source of inspiration for his book, *The Prophet*. Yet for all these attractions its greatest appeal for us was its remoteness. That narrow winding road that took at least two hours from the coast, the frequent heavy snows, and its proximity to the sky gave Bisharri special appeal as a retreat from busy Beirut. It was, however, not

renowned for its quantity or quality of hotels. We found the Bisharri Palace, whose name had nothing to do with its appearance.
We entered through a gate in a high wall at the side of the building and went through a cluttered garden with a birki pool, traditional to Lebanese gardens, as well as grape vines and flowers
potted in discarded oil tins. The owners were a family who lived
on the first floor and ran a hotel on the second and third floors.
They took us up some stairs to the third floor and showed us into
a whitewashed room with two beds, a dresser, and a table with a
large pitcher and bowl for washing. On one wall was a picture of
Christ on the cross and on another a colored photograph of cedar
trees in snow. The proprietors apologized for the modesty of their
establishment, unconvinced by our protestations that this was exactly what we were looking for, or, in other words, all we could
afford.

After dinner we went out to explore the town. Having resigned ourselves to a movieless weekend, we were happily surprised when we came upon a little hole-in-the-wall movie theater
showing, of all things, *Othello* in Russian with English subtitles.
Of course we would see it. We paid our twenty-five piasters each
(about eight cents in those days) and went into a stuffy little room
where we sat down in two of the thirty or so straight-backed
wooden chairs, more or less lined up in rows. Through billows of
cigarette smoke and the cracking of bizr we watched a glorious
rendition of *Othello,* filmed in color in Cyprus. The fifteen or so
other viewers sitting around us, mostly men, made no pretense of
understanding either the Russian dialogue or the English subtitles. There was occasional clapping when anything heroic happened or tittering during love scenes, but they mainly chatted
away throughout the movie, puffing on cigarettes or chewing bizr.

We spent a freezing night in our unheated hotel room but
awoke to brilliant sunshine—the first springlike day the propri-
etor told us, as he served us Malcolm's favorite breakfast of fresh
mountain bread, olives, tea, and lebaneh, a creamy substance
made of drained yogurt. After breakfast, we walked out into the
village where the combination of bright sun and cold air felt wonderful. There were still patches of snow in shadowed corners of the
terraces, and the high peaks above us were completely covered
with snow. But there was the sound of running water everywhere

as melting snows gushed into whatever courses they could find. It seemed surprising that the whole village wasn't flooded.

The leaves on the trees must have known by the date rather than by warmer air that it was time for them to open. Tall white birches were just showing signs of green. The greenest green was in the terraces of winter wheat which made a lovely pattern with the slate-colored terrace walls and the white bark of the birch trees. Bright red poppies and anemones grew amidst the winter wheat, and cyclamen peeked out from the stones of the terraces. Almond trees were bursting with soft white blossoms.

We walked on across the terraces until we could look back and see Bisharri and Hasroon perched at the end of the gorge. A farmer and his family were working on one of the terraces and seemed both startled and pleased when they looked up and saw us. "Ahlan, ahlan," they all called when they overcame their initial surprise at seeing two foreigners in Western dress stomping across their land. We stopped and talked awhile and answered their questions as to why we had come to Bisharri. They were handsome mountain people with ruddy cheeks and bright eyes and the characteristic, not unpleasant earthy smell of village people who work the land and spend much of their time out-of-doors. Their house was too far away to offer us coffee, but being Lebanese and therefore incapable of not offering us something, they pulled up some green onions from the ground and thrust them into our hands. We thanked them profusely in as many ways as we could think of, hoping we weren't hurting their feelings by not eating them on the spot.

Further on we came to a large grassy meadow where a shepherd was leaning against a rock half asleep, while his sheep feasted on the new green grass. The sheep were the fat-tailed variety typical in Lebanon and Syria with bright red-orange splotches painted on their backs to ward off evil spirits. Neither the sheep nor the shepherd seemed to notice our company, so we walked on.

Back in the village at the end of the morning we went into the big Maronite church where people were congregated in observance of Good Friday. Inside, worshippers awaited their turn to kneel by an encoffined plaster-of-Paris figure of Christ draped all in black. During the morning, we were told, the coffin had been carried around the village and then placed in the church to await the resurrection on Easter morning. We watched the village people bestowing flowers and kisses on this pasty-looking figure with rouged lips and cheeks. Incense burned while the brocade-robed Maronite priest chanted sometimes in Arabic, sometimes in Syriac, sometimes in Latin. Children carried beribboned candles to the front of the church to place near the altar. For us, all this ceremony had an aspect of excessive ornateness that was in marked contrast to the simple life and great natural beauty of the land we had just been walking through.

As we drove back to Beirut that Easter weekend, it was not difficult to distinguish the Christian from the Muslim villages. Streets were crowded with processions of children carrying their candles and palm branches, and people milled about showing off their new spring finery. In the Muslim villages the persistent voice of the muezzin calling the faithful to prayer was turned to the highest volume of their loudspeakers, not to be outdone by their Christian neighbors. They were heard five times a day every day, while the church bells pealed only on Sundays and special holy days.

Malcolm's parents were due to retire at the end of the 1960 school year after almost forty years at AUB. We began going to a long succession of parties and receptions in their honor. One especially memorable one was given by the young women in the three new women's hostel buildings constructed on the site of the house with our favorite couch where the Kerrs had lived. The evening was devoted to honoring Malcolm's mother as the retiring advisor to women. Part of the garden where our engagement party had been held remained, and now another family rite of passage was being held here under the same pine trees. The students entertained us with a play mimicking the foibles of their advisor, the strong-minded, enlightened woman who might have remained a rather overpowering figure to me had I not grown to know her so well. They too must have felt they knew her well enough to poke fun at her affectionately, dramatizing scenes of Mrs. Kerr commanding students to follow university regulations or teaching her class on family relations.

The most touching of all the farewell occasions was a presentation in Dr. Kerr's lab by the three women who washed the floors and scrubbed the lab equipment. They presented him a gift which was a picture album with a lacquered black cover decorated in butterfly wings depicting Mt. Fuji. When the cover was lifted, a music box played "Jingle Bells."

The retirement of Malcolm's parents meant the selling of the Ainab house. Since Malcolm's and my plan was to return to the United States after our three-year contract was up, we were not in a position to buy or inherit the house. The bitter pill of selling it was sweetened a bit by the fact that the house was purchased jointly by two AUB families, Mary Helen and Ted Kennedy and Laure and Ralph Crow, who were good friends of ours. We also hoped that as former owners, we would always have first chance to rent whichever of the five houses was vacant each summer.

That summer of 1960 was our first in a different Ainab house. Malcolm's parents and we rented a house on the other side of the hilltop with a view of distant mountains rather than of dense pine forests. Malcolm's younger brother Doug, a recent graduate of Haverford College who was soon to begin medical school, came to join us for a long summer of relaxation and tennis, interspersed with an adventurous driving trip to Damascus, Amman, Jerusalem, and the Dead Sea, and later picnics to favorite sites around Lebanon.

The mountain air had proved to be particularly beneficent that summer, for once back in Beirut at the beginning of the school year, I found that we were going to have a new baby in the spring. This one would be a true Lebanese from start to finish. With this news and the fact that it was our last year in Lebanon for awhile, I decided not to teach but to enjoy the life of a leisurely Beirut housewife.

During the previous two years in Beirut, we had been so involved with our new life at AUB and our first child that we had not been very close followers of the goings-on in our own country. All that changed in the fall of 1960 when the Nixon-Kennedy presidential campaign reached its height. The campaign was covered daily in the Beirut newspapers, always with an eye out for some sign of empathy toward the Arab world on the part of either candidate. Americans were anxious for a balanced view of the Arab-Israeli problem from the White House. Kennedy was the favored candidate among Americans and Lebanese.

Lebanese friends would ask us about the campaign and the

candidates, forgetting that our sources of information were the same newspapers and magazines they were reading. Films of the Kennedy-Nixon debates were shown at the American Embassy for all who were interested. Newsreels at the movies were full of campaign news, and when Kennedy appeared on the screen people would applaud. By election day there was almost as much anticipation and excitement in the air as there was in the United States. Radios were tuned to catch election results as they came in. When Kennedy's election was announced, victory parties began among Americans, with many Lebanese joining in. We were invited to an Inauguration Day celebration in January at the home of some embassy friends. I borrowed a billowy, pink and red chiffon maternity party dress that made me feel somehow lighter than the new proportions I had gained, and Malcolm pulled out his old college tuxedo which fit his still-slim form. When we arrived at our friends' house, a telegram was pinned to the door saying, "We'll be with you in spirit. All best wishes, Jack." Our hosts apparently had a personal connection with the Kennedys back in the United States. Inside was a huge picture of Jack smiling at us. American flags flanked the picture and were hanging from walls around the room along with balloons and streamers. Crowds of guests talked and danced in a mood of jubilence and optimism for the good days that were bound to lie ahead under the leadership of this highly qualified, new young president—little knowing how short-numbered those days would be.

The optimism shared with our host country over Kennedy's election emphasized other things that made those days pleasant for Americans living in the Middle East. Cultural and business relations between Arab countries and the West were healthy and thriving. Ideals of Arab unity, tangibly inspired by Egypt's President Nasser, brought a sense of pride and proper place in the world to his many followers. And the hope of a homeland for the Palestinians was still fresh, a unifying cause for the Arabs, not yet compounded in complexities by decades of failure to find a solution.

Lebanon was again succeeding in that precarious balance of government shared between Christians and Muslims. Some political analysts predicted that Lebanon would be the model of a country that could build a democracy out of diverse religious and political groups. Malcolm, in character, was more doubtful. In an article entitled "Lebanese Views on the 1958 Crisis," he said, "In short, Labanon needs an overhauling of the social attitudes of its citizens and a new crop of politicians. This requires education; but first it requires a collective act of conscience." Those words were remarkably prophetic. Were he writing today, he might make the same comments.

The troubles of 1958—revolution in Iraq, the Marines landing in Lebanon—for any long-range warnings they might have held, had blown over, and Beirut was having a heyday of prosperity. Bankers, business men, diplomats, and tourists flocked to the city. Top academicians from around the world came to AUB where they could work in an atmosphere of internationalism and intellectual freedom. Students from Syria, Jordan, Egypt, Sudan, Iraq, and the Gulf countries developed their particular philosophies, theories of government, and future professions studying alongside Lebanese Christians and Muslims and a smattering of Europeans and Americans. It was an ideal atmosphere for a young scholar of Middle Eastern studies, and Malcolm flourished. Along with teaching and writing articles for professional journals, he prepared his Master's thesis, *Lebanon in the Last Years of Feudalism*, for publication by a local Beirut press. We worked together on the index in Ainab with papers spread across a ping-pong table. When it became apparent that the book needed a map, he asked me to draw one showing the areas in Lebanon where the civil wars of 1840–1860 were fought. His faith in my artistic talents was not borne out when the reviews of his book appeared. "A highly skilled and professional book," one reviewer wrote, "with the exception of the map."

There was plenty of opportunity for Malcolm to indulge his intense interest in Lebanese politics sitting at Faisal's Restaurant across the street from the campus, engaged in ongoing conversations over lunch with other professors and students. A rich pollination of ideas went on in that setting as they discussed the complex events and personalities of a country trying to achieve a workable balance among its many religious and sectarian factions while maintaining ties with both Arab neighbors and the West. In a memorial volume in 1982 for his former student Abdul Hamid Sharaf, who later became prime minister of Jordan until his premature death at the age of forty due to a heart attack, Malcolm somewhat whimsically recalled their conversations in the privileged atmosphere of the American University of Beirut in the 1950s: "Left to ourselves, Abdul Hamid and I could have quickly solved all the problems; without our help the statesmen and thinkers might take a little longer, but we always hoped that they would soon acquire the goodwill and understanding that would assure them success."

Several months before our three years at AUB were up, Malcolm was offered a Rockefeller grant for postdoctoral study at St. Antony's College, Oxford, for the academic year 1961–62 and a contract to teach in the political science department at UCLA, which would take effect after our year at Oxford. Although we were not keen to leave the Middle East, some compelling instinct made me want to make a base for ourselves and our children in our own country, and Malcolm concurred.

Early on the morning of May 21, 1961, a week ahead of schedule, perhaps because of a bout of upset stomach and a vigorous game of mixed doubles the day before, I went off to the hospital and redeemed us in the eyes of some of our more traditional Arab friends by giving birth to our first son. John Malcolm Kerr was born under the same hospital roof where his sister had been born, and his father as well some thirty years earlier. I opened my eyes to see a beautiful blond baby on the table next to me. The birth process seemed as miraculous as it had been the first time, perhaps even more joyful for the confidence gained from having been through it once before.

Babies should always be born in May, I decided after coming home with John to our rooftop garden, full of flowers and sunshine and sparkling ocean view. I appreciated the equinoctial advantages of the season most of all in the early hours of the morning when I got up to nurse our baby and watched the sky behind Mt. Sanneen slowly light up and run through deep to lighter shades of pink, and then burst into brilliant sunlight. The miracle of creation was embraced in this new life I was caring for and in the birth of the new day.

Susie, at age two and a half, had been enthusiastically awaiting the arrival of her new sibling. When John and I arrived home from the hospital, she eagerly wanted to help care for him, a role she played with increasing responsibility as each new brother came along. I have often wondered how we could have raised three boys without her.

Anticipation of adventures ahead and the activity of tending our children and packing up our possessions kept us from dwelling too much on the reality that we would soon be leaving the Middle East. A flow of ongoing parties also helped, and then a month in Ainab before we finally left on August 1 for England. I remember John's bright two-and-a-half-month-old eyes looking up at us as we tucked his small bed in front of us on the airplane, the only one in the family unconcerned about this first of two transcontinental moves we were making as a family. Susie sat on Malcolm's lap, a bit bewildered to have another life change thrust upon her so soon after the birth of a new brother. Malcolm and I were looking forward to the green of England, sampling Oxford life, and living in the country cottage which his future mentor at St. Antony's, Albert Hourani, had found for us. But we knew we were leaving Beirut because we were moving on to a new stage of our lives and that, even with all the new adventures ahead, we would inevitably miss the warmth and color and lifebeat of the Middle East.

PART THREE

Between California and the Middle East 1961–1981

CHAPTER 10

Bonds of Closeness Around the World

*T*he English winter of 1961 set a record as the coldest to date in the twentieth century, but the weather was offset by the warmth of our welcome at St. Antony's College where the two Middle East scholars Malcolm was to be working with, Albert Hourani and Elizabeth Monroe, took us in like adopted family. The familiarity of the academic world provided easy access to Malcolm and me whenever we moved our family around the world. The formation of friendships such as those at Oxford and AUB, and soon UCLA, created a bond of closeness that made a small world out of a large one.

Malcolm benefited from spending the academic year at St. Antony's as a time away from teaching and a chance to reflect on the last three years in the Middle East and to be with colleagues there in the same field. He was invited to participate in college life, which included the centuries-old Oxbridge custom of dining exclusively with other dons or professors at "high table," while the students dined in the same hall at "low table". Wives were not included on these occasions, which had their origins in monastic ritual of the Middle Ages when Oxford and Cambridge were founded. When Malcolm suggested that he would prefer to bring me, Albert Hourani graciously responded, "We are prisoners of our traditions, aren't we? The only way around this outmoded custom is for you to invite Odille [his wife] and for me to invite Ann. One never brings his own wife." This plan was carried out thenceforth, and by the time we left Oxford, the charade of taking someone else's wife rather than one's own was forgotten. A custom of four hundred years had been changed through the cordiality of Albert, whose kindness and hospitality cut through the imprisonment of tradition.

In the fall of 1962, Malcolm began a twenty-year teaching career at UCLA, six of which we would spend abroad on sabbatical or on leave of absence in the Middle East, North Africa, and Europe. It was good to be back in sunny California after the cold of England. We settled down into child rearing and home owning, with the pleasure of my family and longtime friends nearby.

We discovered on our moves around the world that the children adjusted more quickly than we did to new surroundings. They just needed to be plugged in, and we were there to do that for them. They made friends with the other children on the block, and our garage and driveway became the setting for dress-up games, imaginative constructions from the contents of the garage, and processions of bicycle and tricycle riders—much the same kind of neighborhood activities that had filled my childhood.

Malcolm, whom I'd always suspected of East Coast bias, soon learned to appreciate life in my home state for its treasure of ocean, mountains, and deserts. UCLA was a fast growing institution with a good political science department and an expanding center for Near Eastern studies. (The terms *Near Eastern* and *Middle Eastern* are essentially interchangeable.)

In November, 1963, President John Kennedy was assassinated, two and a half years after he assumed the office of president. Like everyone in America, we were drawn into several days of shock and immobility as we sat by our television set watching the unfolding drama of events following the assassination, never imagining that the same tragedy would one day strike our family. The word *assassination* is one that remains associated in my mind more with the Kennedy family than with ours, and one I rarely use in referring to Malcolm's death. The harsh tearing away that it implies is a meaning that can only be absorbed over a very long period of time, if ever.

In the fall of 1964, Malcolm received a grant from the American Research Center in Egypt to spend a year in Cairo writing a book on the political union between Syria and Egypt. He took a two-year leave of absence from UCLA so that we could spend the second year in Lebanon. After a Kerr family reunion on the East Coast, we flew to Cairo via London and Athens with John and

Susie, now ages six and three and a half. It was ten years since I had sailed into Beirut on a Dutch freighter and had fallen in love with the Middle East—and with Malcolm a month later. I had celebrated my thirtieth birthday in Athens and Malcolm would soon be thirty-three. He had filled out a little, which suited him, and retained a boyish look inherited from his father; I had lost my girlish bloom and my hair was not as blond as before, but Malcolm did not seem to mind. Now with the responsibilities of house and career left behind in California, we were excited at the prospect of living in a new Arab country and exploring it together.

We found a spacious ground floor apartment and a housekeeper who went with it in Zamalek, an island in the Nile full of stately but dust-covered buildings and overgrown gardens. The streets overflowed with lively, noisy people twenty-four hours a day in spite of economic austerity and tight government control. The hardest thing for Egyptians to come by in those days was an exit permit, followed closely by sugar, tea, and coffee. Not even the Sphinx could get an exit permit, according to the punch line of one of the jokes circulating in Cairo.

The year 1964 was an interesting time to be in Egypt and one that broadened our understanding of the Middle East. It had been sixteen years since the first Arab-Israeli war and the establishment of Israel, and twelve years since the expulsion of King Farouk ended a hundred and fifty years of monarchy in Egypt. Gamal Abdul Nasser had been president for almost a decade, attempting on the domestic front to shed the vestiges of colonialism and redistribute personal and public assets of the country through severe measures. By virtue of his charismatic personality and a certain historic role of Arab leadership for Egypt, Nasser was developing a following in much of the Middle East as the champion of Arab nationalism and a force for political union among Arab states. The devastating series of short wars with Israel was still a few years away.

Malcolm addressed the common desire among many Arabs to establish political alliance in the first chapter of the book he wrote that year, *The Arab Cold War*, published in 1965.

Ever since World War II, popular political sentiment in the Arab world has been dominated by urgent appeals for Arab

10. Malcolm, Ann, Susan, and John Kerr
at the pyramids in Cairo, 1964.

unity, while the field of activity between governments and parties has been dominated by bitter rivalry. Why the idea of unity is so strong among Arabs—so much more so than among Latin Americans, for instance, or the English-speaking nations—is a mystery that neither Arab nor western historians have satisfactorily explained. In this essay, we shall content ourselves with acknowledging that this obsession, whatever its causes, is an important psychological force, and therefore a political reality, which warring politicians seek to use against each other (1981, 1).

Each new sojourn in the Middle East brought a greater awareness for Malcolm and me of the complexity of similarities and contrasts in its people and of the varying perceptions which we each brought with us as our experiences increased and we matured. For all the similar sights, sounds, smells, and national characteristics of Middle Eastern countries and people, there were also myriad differences which that year in Cairo served to underline for us—for Malcolm as he wrote about the difficulties between Egypt, Syria, and Iraq in trying to form a political union, and for me as I

explored Cairo and observed differences in national character between Egyptians and Lebanese.

Both Egypt and Lebanon had fertile effects on us apparently,
for we found we were to again have a baby born in the Middle
East, due in the fall of 1965. That summer at the end of our
Egyptian sojourn, after certain difficulties in securing exit visas,
we moved our children and our small Volkswagen to Lebanon and
AUB. Immediately after finding a sea view apartment above a
spaghetti restaurant in the little seaside quarter of Ain Mreisseh,
below the AUB campus, we went to Ainab for the summer holiday where we rented one of the houses that was vacant that
summer.

Ainab was a fine place to await the birth of our third child. In
fact, we were enjoying the cool restfulness and beauty of the hilltop so much, with built-in companionship for us and our children
and quiet working conditions for Malcolm, that we were reluctant
to go down to hot, sticky Beirut. Stephen obliged us by waiting
to be born until the same week Susie and John were due to start
school, so we stayed on in Ainab until the last possible minute,
feeling the slight coolness signaling the beginning of fall and
watching the warm pastel colors of summer light change to the
more pronounced shades of late September.

The AUB delivery room had by now become a familiar place
to me, and I went with ease to give birth to our third child,
another beautiful blond baby boy with all the right number of
fingers and toes and a hearty cry. Malcolm stayed with me in my
room throughout the evening after Stephen's birth, but so did my
roommate's family and friends. No chance to be by ourselves to
contemplate the miracle of birth or for me to complain to Malcolm
about the pains of my contracting uterus. Our presence did not
inhibit expressions of such emotions, however, from my roommate. There were effusive greetings and phrases of congratulation
and praise punctuated by intermittent wails of pain. Throughout
the evening, dozens of her family members and friends poured into
the other half of the room bearing the chocolates and flowers for
the visits expected in Middle Eastern culture at major rites of
passage. Malcolm and I sat within the curtained portion of our
corner of the room, in frustrated semiprivacy against a backdrop of
chatter in Arabic and enveloped in billowing cigarette smoke,

11. Ann with new baby Stephen, Malcolm, Susie, and John
in front of the American University of Beirut hospital, 1965.

mixed with the sticky sweet smell of too many bouquets of
flowers. At last there was relief. At 10:00 P.M., the babies were
brought to their mothers for feeding and all guests other than
fathers were asked to leave. My roommate fed her baby and
quickly fell asleep, exhausted from so much social activity. Malcolm and I finally had a chance to contemplate our new son in
peace.

There was not much time for relaxation when Stephen and I
came home from the hospital to our apartment in Ain Mreisseh.
The demands of an enlarged family, long school days for Susie and
John at the Beirut Franciscan School, and Malcolm's increasingly
busy career were overwhelming. I was not happy when he left the
day after we got home from the hospital to go to a conference in
Switzerland on Middle East politics and then returned to begin a
three-course teaching load which required long hours of preparation—along with his research and articles he was writing.

A school bus called for Susie and John every morning at 6:30
A.M. which was usually just when baby Stephen was crying for his
breakfast. Malcolm cooked oatmeal for all of us while I held my

nursing baby with one arm and helped the older children dress with the other, all of us in varying degrees of pre-dawn drowsiness or grouchiness.

A bright light in our lives that year was Najeebe who came back to work for us as soon as Stephen was born. She arrived around 9:00 three mornings a week after she and I had seen our respective families off and just as the smell of fried onions and garlic began wafting up from the spaghetti restaurant below, far too early in the morning to be appetizing. I had the baby bathed and ready for his morning nap so I could take those hours for myself while Najeebe did the laundry and scrubbed the tile floors of our apartment to a state of cleanliness that I was never able to manage. She also made us delicious Lebanese lunches of stuffed cabbage or kibbeh and tabbouleh.

Those few mornings a week snatched from the cares of family life were a chance to experience some of the richness and sophistication of life in Beirut in the mid-sixties. The city was flourishing and reaching its full potential as an international center of business, education, and tourism. The Lebanese had a style in the way they did things and a knack for efficiency in matters of business. Beirut combined a quality of intimacy and sophistication that appealed to all who went there. Rue Hamra, which ten years earlier had been a sleepy street of small stores, now sported speciality shops selling fine china and silver, extravagant toys, and food from all over the world in grocery stores and chic restaurants, along with X-rated cinemas, high-priced prostitutes, and probably some headquarters for drug dealing with the poppy growers in Baalbek.

The belief of many of its citizens in Lebanon's destiny for leadership in the Middle East looked as if it was being realized. The confessional system of government with each of Lebanon's different religious groups proportionally represented was in place, and the country was functioning as a democracy. Ras Beirut, where AUB was located, with its religious mix of Maronite and Greek Orthodox Christians and Sunni and Shiite Muslims and its racial mix of Middle Easterners and a sprinkling of Europeans, Americans, and other internationals, made for an atmosphere of stimulation and creativity. The particular blend of religious and sectarian groups and an absence of imposed authority from any one of them at that time allowed for freedom of thought, distinctive in the Arab world. Tolerance for liberal intellectual ideas flourished in this setting and provided the atmosphere that fostered the growth of AUB. Besides university courses and special lectures, there were plays and art exhibits, concerts and conferences of businessmen, doctors or historians from around the world. AUB was a pivot for the cultural and intellectual life of Beirut which reached out to all the Middle East.

For all this cosmopolitanism there were anomalies, I thought, every time I tried to maneuver the baby carriage around the piles of garbage on our street corner when I took Stephen out for walks in the afternoons or had to hold my nose as I went past more garbage into an elegant shop off Hamra Street. If these people could run hotels and tourist trips and banks so effectively and profitably, why couldn't they organize their garbage?

Economic prosperity did not solve the problems of poverty either, and this problem, like most others in Beirut, had religious overtones. Christians were often better off financially than Muslims. Whatever their economic conditions or religious persuasion, by 1965 many people had television sets, and when I sat on our balcony painting watercolor scenes of Ain Mreisseh, I was uncertain about whether or not to include them, concerned that they would detract from the picturesqueness of the charming fishing bays and old red tile-roofed houses or the street scenes of donkey-drawn carts winding their way among colorfully dressed pedestrians. I also left out some of the faceless cement high rises that were increasingly marring the view. There was no question about excluding the piles of garbage from my paintings or the huge rats that nibbled there, and I had learned to try not to notice the brown streaks of raw sewage that ran from open pipes into the aqua blue water of the bay below us. Everyone knew that a bribe of the right size in the right place could convince contractors to ignore building codes and that substandard plumbing was the result.

Beirut had had all these problems in the past, but with the movement of population from the villages to the city, they were becoming more pronounced. Moreover, we were now living in a mixed neighborhood, less isolated from poorer people, and perhaps were getting a more realistic picture of the city than we had had in the past. Looking back with the perspective of hindsight, it is possible to discern conditions both within Lebanon and regionally that pointed to possible future instability.

In the south, Palestinian guerrillas had become active and were making raids into Israel. Reprisal attacks caused Lebanese authorities to attempt to prevent Palestinian fighters from entering Israel. This drew criticism from pro-Palestinian groups and brought the Palestinian problem into sharper focus in Lebanon. Another event at that time, which was perhaps a sign of problems that lay ahead, was the crash of one of Lebanon's major banks, the Intra Bank, in 1966. This bank had a large number of Palestinian investments and when the Lebanese government did nothing to prop up liquid assets, which might have saved the bank, there was more criticism from Palestinian supporters in Lebanon.

By summer 1966, our year at AUB was finished. It was now time to turn our thoughts homeward and return with our children to our own culture and our house in Pacific Palisades. It would be sixteen years before we would again make a home in Lebanon, though we would spend a short time there in the summer of 1970.

A year or so after our return to California, Malcolm was asked to be chairperson of the political science department at UCLA, which made him pleased and proud—and me for him. Years afterward he claimed this was the most difficult and challenging administrative job one could have in a university. The chairperson was a power among equals whose authority depended on being able to deal tactfully and diplomatically with his colleagues. Not much past his thirty-fifth birthday and looking as boyish as ever, Malcolm was younger than many of his colleagues which added to the challenges of his job. For my part, I liked the idea of being the chairperson's wife and thereby more a part of what Malcolm was doing.

The Middle East entered our lives in California in June 1967, when another Arab-Israeli war broke out, a watershed event in the Arab world which consumed our attention. The June War or the Six-Day War, as it was soon termed, came into our living room on television, showing the tremendous strength of the Israeli army and air force and the ease with which they conquered neighboring land in an attempt to secure their borders. We watched day by day as the Israelis crushed the Egyptian air force, annexed the West Bank of Jordan, Arab Jerusalem, the Golan Heights of Syria, and the Sinai Peninsula, all in less than one week. There were 1,300,000 Arabs living in those conquered lands.

The hero of Arab nationalism, Gamal Abdul Nasser, under pressure from other Arab leaders to stand up to Israel, had provoked the attack by ordering United Nations peace-keeping troops from the Sinai, moving Egyptian troops to the Israeli border, and closing the Straits of Tiran in the Red Sea east of Sinai to Israeli shipping. These actions gave Israel the chance they were waiting for—to extend their lands and gain full control over Jerusalem, which they thought was rightfully theirs. In the wake of defeat, Nasser resigned, but his popularity did not diminish and his resignation was rejected.

We read and listened to interviews with Arab intellectuals who criticized their culture for lacking discipline, for being boastful, and for confusing word and action. Jewish intellectuals worried that Israel might lose her soul in military expansionism. But Israel was exultant in her victory and former hopes for Arab-Israeli peace remained as remote as ever. Malcolm in an irreverent one-liner declared, "Force is one thing the Arabs do not understand."

Although Nasser survived the crisis, his magnetism as leader of the Arab world was weakened and the impetus for pan-Arabism declined, a situation that brought hope to Maronite leaders in Lebanon for increased influence and security. What they could not foresee was that the June War had also brought a loss of faith among the Palestinians in Arab leadership, which would have far-reaching effects for Lebanon. Palestinians would have to rely more upon themselves to regain their land, and in so doing, they would develop their own distinctive national identity. Lebanon had an accessible border with Israel, a sizable Palestinian population, and a certain tolerance for different political groups. Soon the country became a natural base of operations for Palestinian interests.

In July 1968, the fourth child and second daughter we had planned surprised us by turning out to be a boy. The doctor absentmindedly pronounced Andrew to be a girl, but the nurse corrected him politely, saying, "You'd better take another look, Doctor." I could see very clearly that I had brought forth another son, although the perfect features of his face would have made a lovely girl. Any disappointment in not balancing the sex ratio in our family disappeared within an instant. Now we had a baby born not only in California but also in the same hospital as his mother. This was a baby not just for Malcolm and me but for the whole family.

It did not take us long to realize that a family of six was too much for our small house on Haverford Street. After months of fruitless househunting, I finally came upon our dream house, a rambling white house with adjacent guesthouse on a mountaintop overlooking the Pacific Ocean to the west and the city to the east. The property was surrounded by canyons on three sides, and the beach was a five-minute drive down the hill. Directly below, though perhaps a twenty-minute walk, lay the Palisades shopping area known as "the village" and the elementary and high schools.

On another level of the mountain below the house was a huge stone patio with big wooden gates that opened out over the canyon toward the Pacific, evoking the feeling of our Ainab house or a Crusader castle in Lebanon. I phoned Malcolm to tell him that I had found the perfect house for us and that we should go see it together as soon as possible, which we did. It was a March evening in 1969 and an unseasonable Santa Ana wind was blowing, making the view of city and coastline crystal clear. We stood on the lawn outside the house and watched the sky turn coral as the sun set and the lights of the city began to sparkle. Catalina Island was a dark blue silhouette against the coral sky. "I think I can see Formosa," Malcolm quipped as we gazed in awe at the view, barely daring to believe that this house could be ours if only we could get the price down, sell our present house, and borrow enough extra money for a downpayment.

Malcolm, too, thought that the vast, stone patio evoked Ainab and that the simple elegance of the house was reminiscent of Marquand House. Its panoramic view of sea and city recalled the rustic penthouse where we had lived in Beirut. The rusticity was present in this house in the form of peeling paint, an overgrown garden, and a roof that looked like it was sure to leak. These features were to our advantage in bargaining the price down. And so for a sum that would currently not buy one room in Pacific Palisades but which seemed monstrous to us then, we bought the most beautiful house in California.

That home on Chautauqua Street became an anchor for our family in 1969 and has remained so ever since. Every time we returned from our sojourns abroad, we wondered all over again if such a lovely place could be ours. Walks with the dog in the mountains just behind us, basketball in the driveway, barbecues in the patio with family and friends and the feeling of closeness to nature became our way of life. Birthdays, anniversaries, and graduations were occasions to celebrate on the big brick patio, as well as parties for students and friends. "Plant trees," an old gardener friend told me just after we bought the house. "They grow while you sleep." (And he should have added travel.) The pine and eucalyptus trees I planted as saplings in the canyons around our hilltop were noticably taller on each of our returns from abroad and today tower into the sky.

In the summer of 1970, we left for a sabbatical year in France and North Africa. Malcolm thought he was weary of Middle Eastern problems, and we decided we would like to spend some time in Europe. He dreamed up a research project on the politics of higher education in North Africa which enabled us to get a grant to spend the school year in Aix-en-Provence and the following summer in Tunis. This would give our children a taste of Europe and Malcolm and me a chance to spend time in a part of the Arab world that had always appealed to us. We also hoped to improve our French.

Being that close to Lebanon, we could not miss the opportunity for a summer visit to Ainab. After a Kerr family reunion in Goshen, Massachusetts, we flew to Vienna from Boston, picked up the Volkswagen camper we had ordered, and headed for the Balkans, Greece, Turkey, and Lebanon. At the time, that long drive with four young children had very few redeeming features. There was no chance to savor much of the interesting countries we were driving through. By the end of the trip I was shocked that I could harbor such animosity for every member of my family. Malcolm was never willing to stop to see the sights I wanted to see and insisted that we just keep driving in order to get to Ainab sooner. Susie and John argued together, or worse, teamed up to tease me for trying to say hello and thank you in German, the lingua franca of the Balkans, although they showed admiration for their father who admittedly had expertise in the language which I lacked. Their condemnation of their mother ran rampant when they began to challenge my driving abilities, as if there were some transfer from my inability to speak German. How could they overlook the fact that I had been their private chauffeur from the day they were born? And the little boys vied with one another in the front seat for a larger share of Malcolm's or my lap, punctuating their arguments with piercing screams which they underscored with violent jabs at us with their knees and elbows.

Yet when the subject of that trip comes up now, their recollections are of the adventure of crossing the Bosphorus on a ferryboat, eating Wiener schnitzel for dinner in restaurants, staying in old but grand hotels, playing endless games of Geography in the car, and stopping for picnic lunches in the green mountains of Turkey.

We reached Ainab on the evening of July 4, 1970, after ten days of traveling, just as our friends were lighting firecrackers and sparklers on the tennis court, an incongruous atmosphere after the continuous dose of foreign farmlands and village life through which we had been driving.

That was a summer of catching up with friends and with what was happening in the Middle East. In the four years since we had left Lebanon, the June War of 1967 had ensued and Palestinian-Israeli problems were beginning to be played out on Lebanese soil. Palestinian activists, supported by Lebanese leftists and militant students, were gaining increasing popular support. In 1968, Israeli commandos had landed at Beirut Airport and destroyed Middle East Airlines planes in an attempt to tell the Lebanese government to get control over Palestinian commandos and stop them from using the border as an entry into Israel.

During our summer in Ainab, King Hussein was in a power struggle with activist Palestinians in Jordan. This came to a head in September when the King suppressed Palestinian activists with military force and ousted large numbers of them from his country, an episode that became known as Black September. These activists went to Lebanon where their presence among the half a million refugees already present served as a further threat to the precarious political and religious balance of Lebanese society. Lebanon was now the one country bordering Israel from which armed commandos could operate freely. Egypt, to Israel's south, had a well-trained army to control border activities.

The city of Aix-en-Provence, in the southern vacation area of France and its gateway to Mediterranean culture, seemed northern and very European to us after our summer in Lebanon. Ropes of garlic clusters hung in vegetable shops and Provençal olive oil was as fine as could be found, but the cooking smells, though delectable, were not the same as those of the Middle East. The light of Provence, extolled by impressionist painters, was somehow not as brilliant as Middle Eastern light. When we tried out our French, it came out as Arabic, and no one praised us for our efforts as our Arab hosts would have done. Perhaps we had really been fooling ourselves when we decided we needed to spend a sabbatical someplace other than in the Middle East. Too late for such regrets, we set about settling in.

We found a charming but impractical summer cottage near the road to Nice on a pine-wooded hillside where the mistral winds blew down from the Alps. There was a small, drafty room down the hill from the main house which Malcolm made his study. We enrolled the children in the local school, hoping that they would be able to adjust quickly to studying in French, propped up by Malcolm to help them with their homework. Their quick adaptation to French culture was evidenced when we took them to a restaurant for dinner a few months into our stay and they ordered snails, French bread, and Coke. They also switched happily from being baseball to soccer fans and, in the absence of television, to devouring the French comic Tin Tin books.

While I took French lessons, Malcolm worked in his drafty room down the hill, trying without much success to get interested in his new research project. He was also working on a third edition of *The Arab Cold War,* which he often turned to in preference to studying the politics of higher education in North Africa. For all his intentions to spend a sabbatical year away from the Arab-Israeli problem and inter-Arab politics, all of which he had become disgruntled with, he found he could not really be drawn away from the subject with which he had been involved for so many years. This interest was rekindled by the death of Egypt's President Nasser in the fall of 1970 and the possible repercussions to Arab politics, but his discouragement remained.

In the preface of the third edition of *The Arab Cold War* he wrote:

> I do not expect that there will ever be a fourth edition. Nasser's disappearance removes the main character from a story which I

have tried to relate largely in terms of personalities. More particularly, since June 1967, Arab politics have ceased to be fun. In the good old days most Arabs refused to take themselves very seriously, and this made it easier to take a relaxed view of the few who possessed intimations of some immortal mission. It was like watching Princeton play Columbia in football on a muddy afternoon. The June War was like a disastrous game against Notre Dame which Princeton impulsively added to its schedule, leaving several players crippled for life and the others so embittered that they took to fighting viciously among themselves instead of scrimmaging happily as before. This may be instructive for the student of politics, but as one who all his life has had friendships and memories among the Arabs to cherish, I have found no relish in describing it.

In May, we left France and went to spend three months in Tunisia, taking another adventurous journey in our Volkswagen bus through Spain, Morocco, and Algeria. This trip went better than the long drive through the Balkans and Turkey the previous year because we had learned to drive shorter distances in one day and to stop for frequent games of ball or Frisbee. Malcolm's official work in Tunisia would be to continue his research on the politics of higher education in North Africa, but unofficially we wanted the chance to explore what was for us a new part of the Arab world. Tunis was captivating, with its blend of Arab, French, and Berber cultures and striking blue and white architecture accented by bougainvillea and jasmine. We rented one of the blue and white houses with a lovely garden in the Carthage area of Tunis, just up the street from the Punic Ports where other settlers from Lebanon had settled three thousand years earlier. The ancient Phoenicians had landed as colonists, carried on a thriving trading business, and later fought their historic wars with the Romans. Only a few hundred meters from our house was the Toffet, or temple of child sacrifice and burial place of these Phoenicians turned Carthaginians. There were many references to the Toffet that summer whenever the children got out of hand.

The call to prayer rang out five times a day from the tall, rectangular, colorfully tiled minarets of Tunisian mosques, so different from the cylindrical minarets of the Middle Eastern Arab world. The call was to a generally uniform population of orthodox

Sunni Muslims, notably lacking the large religious minority groups found in Lebanon and even Egypt. Just as it had done in those two countries and in Morocco on my first day in the Arab world, the call to prayer sparked a sense of mystery and timelessness, particularly as we walked in the narrow streets of the old section of the city, with its many mosques and wall-to-wall shops full of handcrafted objects in cloth, wood, leather, and copper. I was reminded once again how much I was under the spell of this culture. I spent many days with my watercolors that summer, sitting on the spur of land that separated the two Punic ports, trying to capture some of Tunisia's beauty.

CHAPTER 11

Ulyssean Journeys

A t the end of the summer, we returned to California where, as always on our returns from abroad, my parents awaited us. In our absence they had made sure that everything went well with our house which we had rented to a UCLA family. The Arab world was not yet the dangerous place it was to become, but for my parents, each return was met with relief. Their permanent presence gave us a sense of continuity that counterbalanced all our moving around the world. The children, now ages three, six, ten, and thirteen were delighted to be reunited with their grandparents—and with our dog, Hogie, who had successfully survived being rented along with the house. Those next five years from 1971 to 1976 were golden ones as we raised our children on our Chautauqua Street mountaintop above the Pacific. The Middle East seemed far away.

The relaxed atmosphere of our first year back without many outside commitments or outside involvements continued until Malcolm was asked to be the divisional dean of social sciences at UCLA. He assured me that it would take up much less time than being department chairperson, and he was right. We still managed to keep our Friday morning tennis date and to have lunch afterwards while the children were at school. Malcolm was usually home from work in the evenings by 6:00 to help with dinner and play basketball in the driveway. Stephen, now age six and a couple of inches taller than when we left, showed impressive ability to get the ball in the basket. It was a remarkable sight. Standing with his back to the board he held the ball in his arms at knee height and with a big jump, hurled it up over his head in a backward motion. The ball, so large relative to the small boy throwing it, almost seemed to carry him with it.

Dinner time presented a nightly struggle in the process of civilizing our children. It seemed only fair to me that we should spend at least as long at the table as I had spent in the kitchen preparing the meal. And along with reasonably respectable table manners, I wanted interesting conversation. With a father who was a professor of political science and by now a leading Middle East specialist, this seemed only natural. But somehow, even with candlelight and a decorous atmosphere, my hopes were usually dashed. More often than not, the conversation turned to silliness and jokes or the latest Dodger game, reflecting not only the inclinations of the children but the irrepressible sense of humor of their father and his greater interest in discussing sports than world affairs. By the end of the meal, during an interval between the effort of elevating the dinner conversation and enforcing an equitable distribution of dishwashing, the little boys climbed onto our laps, or we all stretched out on the floor for backrubs and roughhousing with the dog.

During those five years of domestic tranquillity at our Chautauqua Street hilltop in the midseventies, Lebanon was becoming embroiled in the civil war that would soon tear it apart and bring tragedy to so many. The fragile country, fabricated at the end of World War I out of feudal areas which had for centuries been part of greater Syria, could not withstand the tremendous pressures facing it from within and without. The confessional or representational system of government accommodating many different Muslim and Christian sects was already precarious. Now it was being thrown off balance by increasing disparity between rich and poor, by the presence of hundreds of thousands of Palestinian refugees amidst a Lebanese population of only three million, and by the spilling over of regional problems into Lebanon. An overlay to these problems was the extreme freedom and openness of Lebanon.

This openness, particularly in relation to the rest of the Arab world, had brought both blessings and problems, blessings in that it had allowed Lebanon to become the business, tourist, and recreational capital of the Arab world, problems in that it spawned flourishing trade in narcotics, pornographic films, high-priced prostitution, and the flagrant violation of zoning laws that was fast allowing graceful eighteenth- and nineteenth century buildings to be replaced with wall-to-wall high rises. This open atmosphere had also fostered the liberal intellectual climate in which AUB could develop, as well as a hospitable environment for artistic and cultural expression that made Beirut one of the most stimulating and cosmopolitan of Middle Eastern capitals.

But the excesses of freedom and political and geographical vulnerability of Lebanon were turning the country into a region where interpolitical and interreligious rivalries boiled and tempted meddling from neighboring countries for their own gains. Arms were as accessible as the opium poppies grown in Baalbek, and killing other human beings was becoming common. Malcolm had a sabbatical year coming up in 1976–77 which we wanted very much to spend in Lebanon, but it seemed out of the question to take children there when there was such instability. When he was invited to be a distinguished visiting professor at the American University in Cairo, we accepted—delighted at the prospect of being back in the Middle East, even though it could not be Lebanon.

"You're not going to like Egypt very much," I warned the children. "The food is terrible, the weather is hot and sticky for months on end, everything is always dusty, and the TV is in Arabic." Almost as an afterthought I added, "but we'll learn a lot and it will be a great adventure." If the first description hadn't discouraged them, the motherly adage probably would.

It was eleven years since we had lived in Egypt. Stephen and Andrew had not existed then, and Susie and John had been too young to be able to remember much of that time. I thought that, if I prepared them for the worst, they wouldn't have much to complain about when we got there. John and Andrew, adventuresome by nature, were eager to go, even though John would have to leave behind Stella, his beloved pet boa constrictor who felt as much at home coiled around John's right arm as he did having her there. Susie, by natural inclination the bearer of family interest in the Middle East, would take her freshman year of college at AUC. Steve, whose interests lay more in sports than foreign travel, kept stoically shooting baskets in the driveway, showing little interest in our forthcoming adventure.

After an August reunion with the Kerr family in Goshen,

Massachusetts, we flew to New York and joined an AUC charter flight to Cairo. We must have been quite a sight to the Egyptian customs inspectors, Malcolm and me with four stair-step, blond and suntanned children, ages eight to seventeen, in procession behind us, carrying "boogie boards," tennis rackets, a basketball, and suitcases stuffed with a year's supply of clothes. The airport was sweltering hot and chaotic with crowds of arriving passengers being met with charming inefficiency. "It wouldn't be like this in the Beirut airport," Malcolm grumbled. But we were soon met by AUC officials and driven in a small bus down the Nile Corniche about eight miles south of Cairo to our AUC apartment in Maadi, the suburb where the American school was located.

I remembered the last time we had driven down the Corniche twelve years earlier when the residential suburb had to be separated from Cairo by farmlands where children tending water buffaloes wove garlands of flowers between their horns from the flame trees that grew along the Nile. But the agricultural land was now being invaded by construction. Ubiquitous Third World cement block buildings were rising up among the cotton and alfalfa fields where piles of rubble and construction debris were carelessly dumped. Inside the community of Maadi, there was still the sleepy, countrified, rather neocolonial atmosphere that I remembered. Galabiya-clad bawabs, or gatekeepers, looking unconsciously decorous in their flowing but utilitarian gowns, sat on benches in groups of two or three somewhere in the vicinity of the house they were guarding. An occasional flock of goats meandered along the dusty streets led by a woman in long black garb with colorfully dressed children at her side. Peeking through high hedges were vast gardens full of mango, guava, and jacaranda trees along with unfamiliar varieties of flowering trees. The smell of jasmine filled the hot air. For me, that smell evoked the Middle East, conjuring up a jumble of images more vividly than any other sight or sound. Despite the encroachment of tasteless modernization, the old magical attraction of this part of the world came back to me as forcefully as ever.

Malcolm did not share my instant attraction to this part of the Middle East, similar in many ways yet different from the Arab country further north where he had been born. He complained about the sticky heat, the flies, the dust, and the bumpy bus ride.

Abdu, the cook employed for us by the university, had laid

the table with white tablecloth, pink roses already withering in the heat, dried out roast beef, and mushy vegetables. My warnings to the children about Egyptianized Western cuisine were confirmed, but they hardly noticed. Abdu, whose talents obviously lay more in human relations than in cooking, charmed them with his good humor. His jokes in Arabic English became the foreign language the children picked up rather than the real Arabic we would have liked them to acquire. A ride on the back of Abdu's bike was a treat for Andrew who soon learned that it was easy to talk Abdu into picking him up from school in the afternoon.

We had to adjust to a house about a fourth the size of ours at home with one bathroom for the six of us and no possessions except our clothes and our sports equipment. Malcolm, being adaptable by nature, put up with the crowded conditions, although he missed the more gracious living of our home in Pacific Palisades. For me the reduced scale of living with a cook in the kitchen was a welcome change from housewifely chores and the responsibility of material possessions. My independence was further enhanced by the fact that from the first day John, Stephen, and Andrew took to their new school with enthusiasm. We had discovered the previous year that Andrew had fairly severe dyslexic problems, so we decided to have him repeat second grade, hoping that his ego would not be tarnished in the process. Our fears were put to rest a few weeks later when we overheard him responding to someone who asked him what grade he was in. "I'm in second. I should be in third, but I skipped," a dyslexic reply, perhaps, but with a flavor of inner confidence.

Cut free from household responsibilities, yet with the pleasures of my family around me, I felt as though I had been miraculously delivered into the existence I had long deserved. Along with the delights of my new freedom I was rediscovering the Middle East, feeling as I had when my love affair with Lebanon began more than two decades earlier. But this time the magical reactions had an underpinning of experience and knowledge of the area. I had studied Egyptian and Islamic history and art at UCLA for the previous two years, and I was eager to explore the monuments of those civilizations. I was also considering how to prepare for a future career now that my children were all in school. This year of freedom from domestic responsibilities was a time to get started.

Susie, Malcolm, and I made the eight-mile commute into

Cairo to the American University each morning in the green and white Volkswagen bus we had had shipped from Germany—Susie to freshman classes, I to classes in Islamic art and architecture, and Malcolm to his office where he assumed the lofty role of distinguished visiting professor. On those daily commutes, five thousand years of the monuments of Egyptian history passed before our eyes—the pyramids across the Nile to the west, striking in the almost abstract-modern straightness of their ancient forms, Coptic churches with their decorative eastern crosses, and the showpiece Citadel of Salah-ad-Din, the Muslim victor over the Crusaders, with the slender minarets of its central mosque, the Mosque of Mohammed Ali, marking the Cairo skyline.

Egypt offered fertile fields of study for a political scientist of the Middle East. For twenty years, Malcolm had studied Egypt's politics; now, he had before him a living laboratory of the development problems of the Arab World. The process of moving from a long period of colonialism to independence was being played out in countries around the Middle East. In the twelve-year interval since we had lived in Egypt under Nasser in a period of economic austerity and fervent Arab nationalism, Egypt under President Anwar Sadat had become a more industrialized state with an open economic policy and friendly relations with the West.

In 1973, another Arab-Israeli War had taken place when Syria and Egypt made a secret military plan to regain their respective captured lands, Golan and Sinai, from Israel. Their initial attack was successful, but the Israelis later gained the upper hand, and a cease-fire was eventually negotiated by the United States. Sadat had succeeded in his objective of a limited war to get across the Suez. Though they had not won a complete military victory, the Arabs took the success of their surprise attack as a psychological victory. From this time Sadat gained the confidence to pave the way for his peace initiative, which would be realized in his trip to Jerusalem in 1978.

With a complex mix of economic and political circumstances at hand, Malcolm began a project in 1977 to study Egypt in the context of rich and poor Arab states. It became a joint effort sponsored by the Center for Political and Strategic Studies of the *al-Ahram* newspaper along with the Ford Foundation in Cairo and the Von Grunebaum Center for Near Eastern Studies at UCLA. Over the next few years, Arab and American professors traveled between the Middle East and UCLA studying the effect on Arab states of oil wealth, labor migration, and liberalized national economies. The outcome was a collection of their papers edited by Sayid Yassin and Malcolm, published in 1982 called *Rich and Poor States in the Middle East; Egypt and the New Arab Order.*

In December, Malcolm attended a conference in New York which he combined with a pre-Christmas visit to his parents. Sadly, his itinerary was timely, for during that visit in early December of 1976, his father suffered a heart attack and died within three days. Malcolm was able to stay with his mother, brother, and sisters for a while and be part of the memorial service. I received a telex from Malcolm at AUC and took the sad news home to the children. This was the first death of a close family member we had experienced. It was not easy to accept the fact that this energetic man so full of life to the last was suddenly gone; he had led a long and rich life for eighty-three years. Malcolm's equally energetic mother, then eighty, lived on for nine more years, tragically to have to know of the assassination of her son a year before her death.

Malcolm returned for a family trip to Luxor for Christmas in the bright winter sunshine of upper Egypt followed by a blustery, rainy New Year's weekend in Alexandria. The pounding waves, the clear air, and the Mediterranean atmosphere of the city was a reminder that Lebanon was only a short boat ride away.

In January 1977, a truce was signed in Lebanon which many thought would bring a permanent end to the civil war, but, like so many others to follow, this one ultimately proved futile. Susie and I seized the opportunity to go back and visit Beirut, her birthplace, during the midsemester break in February. She had not been there since she was thirteen. Malcolm had been to Beirut a couple of times for conferences in the years since our summer in Lebanon in 1970, and he decided to stay home with the boys and give us a turn. As the airport was not yet functioning after the war damage it had sustained from repeated fighting the previous year, we flew to Amman, where we stayed with Widad Irani Kawar, the AUB classmate with whom I had spent that Christmas in Bethlehem so long ago. From there, it was a bus ride to Damascus, and then a taxi ride up over the familiar route through the interior

Lebanon range to the Syrian-Lebanese border. The air was as crisp and pungent as I remembered, and we took great breaths of it while waiting for customs to clear our passports. The inspectors had not seen many American visitors in recent months and were very welcoming. The presence of foreign visitors portended a return to normalcy. We continued down into the tranquil Beka'a Valley, then up through the snowy Lebanon range, and finally down to the coastal plane and Beirut.

As we neared the city, there was abundant evidence of the recent fighting between Christians and Muslims. The taxi driver pointed out the damage—mostly shrapnel holes in the walls of buildings but also large, gouged-out hollows where shells had hit directly. Closer to AUB in West Beirut, there was less evidence of damage. Glaziers were doing a record business repairing broken windows and, except for a few shrapnel holes and the familiar piles of garbage on street corners within smelling range of upscale shops, that part of town looked in good shape. But gone were the usual shoppers who used to fill the streets in the late afternoon. Only a few people walked to or from their homes, and the shutter doors on most of the shops were pulled down tight.

Malcolm had made reservations for us by telex at the Mayflower Hotel. Like many other Beirut hotels, it had remained open throughout the civil war, and the efficiency with which it was run, even under difficult circumstances, was a reminder of the business skills of the Lebanese.

Susie and I dropped our bags in the room and set off to walk the short block to the campus, impatient to verify that that beautiful place had remained unscathed. The same old gentlemanly guard who had been there in Malcolm's and my student days, now even older, greeted us effusively. "How is Dr. Stanley, and how is Mrs. Kerr?" he asked. "And how is the young Dr. Kerr?" I had to tell him of the death of Dr. Stanley two months earlier. The guard reacted with shock to the news that the engaging professor with the hint of humor always in his eye, whom he had seen daily on the campus for so many years, was no longer living. "Allah yahormou" (God have mercy on him), he said quietly. Death was a subject that was close to most Lebanese after the violence of the past several years of civil war. The old guard talked sadly about friends or friends of friends who had died as victims of the war.

We walked through the campus to the home of old friends, the Lebanese dean of arts and sciences and his American wife, who had invited us for dinner. Susie and I were enthralled with the unchanged beauty of the campus; the old stone buildings with their red tile roofs were reassuringly the same. The air still smelled of sun-warmed pine needles and sea breezes, and, as always, the brilliant aqua-blue of the Mediterranean formed a backdrop for the entire length of the campus. The civil war had not visibly intruded, although an unnatural quiet prevailed inside the campus as well as out.

As we sat sipping tea in their living room overlooking the sea, our hosts described life at AUB. "It's been months since we've gone outside the campus in the evenings. Everyone shops in the morning and then goes back home again. Since the truce was signed last month, the curfew has been lifted, but people are so used to the idea that it's dangerous to go out after dark that few go further than across the street." It was difficult for me, and for Susie, to internalize this fear, fresh as we were from the chaotic bustle of Cairo where simply crossing the street was a risky proposition, and where the dilapidated condition of many buildings was far more suggestive of war damage than what we had seen in Beirut.

With so many old friends to visit and the pacifying quiet of the streets of Ras Beirut, Susie and I freely accepted invitations for any time of day or night and walked the short distances to where they lived, unable to feel any danger in what we were doing. I delighted in seeing people and places from the past through the eyes of Susie, now herself a college student as I had been when I first saw Beirut, and to introduce my almost adult daughter to that world.

My Beirut was familiar within the campus and the warm circle of old family friends, but underneath so much had changed. War had sobered people, although our Lebanese friends sounded hopeful that the worst of it was over, that life might go back to what it had been before, that the indomitable resilience of the Lebanese people would pull the country together and put it back on its feet. Steeped in the family lore of Beirut and as susceptible to its seductive charms as her parents, Susie relished the beauty of the campus and the hospitality of friends much as I had twenty-two years earlier. It was easy to brush the dust under the carpet and listen to the optimists among our friends, who said that things were soon going to be better. Back in Cairo a week later, we regaled an envious Malcolm with stories of our trip and related friends' predictions that Lebanon would soon return to normal.

.   .   .

Involvement in Cairo life and affection for Egypt increased with each month of our stay, mine more than Malcolm's but his as well. In the second semester a chance came along for me to fill a teaching post in the freshman writing program at AUC. From the first day, I found this work brought tremendous enjoyment and satisfaction. The students were responsive, and through our daily classroom encounters and reading their compositions, another dimension was added to my understanding of Egypt. Malcolm's research for his book was going well, and through it we were becoming reacquainted with many of the Egyptian academics he had worked with during our previous stay in Cairo. When the president of AUC confided to Malcolm that he was planning to retire the next year and wondered if Malcolm would be interested in being a candidate for his job, we had to think long and hard, weighing the pros and cons for each member of our family and for our relatives at home. Finally, we decided that, if we were to move our family away from our Pacific Palisades hilltop for a long-term job in the Middle East, it should be to AUB rather than AUC.

As the end of the school year approached, we began thinking about how we would travel home. Intrepid as usual in planning our itinerary, we decided to drive along the coast of Egypt and Libya to Tunisia. Through a friend there, we arranged to rent a house in the small fishing village of Kelibia for a month. The succession of exquisite, ancient Roman cities along the coast of Libya, Cyrenia, Sabrata, and Leptis Magna, gave the children good reason to cry the familiar accusation, "Oh, no, not another Roman ruin, Mom." But Malcolm was almost as impressed as I with the splendor of vast, columned cities spread along the North African coast above the Mediterranean, founded by Phoenicians and added to by Greeks and Romans. Together we steered our children through these relics of past civilizations, and also into the outrageously expensive and ill-kept hotels of Libya where we threw our own blankets over unchanged sheets after brushing away the pistachio and watermelon seeds of the previous occupants.

Soon after crossing the Tunisian border, we visited the island of Jerba, just off the coast, where, according to history, Ulysses was attracted by the Sirens or sea nymphs who interrupted his voyage. We lingered there a few days to enjoy the long, white beaches and warm sea in a comfortable hotel in the midst of our own Ulyssean journey before heading on to Kelibia for a month of rustic living in a house on the beach close to the life of the local fishermen.

CHAPTER 12

Home Fires

*H*ome again in California in the fall of 1977, there were many changes that made the readjustment more jarring for me than on our previous returns. Our nearest neighbors had moved away and sold the bottom half of their lot, which meant a new house would replace the wild canyon on one side of our property. Malcolm had become the director of the Von Grunebaum Center for Near Eastern Studies at UCLA, a job that kept him working long hours and took him away on frequent trips. The boys were now in three different schools which required complex car pooling, and they were not home much because of after-school and weekend sports. The most drastic change of all was having Susie go off to college, causing me to lose my female ally in the family. I did not like being back in the kitchen when I had just discovered a new career and a new stage of life in Cairo. Our magnificent house and all its modern appliances were unwanted possessions and our beautiful garden no longer fun to work in without the children playing there. And as before on our returns, I missed all the smells and sights and sounds of the Middle East. I kept thinking that, if we had agreed that Malcolm be a candidate for the AUC presidency, we might now be living in Cairo, and I could be leading a stimulating life as teacher and president's wife.

That longing was intensified when Anwar Sadat made his dramatic trip to Jerusalem in the fall of 1977 with a peace initiative followed by the return visit of Menachem Begin to Egypt. How interesting it would have been to be in Cairo to witness the reactions of people to this momentous event. We watched Sadat on television making his speech in Arabic to the Israeli Knesset, declaring his wish to establish peaceful borders along the Sinai peninsula with Israel. Malcolm was immediately critical that a unilateral peace agreement of one Arab country with Israel would throw off balance the efforts for a general settlement of the Palestinian problem. What would happen now to the painstakingly slow but steady progress being made for peace talks in Geneva between representatives of Israel and all the Arab countries? Would they settle the question of national rights for the Palestinian people of the West Bank and Gaza and the right of Palestinians outside to return? I could not completely agree with Malcolm. I thought how natural it was for Sadat to try to make peace for his war-weary people, if he could, with the enemy they had fought in three different wars, the Suez War of 1956, the June War of 1967, and the October War of 1973. Yet with the interruption, or perhaps discontinuation, of plans for a general conference in Geneva, chances for a solution to the Palestinian problem grew even dimmer, and with it the chances for peace in Lebanon.

On the heels of our return that fall, President Carter had appointed Malcolm to be one of a group of consultants on the Middle East to be on call should the President want the advice of academic area specialists. This news apparently did not please a group of people in Los Angeles who were extremist members of the California Jewish Defense League. Deeming Malcolm to be their enemy, they set fire to our car one night in the driveway just outside John's bedroom window. This turned out to be a single incident with no further ramifications, but there was a certain irony in this terrorist act occurring in our own home after we had traveled thousands of miles in the Middle East without mishap.

In an effort to find a career niche for myself in California in something involving the Middle East, I began to look for Los Angeles-based companies that did business in the Arab world with the idea that I could develop cultural and language orientation programs for their employees going to the Middle East. Armed with an employee survey which I had drawn up and some literature on the importance of cultural training before working overseas, I called on company executives. My request was to be allowed to interview their employees in Saudi Arabia, Egypt, and Lebanon in the coming summer, when I would tag along with

Malcolm on a business trip, in order to learn their opinions on how their employers could best prepare them for living in the Middle East.

Since I was essentially offering these companies free information about a subject that might improve their profits, it was not difficult to obtain consent for the interviews. Malcolm and I went off the next summer on an exciting three week Middle Eastern adventure by ourselves that would take us to Saudi Arabia, Egypt, and Lebanon. We left Susie, home from Oberlin College, and John, soon to be a senior at Palisades High, in charge of the household and running a neighborhood summer day camp on our mountaintop with Steve and Andrew as assistants.

While Malcolm met with bearded shaykhs from an Islamic university in Riyadh to establish a linkage program with the UCLA Near Eastern Center, I visited the sterile compounds of American companies to listen to a torrent of complaints that employees felt free to unload on an uninvolved third party. I thought it was a great accomplishment when one company offered to fly me to the southern province of Khamis Mushayt to interview their employees there. Women did not usually travel alone in Saudi Arabia, so I adopted my most conservative demeanor, wore my longest skirt, and made the side trip without Malcolm and without a hitch, except for having to subdue an overly friendly taxi driver on my return to Riyadh.

We went on to Cairo where Malcolm consulted with colleagues on the project he had initiated the previous year between UCLA and the al-Ahram Center for Political and Strategic Studies on rich and poor Arab states, while I conducted interviews, visited friends, and exulted in being in Egypt. We were anxious to learn about the mood of Cairo after the Sadat-Begin visit. Reactions were fairly predictable: our academic friends, Egyptian and American, believed that, in spite of plans outlined for a settlement of the Palestinian problem in the upcoming Camp David talks, which were the outgrowth of the Sadat-Begin visits, the Israelis would manage to stall and stonewall, and nothing would be done. Egyptian taxi drivers, my bellwether of public opinion, were relieved that they would not have to fight in any more wars with Israel and held a certain curiosity at the novel prospect of exchange between the two countries.

While Malcolm and I wanted to talk about Egypt, our friends wanted to know about the fire bombing of our car the previous fall in our driveway in Pacific Palisades. In reports in international newspapers they had read, the incident sounded worse than it had actually been. "Why did they do it?" our friends asked. "You've written as critically about the Arabs as you have about the Israelis." We ourselves, of course, had been trying to figure out the answer to that question. Malcolm's outspoken ideas on the need for recognition of Palestinian rights made him unpopular in Israeli circles, just as his often expressed exasperation with Arab inability to get organized and cooperate with one another in their own best interests made him suspect among some Arabs.

It was eight years since Malcolm and I had been in Lebanon together. Now in late June 1978 Malcolm, as a newly appointed and very proud trustee of AUB, was to go to Beirut for a meeting of the board. We flew into Beirut, holding hands tightly and peering out the window with anticipation as we were landing—and trying to spot Ainab in the mountains southeast of the city. The airport was filled with soldiers armed with machine guns and looking much more serious than the sleepy soldiers guarding official establishments in Cairo who gave the impession that, although they were holding a gun, they weren't really interested in using it. A multi-Arab peace keeping force had been established in Lebanon in 1976 consisting mostly of Syrians. The invitation for them to stay had to be officially reissued by the Lebanese government every six months.

We stayed with friends on the campus and relished awakening in their upstairs bedroom to the chimes of the College Hall clock tower in the pine-scented air from the treetops all around us. The backdrop was an expanse of blue so close that it seemed as if we could jump into the sea from our bedroom window. While Malcolm attended meetings, I visited insatiably with old friends—former classmates, professors, and the shopkeepers I knew, most of whom were in the same shops I used to frequent and who were full of stories about how many times they'd had to replace the glass in their windows after shells had hit nearby. "El hamdulillah (praise God), we are still here," each one said at least several times during our conversation.

Unlike the old, carefree days of bustling business and relatively low prices, inflation now impeded local business, and a shortage of foreign visitors afflicted hotels and other tourist industries. The Lebanese pound, which had remained stable at three to the dollar for many years, had doubled to six to the dollar. "But these are not our most serious problems," explained a Middle Eastern artifacts and antiquities dealer on Rue Bliss across from the AUB main gate. "Every month, I have to pay out hundreds and hundreds of pounds in protection money to people from different militia groups who come around and say they are in control of this neighborhood. Some force me to buy their propaganda sheets. Others just ask directly for their monthly payment." What will happen if you don't pay?" I asked. "They might break into my shop or encourage others to do so—or they might throw a bomb in one night." So it appeared that the term "protection money" was a misnomer.

But the always threatening civil war in that summer of 1978 did not stop Beirut social life, and the trustees and their spouses were entertained royally. One very rich Lebanese trustee invited us to his small palace in Yarzi, a wealthy residential suburb in the mountains to the north of Beirut. Tables beside his swimming pool groaned with the weight of huge platters of every kind of Lebanese delicacy imaginable. There were occasional sounds of distant shelling, but our hosts assured us that the noise came from the south and was never a bother in their locality. I was reminded of friends back home from different parts of Los Angeles who claimed to live in the one smog-free area of the city.

The trustees were invited by the president of Lebanon, Elias Sarkis, to visit his palace in Baabda. We were ushered into the visitors' salon where brocade-covered chairs encircled the room. Once we were assembled, the president walked in and proceeded around the room, shaking hands with each one of us as photographers flashed their cameras. It soon became evident why Sarkis was known as a do-nothing president. When we all sat down, he looked at us with heavy-lidded eyes and spoke in a voice that was so soft we could hardly hear him. When we could, the content was not noteworthy. Sarkis, a Christian who was acceptable to Muslims, had been chosen as a compromise president, and it was apparent that he was disinclined toward action, particularly the dynamic action needed to force diverse Muslim and Christian groups to negotiate and compromise.

For the first time in several years, the AUB commencement was to be held out-of-doors in the traditional setting on the athletic field at the bottom of the campus next to the sea. The presence of dozens of security soldiers on the hillside leading up to the main campus was a reminder that the atmosphere of peace and tranquillity on the campus was deceptive. Yet parents gathered by the hundreds to see the grand pomp of an AUB graduation and to watch proudly while their children received the degree from the university that was considered the best in the Middle East. Professors in a variety of different colored academic caps and gowns representing universities from all over the world marched in stately procession amongst almost a thousand students from undergraduate and graduate programs. The final party of the week was on the Marquand House Terrace, which, of all the places we had been entertained, Malcolm and I agreed was the most beautiful. Dinner was served at small tables, and afterward we danced late into the warm evening underneath the cyprus trees that Daniel Bliss had planted seventy-five years earlier. Beirut and AUB had recast their seductive spell over us, and the war seemed far away.

Once back in California, the results of my efforts to find a job took form in an offer from the Northrop Corporation to develop a cultural orientation program on Egypt for their employees going there to provide flying training and maintenance of their F-18 airplane. I started to work within the week. The immediate involvement would be an opportunity to inform people better about the Middle East. I tried not to think too much about the fact that I was working for an organization that made "weapons for peace."

Joining the ranks of freeway commuters and other mothers with full-time jobs had its drawbacks, but with Malcolm making breakfast in the morning and my ultimatum to the boys that from now on they would do their own laundry, we managed. I wrote handbooks, devised an orientation program, coerced vice-presidents to get me some money from their budgets to buy audio-visual equipment, and with the help of Arab friends from UCLA, developed simple Arabic lessons in Egyptian and Saudi dialects. The program was successful, but in spite of its positive results, constant vigilance was required to keep it from being a victim of budget cuts when executives were looking for dispensable parts of their programs.

One afternoon in late October, just as I was about to leave

work to go home, a secretary came in to tell me that a big brush fire was burning out of control in the Santa Monica mountains near Pacific Palisades. I rushed out of the office to make my way home. I could feel the dry Santa Ana wind, which so often blows in the fall in southern California and has caused tremendous fires over the years. This fire was to inflict overwhelming damage and loss to people all over Los Angeles County and be an experience for me that would be of value later in understanding the process of loss, devastation, and regeneration.

When I reached home, flames were leaping into the air at the top of the mountain and beginning to make their descent into the canyon beside our house. Malcolm and John were on the roof watering it with the garden hose and wet towels. Steve had not been allowed to leave Paul Revere Junior High School because of fire danger on the route home along Sunset Boulevard, and Andrew had been picked up from the elementary school by a friend. From Palisades High School, down near the ocean, John could look up into the mountains and see the fire coming closer and closer to our house. As soon as students were released, he ran the mile straight uphill for home, the last portion on a mountain trail. He and Malcolm had immediately started loading one of our two cars with crucial documents and business papers and a change of clothing for each of us.

I at once set about loading the car I had been driving with family pictures and souvenirs and my water colors of the Middle East. Soon after, my parents arrived and took to their car our meager silver and china collection and various practical items they thought we would want in the new home it appeared we might have to construct from scratch.

We drove all the cars to the home of friends in a safe part of the Palisades. They then drove Malcolm and me back up to our house where we would stay as long as we could to keep the fire at bay. We had our bicycles ready for a quick exit. From the looks of things, we would need them very soon. The flames had progressed down to the bottom of the canyon right below us and were starting up toward our house. The fire advanced toward us with its crackling and roaring noise and the raging wind of its own creation, blowing fire balls of burning chaparral into the air. When it reached the high stone walls of the patio and leapt over them with

ease onto the dry wood-shingle roof, Malcolm and I decided that
we were ready to obey the insistent orders of policemen coming
over loudspeakers from patrol cars to abandon our houses.

We rode our bicycles down the hill through the smokey chaos
of police cars and neighbors making their retreats. There were no
fire engines in sight; it was thought that they hadn't yet arrived
from the five other brush fires that were raging in southern California. It must have been about 5:30 or 6:00 in the evening but in
the eerie light of the fire it was hard to tell. Assuming our children were in safe hands though uncertain where, Malcolm and I
sat like the refugees we were on the curb of a street corner on
Sunset Boulevard where we had a clear view of the mass of flames
surrounding our house. "If our house burns down, then you won't
have so many material possessions to take care of," Malcolm tried
to console me, only half jokingly. The thought of moving back to
Cairo into an AUC apartment with a cook and nothing to take
care of brought momentary consolation. We continued to watch
with numb disbelief, knowing there was nothing we could do to
save our house.

After perhaps half an hour, flames subsided and the smoke
cleared a bit. We both thought we could see our two white chim-
neys. Perhaps they were still standing after everything else had
burned down? We walked to the home of our friends where our
cars were and our children had gathered and then drove home.
Miraculously, the house was undamaged, although the patio, some
of our garden and wide areas of trees in the canyons right up to the
wall of the garden had burned. In piecing together later some
evidence as to what had saved our house, we found it had been a
combination of the work of a good neighbor, who was a UCLA
biology professor and a talented volunteer fire fighter, the late
arrival of a fire engine, the dumping of water in the canyon by a
helicopter, and a beneficent change in the wind.

We went to bed that night, grateful to be under our own roof
but barely able to sleep because of the penetrating odor of smoke.
The next morning we awoke early to go out and observe the damage by daylight. The high chaparral on the hills as far as we could
see had been reduced to a surface of ash a couple of inches deep.

In the weeks and months that followed, we witnessed a spectacle of devastation and rebirth in those mountains where we walked

almost daily with our dog. The process left a lasting impression on me which, after Malcolm's death, became a metaphor in my mind for the devastation I was going through and for the signs of rebirth that slowly occurred.

Signs of regrowth started gradually and in a variety of ways. Some plants that had shallow, far-reaching roots swallowed the evening dew and the first drops of rain and began to send up green shoots. Burned stumps of native toyon and ceanothus eventually began to sprout new growth. People came to walk in the hills to observe the phenomenon of life growing out of the ashen soil, creating in the process new paths beyond the old ones that had been impassable before. By spring, the most impressive of nature's surprises made itself evident. Wildflowers bloomed in varieties never seen before, some from seeds germinated only by intense heat, others from the unusual ashen content of the soil.

The new growth continued, restoring life to the mountainsides, all the while creating a landscape different from the old. The vegetation returned but in different patterns and forms than before. Little by little the intricately curving black trunks and branches that had stood standing in the ash became enveloped by new growth. But one had only to look among the leaves to see the blackened stalks and branches that remained at the heart of that new growth, reminders that would not go away.

I learned that new forms of life could spring out of what had come before, dependent on the past as their source but generating their own new paths in the process of growth. Separation from the past was impossible and the onset of new forms of life inevitable. Now, many years after the fire, the blackened branches of chaparral have bleached white and taken on the delicate form of reindeer antlers. There is a particular ceanothus where I stop on my daily walks with my new dog where the bright green new trunk has entwined itself around the old darkened one, both reaching into the sky.

CHAPTER 13

Cairo Sojourn

*I*n the winter of that rebirth after the fire, Malcolm had a chance to apply for the position of director of the University of California Study Abroad Program in Egypt at AUC. Although it was not quite two years since he had become director of the UCLA Near Eastern Center, there were practical reasons why we wanted to return to Egypt, apart from the Middle East's irresistible hold on us. The advantages were greatest for Andrew and me. I could go back to the teaching at AUC that I loved and study for an M.A. in applied linguistics to improve my professional status. Andrew could return to the American school in Cairo, a school that was better able to address his special learning needs than Pacific Palisades Elementary School. While I missed Egypt more than Malcolm did, he was willing to go for our sakes, and it would also be advantageous to him in finishing the research project he had started in Cairo on rich and poor Arab states. John, soon to be a freshman at Swarthmore College, and Susie, a junior at Oberlin, were delighted at the thought of trips back to Cairo for Christmas and summer. Only Steve was gloomy at the prospect of having to leave home and his school and community basketball teams where he was becoming increasingly successful.

We were reduced to a family of four as Susie and John saw Andrew, Steve, Malcolm, and me off at the airport in late August 1979. They still had a week before leaving for college, so they would see that the house and dog were properly turned over to our fourth set of tenants in ten years. I hoped that John, having recently decided not to take his snake with him to Swarthmore,

175

would succeed in discharging Stella to the care of a friend and then dismantle the huge cage he had built for her now six-foot length which took up a third of his room.

Our new home in Cairo, another AUC apartment in the suburb of Maadi where we had lived in 1976–77, was more spacious than the last and ideally located opposite the entrance to the Maadi Sporting Club for easy access to swimming and tennis. Well experienced at settling in, we got the boys into school, regained our club membership, and found a cook within a week. These trappings of a neocolonial existence were a tradeoff for more rustic living conditions than we were accustomed to at home. The new cook, Ali, even more than our previous cook, Abdu, was to become an integral part of our family for those two years, and later, when Andrew and I moved to Cairo from Beirut after Malcolm's death, Ali would come back to work for us for five years. His loyalty and honesty typified the race of darker-skinned southern Egyptians and Nubians who came in large numbers to Cairo to work as cook-sufragis (table waiters) and general housekeepers.

Once again I was freed from household cares to teach at AUC and now to begin studies toward a Master's degree in applied linguistics, a career path that I was more than ready for after twenty years of child rearing. Malcolm, noting my enthusiasm for my new academic pursuits, commented that he wished his students would study as hard as I did. He was teaching two courses on the Middle East and one in the cultural studies program, which gave him a chance to read a lot of old classics. And he was concluding the editing of his book, *Rich and Poor Arab States.*

It was a year since Sadat had met with Carter and Begin at Camp David in the fall of 1978 to sign the accord that had brought a semblance of stability to Egyptian-Israeli relations, perhaps best called a cold peace. This stability made possible the continuation of Sadat's infitah or open door economic policy, the effects of which could be seen in the abundance of imported goods on the shelves of Cairo shops and in the increasing construction of new apartment buildings. The gas station where we filled our tank now sported a mini-market which sold, among other things, European chocolate bars and American car polish in aerosol cans. Gomaa's, the major Maadi grocery shop, now sold American Frosted Flakes along with Japanese television sets and Taiwanese electric fans. This facade of affluence for the few who could afford luxury items did not alter the long lines of people who stood in front of the government stores waiting to buy bread, chickens, cheese, or milk at subsidized prices. The difference between rich and poor was underscored by the ever more conspicuous consumption of the rich. Even though these subsidies cost millions of dollars a year from American aid and international funding agencies, the government could not politically afford to remove them for fear of causing a recurrence of the food riots of February 1977, when some basic subsidies had been removed.

Anwar Sadat, whom we recalled being referred to as the suffragi in the Nasser regime for his village origins and dark coloring, now, twenty-five years later, had quite a different image. He sported well-cut uniforms with colorful braid and medals, and inhabited palatial homes in many parts of Egypt. His visionary qualities and his international reputation as a peacemaker were not appreciated at home as much as they were abroad. Nor were the very visible efforts of his wife Jihan to improve conditions for women appreciated in a country where traditionally the wife of a public figure remained out of the public eye and women's rights was not a popular issue.

President Sadat introduced multiparty elections, yet the legal parties were not entirely free to organize support, for he kept tight control over the opposition. Election results always came out around 98–99% in favor of his National Democratic Party and the jails were more full than usual with political prisoners. In these years, which were to be his last, Sadat was also becoming more ascetic. Meditation was part of his daily routine, and it was rumored that he was planning to build a holy shrine on Mt. Sinai where Muslims, Christians, and Jews could worship together. He fasted regularly and allowed himself much time for visionary pursuits, becoming less in touch with the increasing economic, social, and religious complexities of Egypt.

Rigid political control continued and even Malcolm, we later learned, was blacklisted after we left. He had been forthright in writing his criticism of the fact that Sadat's peace policies had sidestepped painstaking efforts being made to use talks in Geneva as the framework for settling the question of Palestinian rights. Religious fundamentalists, though not numerous in the already traditional society of Egypt, were kept under strict surveillance by security police and were well represented among the political prisoners of Egyptian jails.

At the end of the 1980 academic year, Susie graduated from Oberlin College. She had written her senior thesis on her grandfather, Stanley Kerr's volunteer work with the Near East Relief in Turkey, using his letters home to his parents. Now she was going to come out to the Middle East for a year to teach at St. George's School in east Jerusalem. She and John flew together to Cairo to spend the summer with us, crossing paths with Steve who went back to California to stay with friends in Pacific Palisades through the fall school term so he could play basketball at Palisades High School.

Late in the summer Malcolm had to go to Beirut for meetings, and John went along. They had an unexpected adventure when one of Malcolm's former students, who was now working as an adviser to Yasser Arafat, contacted Malcolm to invite him to visit the leader of the PLO. Not sure of whether or not John was invited, Malcolm went alone. The former student picked him up at the home of friends where they were staying. Since Arafat slept in a different place each night for security reasons, the aide wasn't sure where they were going. In fact, when they arrived at what they thought was their destination, they discovered that their elusive host had decided to spend the night elsewhere. Eventually they found him in a drab apartment building in a crowded Muslim quarter of west Beirut. Arafat was sitting on a big couch with two children on his lap. As he welcomed Malcolm he leaned over to push a large AK 47 gun out of the way to make room for him to sit down near them. The opening conversation centered on children, as it usually does in the Arab world; when Arafat discovered that John was also in Beirut but had not come with Malcolm, he sent his driver to pick him up immediately.

Malcolm's previous impression of the controversial leader with nine lives was confirmed. Arafat possessed a single-minded dedication to his cause. Likewise, he demonstrated a monastic-like austerity by shunning many of life's amenities and pleasures, and this personal preparation gave him the staying power to survive as leader of disparate PLO factions.

Arafat told Malcolm and John of his respect for AUB and of

his intention that the PLO continue to provide protection for the university. With the PLO militias controlling west Beirut at that time, it was better to have them on your side than against you. This bestowal of friendship did nothing to endear AUB to some Maronite Christians who already looked upon the university as a breeding ground for Arab nationalists whose rallying cry was the cause of the Palestinians. Many Maronites, feeling that they were an island of beleaguered Christians in the sea of the Muslim world, feared AUB would become a predominantly Muslim university. And there were American congressmen, on whose vote depended further aid for AUB. An association of the university with the name of Yasser Arafat did not incline them to want to contribute U.S. government funds. The university, from the day it was founded, had had to walk a fine line on religious and political issues, but these new complications were unprecedented.

During his stay in Beirut, Malcolm learned that AUB might be searching for a new president. Several board members had alluded to the possibility of a change in leadership in the next year or two and queried Malcolm on whether he might be interested in being a candidate for the job. The possibility was at once thrilling and something that seemed like a natural next step. The seed was planted and, since it was indefinite and something for the future, we could put the idea in a pleasant place in the back of our minds and go about enjoying our second year in Egypt before returning to California.

The Camp David talks had opened the border between Israel and Egypt, which had been closed since 1967. Malcolm and I had taken Andrew and Steve and a group of University of California Education Abroad students on an adventuresome overland trip from Cairo to Jerusalem in March 1980, shortly after the border opened. Now Susie became a frequent traveler on this route as she traveled up to Jerusalem to her teaching job at St. George's School and home again for vacations in Cairo. Malcolm and I too traveled back and forth to see her when we had a long weekend. In a series of three taxi rides and a long stop at the border, it was possible to reach Jerusalem in a day for about $20.00. The first part of the drive took us across the eastern desert to the gentle farmlands of Ismailia and the Suez Canal where we left the first taxi and boarded a "lunch," the local pronunciation of launch. As soon as our feet touched ground, we were bombarded with offers from more taxi drivers to haggle with them over the price of the drive across the top of the Sinai Peninsula to the border of al-Arish. It was a harrowing ride with drivers who sped along the narrow two-lane road, unmindful of the need to slow down for windblown piles of sand along the side of the road or passing Bedouins with their camels and sheep. Along the roadside, poking out of the sand, were the rusty ruins of Israeli and Egyptian tanks from the wars of 1967 and 1973. If one could dig down into the sand through the layers of history, there would surely be evidence of the Romans, Greeks, Assyrians, and Pharaonic Egyptians who also passed this way.

From the muddle of the recently opened border station, after going through lengthy security and passport procedures, we went in another taxi up the shores of the eastern Mediterranean through the Gaza Strip, heavily populated with Palestinian refugees. There the desert landscape began to change to gentle hills and fruit or-chards. The last twenty miles of the drive took us to a higher altitude through pine-strewn, rocky hills and up a final climb to the pristine city, all beige white stone against a bright blue sky. Had we been able to keep going, we could have been in Beirut in less than two hours, but that had not been possible since 1948.

At Christmas time, John came to Cairo to spend the second semester of his sophomore year at AUC, making us fellow students at the same university. And soon after, Steve returned from his time at home in Pacific Palisades in the company of my parents who were celebrating their fiftieth wedding anniversary with a trip to Egypt. It was good to have our three boys at home together again and Susie only a day's drive away in Jerusalem. We took advantage of the time for trips in our Jeep Wagoneer into the desert and to the Red Sea for snorkeling and camping.

Along with those family adventures, another of my favorite memories from that time in Egypt was the train ride between Cairo and Maadi. The price of a ticket was five piasters, less than two cents, which was the same price as a round of local bread, but this train was often so crowded that the conductor couldn't reach all the passengers to collect the fare. It was almost impossible to board the train in the morning when much of the population within twenty miles of Cairo was trying to get to work, and when one did, it was rib cage to rib cage. But in the afternoons there was room to look around and observe the expressive faces of the people of Egypt, which to me seemed both strong and acquiescent, full of humor and warmth while at the same time long-suffering. People often carried the live chickens or ducks that they had bought in the central market, along with huge leafy cabbages or bags of tomatoes and greens to eat inside flat, double-layered bread made of coarse wheat flour. Mothers trustingly handed their babies out through the train window to someone with a friendly face so that they could more easily push their way through the crowded door and retrieve them. School children, always in neatly ironed uniforms and well-combed hair, no matter how poor their families, flocked onto the train carrying their books. Blind people wandered in to beg for money, usually guided by a child; salesmen offered such items as miniature Korans, pencils, or lottery tickets. I relished those train rides in the afternoons after a day of teaching and studying in the relatively affluent environment of AUC as a chance to sit back and observe how the vast majority of Egyptians lived—a way of life from which we were so far removed.

In June 1981, after the completion of my Master's thesis and final exams, Malcolm and I went up to Jerusalem to help Susie move her belongings to Cairo and to have a last look at the beautiful city we both loved before returning to the United States. Malcolm gave a lecture at Tel Aviv University where Shimshon Zelniker and Itamar Rabinovitch, two of his former Israeli graduate students at UCLA, were now teaching. At a dinner party after the lecture, news came of the Israeli bombing of a nuclear plant in Iraq. I remember vividly the shock and frightened reactions of our Israeli friends, which seemed to be a mixture of horror that their government had perpetrated such a deed and relief that they were able to protect themselves against surrounding countries who wanted to harm them.

During our trips to Jerusalem over the past two years, we had become at once more aware of the blatant harrassment of Arabs under Israeli occupation and also of the enormity of Jewish fear of persecution, which had historic roots and now took national proportions in the small state, which felt constantly threatened by its neighbors. For so many years I had lived among Arabs who felt frustrated and impotent in the face of Israeli power. This glimpse into the fears of both sides and the terrible hatred and violence it led to made the Arab-Israeli dispute seem all the more tragic.

We got back to Cairo in time for my graduation ceremonies. I marched in the procession with Malcolm and my children sitting in the audience making faces at me, reluctant to admit that I was really moving beyond the role of wife and mother where they, and I, were so accustomed to thinking of me.

We traveled home that summer, stopping for a visit with Malcolm's family at the vacation home in upstate New York of his brother and sister-in-law, Doug and Mary Ann Kerr. While there, we celebrated our twenty-fifth wedding anniversary, full of feelings of satisfaction and good fortune for all that had happened to us in our first quarter-century and looking ahead to the next quarter-century when we would enjoy the fruits of our labors and have more time together.

PART FOUR

The AUB Presidency
1981–1984

CHAPTER 14

A Time of Decisions

Home again in California, Malcolm, Steve, Andrew, and I became the ideal nuclear family of four as John returned to Swarthmore for his junior year and Susie went to Harvard to begin a Master's degree in Middle Eastern studies. Malcolm's two years heading the University of California Education Abroad Program in Cairo added to his accumulation of credit toward sabbatical leave, and he decided to take the fall quarter off to accept a Phi Beta Kappa lectureship and do some writing. I decided to take my own sabbatical to be at home with Malcolm and travel with him when his lectures occasionally took him to different universities around the country. With my new Master's degree I didn't mind the life of a housewife nearly so much as on former returns from the Middle East. In fact it was something of a pleasant novelty to rediscover the delights of home and garden after two years of studying and teaching. I would take my time looking for a job that would begin after Christmas. Andrew, now a teenager too, was catching up with Steve, and the two were discovering each other as more grown-up brothers. We all basked in the pleasure of being home again, of taking walks with Hogie in the mountains above our house, playing Frisbee on the beach, and having barbecues in our patio with family and old friends. The highlight of the week was watching Steve play basketball for Pacific Palisades High. Once again, caught up in home life in California, the Middle East seemed far away, though in the back of our minds was the knowledge that the trustees of AUB were searching for a new president and that Malcolm's name was high on their list of candidates.

185

In October 1981, President Sadat was assassinated by Islamic fundamentalists as he sat with other members of the Egyptian government at the observation of the eighth anniversary of the October 6th war with Israel. At the time it happened, we were in the midst of preparing to celebrate Malcolm's fiftieth birthday with an evening barbecue at home. Added to the circle of family and close friends were his mother and sister Marion, who flew out from the east coast, but sadly Susie and John could not leave their classes so early in the school year. Malcolm would be on a visiting committee at Harvard the next week anyway and would have a late celebration with Susie, but John was left out of the festivities. In a letter to Susie he wrote:

> I know I owe you a letter but I'm afraid I don't have time for a real one. I spent all yesterday depressed and got homesick last night thinking about not being at Dad's birthday party, and now I'm way behind. I started writing a paper tonight but it was one of those in which every word just comes out badly, so I have to do something else for a while. I think this may be a real letter after all. . . . Tell Dad [when you see him] that I think he's the best Dad imaginable. I think last night was the most homesick I've ever been. It sure was neat to see his name in the *New York Times* yesterday, although it's too bad it had to be because Sadat died. . . . I have to admit that part of the reason I've been depressed the past few days is because hearing about Sadat has made me nervous about [the possibility of] Dad going to Beirut. It's sort of reminded me that if someone doesn't like you they just might shoot you. Whoops, now I'm depressed again! Maybe I'll have to write some more! I think I'll be okay. See you pretty soon Susie.

In Egypt after the assassination there was a remarkably smooth transition to a new government, due in part to general stability among most segments of the Egyptian public and to safe boundaries with Israel. There was also a well-established and effective security system which kept a tight rein on radical elements in the country. Their job was made easier by the traditional values of the population who were, on the whole, not susceptible to promptings for radical change offered in the name of Islamic fundamentalism. The basically Sunni Muslim population did not have the religious and ethnic diversity of some Arab countries, and they tended toward accommodation rather than violence. Conditions surrounding Egypt's Arab neighbors to the north in Lebanon were very different.

The historic and shifting sectarian divisions of the Lebanese, which were as intrinsic to the fabric of that society as Nilotic stability was to Egypt, had not reordered themselves since the outbreak of civil war in 1975. Both internal and external factors interfered. Internally, the modus vivendi that had existed between diverse Christian and Muslim groups in the fifties, sixties, and early seventies had been unbalanced. When King Hussein expelled Palestinian activists from Jordan in 1971 in the uprising referred to as Black September, they moved to Beirut. Arafat made his PLO headquarters in West Beirut and virtually created a state within a state which the fragile government of Lebanon was too weak to withstand. The Shiites, long a sizable and impoverished minority in Lebanon, were increasing in number. Their poverty and inferior status left them open to radical influences of Iranian Shiites who were coming into Lebanon carrying the message of Khomeini. A number of them had a stronghold in Baalbek in the Beka'a Valley, the site of the exquisite Roman temple where Malcolm and I had had so many picnics and evenings at the summer music festivals.

The Maronite Christians, who predominated in East Beirut and in the central mountains of Lebanon, were feeling increasingly threatened as they observed the increase in Muslim and particularly Shiite Muslim population and strength. With the combined Christian population of Maronites, Greek Orthodox, Catholics, and Protestants numbering only a third of the population of Lebanon, the ruling Christian Phalangist Party saw alliance with Israel as a means to survival.

Unlike the more homogeneous population of Egypt, which tended to work toward accommodation, the diverse population of Lebanon tended to splinter and grow more violent. Each religious or sectarian group developed its own militia so that ultimately there were dozens of different militias, each controlling the particular part of the city where they held sway. In Ras Beirut, where AUB was located, the Palestinians were in control, and it was their militia that "protected" the university.

Externally, Israel and Syria were causing problems for Lebanon. Israeli leaders were devising plans for attacking Arafat and the PLO in Beirut and creating a "security zone" against PLO forays by expanding twenty-five miles into Lebanese territory to the Litani River, which some Israelis saw as the natural northern border of Israel.

Syria's President Assad, a major power broker in Lebanon, was suspicious of Israeli ambitions in Lebanon. He was on bad terms with both the United States and with fellow Arab countries, and he had his problems with the PLO too. He backed a faction of the PLO that were rivals of Arafat's and pulled the strings that set off battles between them within Lebanese territory.

The U.S. government, though well supplied with highly qualified Middle Eastern specialists, did not have a coherent policy for the area. President Reagan looked at the region in a U.S.-Soviet context and showed little awareness of the differences among Arab countries and the necessity of paying careful attention to the separate needs and interests of each in planning an effective foreign policy. In dealing with Lebanon, the Reagan administration seemed to disregard the intersectarian makeup of that country. Nor was it willing to come to grips with the issue that had helped spark the civil war and was at the heart of instability and unrest in the Middle East: the unresolved problem of a homeland for the Palestinians. Reagan seemed to follow two popular misconceptions: one, that Israel was the only worthy U.S. ally in the Middle East, and two, that Lebanon should be upheld as the rightful stronghold for Christianity in the Muslim world.

In the absence of a well-founded American policy, the Reagan government let Israel take the lead in actions that would result in disastrous effects for Lebanon, as well as for the United States and Israel. The timing of these actions and their interaction with civic upheaval in Lebanon brought tragedy to our family and to hundreds of thousands of others. In June 1981 when Israeli Prime Minister Begin had used American planes to bomb Iraq's nuclear reactor just before election time, President Reagan responded, "It is very difficult for me to envision Israel as being a threat to its neighbors." Malcolm and I remembered from being in Jerusalem at the time how concerned the Israeli friends we were with at Hebrew University felt at the bravado of Begin's action and the warlike connotations of this "defensive" attack. A month later Israel had again used American-supplied planes to bomb residential areas of Beirut in an effort to knock out PLO headquarters, in the process killing and wounding hundreds of civilians. The United States sent its Middle East envoy, Ambassador Philip Habib, to negotiate a cease-fire between Israel and the PLO. Though shaky, the cease-fire held, and some even dared to hope that a new absence of PLO aggression toward Israel confirmed a growing moderate stance from Arafat.

In October 1981, Secretary of State Haig attended the funeral of President Sadat where he met Prime Minister Begin. Haig wrote in his memoirs: "Begin told him that Israel had begun planning a move into Lebanon and would not draw Syria into the conflict." Haig responded, "If you move, you move alone. Unless there is a major, internationally recognized provocation, the United States will not support such an action." Over the next eight months further conversations on this subject took place between Haig and Israeli representatives who claimed that no one had the right to interfere with their country's self-defense. The U.S. government continued to proclaim that without an internationally recognized provocation, an Israeli invasion of Lebanon would have a devastating effect on the United States.

The next month, in November 1981, Malcolm attended the AUB Board of Trustees meeting in New York where, as we had anticipated, he was officially nominated to be a candidate for president of the university. "If the AUB presidency ever comes my way, I could never turn it down," Malcolm had said on various occasions, and I had concurred, believing firmly that he was made for the job and also remembering my feeling of missed opportunities when we had turned down the chance for him to be a candidate for the AUC presidency.

At the departure of the previous president of the university, Vice President David Dodge had become acting president, and now he and Malcolm were the leading candidates for the presidency. Malcolm and David, a few years apart in age, shared the bond of having grown up on the AUB campus and of going on to Princeton for their university education. David's father, Bayard Dodge, had been the third president of the university. His maternal great-grandfather was Daniel Bliss, the founder of AUB. His grandfather, Howard Bliss, had been the second president who carried the university through the difficult days of World War I when the United States was officially at war with the Ottoman rulers of Lebanon. David had only recently gone to work for the university as vice president in charge of development after a long career with a Beirut-based oil company. He fitted very naturally and happily back into the AUB environment.

During the next months, we reveled in anticipation of the real possibility of Malcolm's becoming president of AUB. We would be able to have our cake and eat it too—the school year on the AUB campus and a month or two every summer at home in Pacific Palisades. Although Lebanon was unstable, there were plenty of reasons to feel positive about going to AUB. Neither the campus nor anyone on it had ever been directly attacked in a way related to the civil war. In fact, AUB seemed to have a special halo of esteem and respect that made it sacred to all the disparate groups in Lebanon. Each of those groups, by virtue of having children studying there, had a vested interest in sustaining the university, still considered the best avenue to a successful future. The civil war could not go on forever, and when it ended, AUB would be in the forefront of reconstruction. It was an exciting prospect to think that we might be part of that.

The trustees went through a lengthy search process exploring the qualifications of the final candidates, sending each of them to Beirut to meet with faculty and administrators on the campus. With David Dodge as a highly competent acting president, there was little impetus to rush the proceedings. Malcolm went to Beirut for a week in late January 1982 and returned elated at having been with so many old friends there. During his absence I had written to Susie and John that my thoughts kept changing about whether we should move to Beirut, but that "while I was down on the hillside planting trees the other day I decided that with so much crime and violence constantly present in our own neighborhood, the only reason not to take the AUB job would be if the financial problems of the university were insoluble." It is easy to fit facts to get the answers we want.

When Malcolm returned, he had little to say about any new insights into the political situation. In any case, if we had had the discussion, it probably would not have changed our overriding feeling that it was impossible to turn down the AUB presidency.

Malcolm often told friends that living in Beirut would be no more dangerous than living in New York City, a view that still had some truth to it in the spring of 1982.

In the early months of that year, there were periodic reports in the press that Israel was planning to invade Lebanon to secure her northern border against the PLO. Malcolm speculated that such announcements might be leaked by the Israeli government to prepare public mentality for that eventuality, but that they would have to wait for some sort of provocation. The PLO had been unusually quiet since the U.S.-negotiated cease-fire the preceding summer, and there seemed to be no reason for an attack. Friends from Beirut reported the speculation there that Israel was waiting till spring after the winter rains were over. I remember thinking vaguely that if there were going to be such an attack, I hoped it would be before March 20 so we could know the effects on AUB and Lebanon, because March 20 was the day the trustees would meet to choose the new president. Malcolm, not one for long deliberation, was by this time getting impatient with the lengthy search process. He was anxious for a decision to be made in New York so we could move forward.

John was unable to get away from Swarthmore to join Malcolm in New York that fateful weekend. I was midway into the semester teaching English language part time at the University of Southern California, but Susie came to spend the weekend with Malcolm.

She wrote movingly about how she and Malcolm spent the evening after the meeting where his selection had been debated drinking champagne in the bar of the Roosevelt Hotel—and then later up in their room how Malcolm, with the help of the champagne, opened up his fears to her. "Do you think I should take this job if they offer it to me?" Susie replied that she thought he really wanted to, and that he would be great for it, and it for him, and that therefore he should. They talked and joked at length, with the jokes getting sillier and turning into giggles, at first a little and then uncontrollably. "But there was NOTHING funny at all," Susie wrote. "Finally we were about to go to sleep and I heard Dad say, 'I figure there's a 25 percent chance that I'll get knocked off and that it will happen early on'. . . One minute we were laughing and the next minute we were crying."

The debate over the merits of Malcolm as a suitable president, we learned later, was long and spirited. There were fears that the same problems would arise as had some years earlier at AUB when he was being considered as a candidate for the job of dean of arts and sciences. Someone in Beirut made available to the press passages out of context from a pamphlet Malcolm had written. The author of an article in the campus newspaper concluded that "Kerr hates the Arabs and of course works for the CIA."

It was not difficult to come up with quotes from Malcolm's writings which portrayed him as a critic of the Arabs, or a critic of the Israelis or of the United States, depending on one's point of view. Malcolm's inclination toward forthrightness and candid expression of his beliefs coupled with a terse and sardonic style formed a side of his personality which could be misunderstood even in the Arab world, a world that he had grown up in, loved, and understood with the perspective of both insider and outsider. His writings were a product of this perspective and of his extensive education as a political scientist and Arabist. It could be said that his position as insider made him feel free to be openly critical of Arabs, and yet he, more than others, knew that especially in that culture one did not criticize openly. Perhaps his outspoken pronouncements on Arab policies derived from his position as an outsider, and also as an academic, an idealist, and a man born to say what he thought, always succinctly, for he had no patience for verbosity, in himself or others.

The next morning Susie waited for him at the Princeton Club to hear the outcome. When he came down to the lobby to meet her, he said with a big smile on his face according to Susie, "How would you like to hug the new president of AUB?" After much debate about the possible ill effects of Malcolm's outspoken writings on Middle Eastern politics, the trustees had decided that the advantages of his selection outweighed the disadvantages. His long university experience, his successful academic career, and extensive knowledge of the Middle East, and his sureness in making decisions made him the best candidate for the job.

In her diary on March 21, Susie expressed it for all of us:

Dad is really president of AUB now. For such a long time it was a possibility and now that it's really true it hits home with quite a thud. Of course, it's very meaningful for my parents to be able to return to Lebanon. As Dad said, "Granny and Grandpa lived there, Mom and I met there, and my children were born there! That's where everything happened! How can I not go?" Well, it's terrifying as well. During the last month there have been some articles in Syrian-controlled newspapers about Dad, all of them completely fabricated out of thin air, talking of interviews that never took place, etc.—portraying Dad as an enemy! It's the extremists in every corner who think he isn't pro-Arab enough and who fly off the handle. So it's a dangerous place simply by virtue of the Civil War that's getting worse, but on top of that Dad is an especially visible target. John and I talk to each other about how scary it is, but whenever I've approached Mom and Dad about it they say, "Yes it's very dangerous, but we could never turn it down."

Malcolm's new job was to begin on July 1, giving him time to finish out the spring quarter at UCLA. The impact of our decision sank in when he had to begin resignation procedures from the university where he had taught and been deeply involved for twenty years. More perplexing was how we would organize our family for the coming year. In my grand scheme of things, we were not supposed to go off to Beirut until after Steve finished high school. He was entering his senior year and, judging by the success he was having on the Palisades High basketball team, he might be a candidate for a university athletic scholarship. We would not want to abandon him during this year of important decisions. But Malcolm liked having his family around him, and it would be particularly important during his first year in so demanding a new job. We thought of dividing the boys and letting Andrew go with Malcolm while I stayed with Steve, but that didn't seem like such a good plan for Andrew, whose education needed careful attention.

Susie came to our rescue. She offered to take the fall semester off to stay in California with the boys while Malcolm and I went to Beirut to spend the first half of the year together. Susie's offer meant that Malcolm and I could begin this new job together with two pairs of eyes and ears and two sets of reactions to people and events, something important in any new job, but particularly in the Byzantine world of Beirut.

Meanwhile in Lebanon, plans were being made for a national election in August. It looked like the one person who might be able to hold the country together was Bashir Gemayel, the young heir to the leadership of the Gemayel clan whose roots went far back in the Maronite heartland of Lebanon. Bashir had a reputation for being tough and brutal and well experienced in the feudal tactics of getting things done in Lebanon. For the Israelis, Gemayel's election would insure a strong Christian ally with common interests in vanquishing the PLO and securing influence over the Muslim population. To pragmatists among the Muslims, his election would mean a president with enough power to provide effective leadership over the seventeen or so officially recognized sects of Lebanon, more or less in line with the constitution established in 1936.

In April, when an Israeli officer was killed by a landmine in Lebanon, the Israeli air force bombed suspected PLO positions in retaliation. A few weeks later, following a suspected PLO attack on a bus in Jerusalem, Begin formally renounced the cease-fire agreement negotiated a year earlier by Habib. In early June, a radical anti-Arafat group of the PLO headed by Abu Nidal shot and wounded the Israeli ambassador to London. Though perhaps questionable as internationally recognized incidents in the sense Haig had intended, they provided the provocation the Israelis needed to invade Lebanon.

Malcolm wrote to his long-time AUB friend, David Gordon, on June 9, three days after the Israeli invasion:

> Like you no doubt, we are engrossed in the Lebanese news these days and wondering where it will all end. I have a number of scenarios in mind, none very good. I do not like to imagine a Lebanon in which order is maintained by the tight grip of the Phalange with Israel's encouragement, but this seems to be the most optimistic possible outcome, while deepening chaos is the most pessimistic. AUB risks being physically occupied by armed units or else by refugee squatters, neither of which it can defend itself against . . .
>
> It is still my firm intention to arrive in Beirut before July 1, if it is physically possible to do so, but we will have to wait and see how this can be accomplished, and what kind of job can be done at AUB thereafter. One thing is for sure: there will be no champagne. Please wish me luck.

During the next month we, like so many Americans, watched our television in horror as the evening news brought us vivid images of U.S.-made bombs dropping on Beirut. From those pictures of building after building going up in flames and smoke, it seemed as if nothing would be left of the city that we were planning to make our home. How could the American government be allowing such a thing to happen? Along with our feeling of horror was perhaps a heightened measure of excitement at having our own stake in these events upon which the whole world was focusing attention. I remember that mixed with our disgust for what was happening in Beirut and a certain fear for our own safety, there was a sense of anticipation that we were about to embark upon an adventure of international importance.

The AUB campus and the American Embassy close by were not part of the area being heavily bombed by the Israelis, but the stress of war was felt by them along with the entire city. The Israeli Army had trapped 6,000 Palestinian fighters in West Beirut, and in order to bring pressure on them had blocked traffic into the area. Electricity outages, water and gas shortages, and a cut in supplies of fresh foods from outside the city affected everyone. The AUB Hospital became overcrowded with war victims and was unable to obtain enough medicine and equipment to treat them. In retreat from the Israeli attack or searching for water, PLO militias moved from their former stations around Ras Beirut close to and even onto the campus, setting up armed checkpoints wherever they chose. Refugees, Shiite and Palestinian, moved from their bombed-out homes to the still safe area around the university, sometimes overflowing onto the campus.

Acting President David Dodge, in the tradition of his forebearers, kept the university going through all this. He had the support of his staff and two Lebanese trustees who lived in Beirut. One of these trustees was Salwa Said, a dynamic woman who had run the Red Cross in Beirut and the Baalbek summer festival. She was one of AUB's most active and committed trustees. Another hero who proved his staying power at this time was the head of the university motor pool, Omar Faour. Affectionately known as Haj Omar (the designation for a Muslim who has made the pilgrimage to Mecca,), this loyal AUB employee made the dangerous drive to Damascus several times a week to bring back supplies for the hospital. With the airport closed, he was also called upon to drive university travelers to the port of Jounieh, north of Beirut, where they could take a boat to Cyprus. For Haj Omar, like so many others over its 120 year history, AUB was a cause that inspired complete devotion. Haj Omar's commitment to AUB continued to the end of his life, which ended prematurely, like that of so many in Lebanon. He was killed by a sniper's bullet in 1985 while crossing the Green Line dividing east and west Beirut.

The trustees who had selected Malcolm in March were to gather in New York at the end of June to decide whether or not it was advisable for him to meet his intended goal of arriving in Beirut by July 1. Susie and John were home from college and ready to take over running the household. Susie would stay home in California until Christmas if we needed her. Malcolm and I prepared for all eventualities, not certain of whether or not we would really be going to Beirut. We each packed one suitcase of summer clothes and another of winter clothes. In the bottom of mine, I laid all the extra pictures, watercolors, and family photographs we had around the house to take to Beirut to decorate the barren walls of Marquand House, which had not had a resident president for two years.

"They always look like gypsies when they travel," my mother observed to my father in a remark that didn't do much to conceal their great concern over the extremely adventurous move we were making. Once again we were leaving our idyllic existence in California to go off and live in the Middle East, but this time it was for an indefinite period and conditions were certainly dangerous enough to justify their concerns. Their fears for our safety remained unspoken to us. As always, they accepted our decisions and spoke with pride as they told their friends about Malcolm's appointment to the AUB presidency.

Malcolm did take up his new job on July 1, 1982; but on the advice of the trustees, it was in the New York office of AUB rather than on the campus. In New York, we moved into an apartment loaned to us by a friend and easily resumed the living patterns of our pre-children days twenty-some years earlier, snug in the knowledge that Susie, John, Steve, and Andrew were taking care of one another in the safety of our home with my parents nearby for family unity. We would stay there and await the turn of events in Beirut. For a while longer we could anticipate the adventure ahead of us without actually embarking upon it. David Dodge, in the tradition of his family and perhaps in even more challenging circumstances than any of his ancestors had faced, courageously carried on as acting president in Beirut. While much was to be done in the United States with public relations and fund raising to make the mission of AUB and its special wartime needs known to Americans, Malcolm was concerned that it was his responsibility to be in Beirut on the AUB campus.

We made a trip to Washington where he testified before the House Foreign Relations Committee on conditions at the AUB hospital and spent some time with Najeeb Halaby, the chairman of the AUB board of trustees, and with various alumni who lived there. On July 19, just following an alumni lunch meeting, we learned that David Dodge had been kidnapped as he walked across the campus on his way to Marquand House. Soon after, the Islamic Jihad claimed responsibility. David's kidnapping was a devastating blow.

The Reagan government, still not sure what its stance should be relative to Israel's extensive use of American weapons for non-defensive purposes in Lebanon, sent Ambassador Habib to attempt to negotiate some sort of settlement. The Israelis had succeeded in surrounding the PLO and trapping them in a small area of West Beirut, blocking their supply lines for food and water. The Israelis did not want to enter this area where the PLO were so securely bunkered that an offensive ground attack to root them out would mean too many Israeli casualties and where it appeared the PLO could hold out for a long time. What was needed now was some sort of supervised exit for the Palestinians.

Habib went into frantic shuttle diplomacy working on many aspects of the problem at once. Under what conditions would the PLO agree to leave? What would happen to the families they would leave behind? What host countries could be found to take them? Such questions brought sadly to light part of the underlying cause of the turmoil ensuing in Lebanon, the need for a homeland for the Palestinians.

A peacekeeping force had to be established to oversee the safe exit of the PLO back to their respective countries. It was difficult to get agreement from concerned parties. The Soviet Union would support a United Nations force in Lebanon but would object to a

U.S. force, while Israel would only agree to a force with an American contingent. There was a great deal of public sentiment in America against getting involved in another potential Vietnam situation. Many key members of Congress thought it unwise to commit Marines to the Middle East. Peacekeeping forces were more effective when they did not represent superpowers, and who could foretell how easy it would be for our Marines to get out of Lebanon once they were installed there? But Israel rejected a United Nations force, and President Reagan, under pressure to end the bombardment of Lebanon, reluctantly agreed to an American contingent in a multinational peacekeeping force.

On August 25, 800 Marines were sent to Beirut to join units from France and Italy. Their task was to provide a safe exit for the PLO and thereby end the bloodbath in Lebanon. The Marines were to stay no longer than thirty days and were to be deployed only in areas where there was little danger.

There was still no firm decision on when Malcolm would go to Lebanon. Perhaps these changing events would make the situation clearer.

As the summer wore on in New York, Malcolm and I gradually came to the conclusion that we couldn't both go to Lebanon and leave our children. Susie should continue graduate school, and I would spend the school year in Pacific Palisades with Steve and Andrew. I went back to California early enough to be with Susie and John for a few weeks before they had to return to college, and Malcolm soon joined us for a week's vacation to coincide with our twenty-sixth wedding anniversary. The joy and fun of all being home together again and the likelihood of Malcolm's departure gave us pause to doubt the course we had set. But there was still a tremendous sense of exhilaration about our pending adventure and to have dropped out then would have been dishonorable.

In Beirut, bunkered in the residence of the American ambassador, Habib and his negotiating team were at work around the clock trying to make arrangements for the arrival of the multinational force and the safe departure of the PLO. With the likelihood of a break in the log jam, Ambassador Robert Dillon phoned Malcolm while we were having breakfast one morning in Pacific Palisades to say that AUB was badly in need of leadership and could he come at his earliest convenience? Local administrators and trustees were struggling in the midst of Israeli bombing to keep the university supplied with food, fuel, and medicine for the hospital, and they needed his help. In the absence of David Dodge, Trustee Salwa Said and Vice President Samir Thabet led the university and kept in telex communication with the AUB office in New York. The ambassador would phone back the next day for Malcolm's reply.

That phone call dropped like a bomb into the tranquillity of our home, which had seemed for the past few days so far from the turmoil of Beirut. Almost as soon as Malcolm hung up the phone, he began to contemplate the possibility of leaving the next day.

The year-long separation suddenly loomed in front of us for what it was, and the dangers of living in Beirut began to cancel out the virtues of returning to AUB. In that brief phone call, the ambassador had disrupted the exclusiveness of our family life. I remember resenting Malcolm's readiness to leave us so quickly, knowing full well that we had both committed ourselves to this endeavor and that his eagerness and impatience to get on with things were very much in character. Malcolm was not one to get cold feet, but I was getting cold feet for him, and I wished illogically that we could be out of all this. The job I had so looked forward to as something we were going to do together was now pulling us apart, and I was the one who was going to have to stay at home. It would have been much easier not to worry about Malcolm if we were together in Beirut working for something we both believed in. The old division of labor that I thought I had broken away from was still there. I would run our household and Malcolm would run AUB. "You can't go tomorrow," I protested. "That's our wedding anniversary." "That's right," Malcolm said, with a quick change of expression as he remembered that we had never been apart on August 18, and now was no time to start. After a pause he said, "I'll go on the 20th."

CHAPTER 15

Up to the Mountaintops

The frantic shuttle diplomacy of Philip Habib to provide an exodus for the Palestinians from Beirut had finally jelled. As the PLO survivors were being evacuated from Beirut Harbor, firing their weapons in the air in claims of victory, Malcolm made his way circuitously from Los Angeles to Lebanon, first to New York, where Susie escorted him on her way to Cambridge to bid him farewell and see him off to Jordan. In Amman, King Hussein invited him to the palace for dinner in a gesture of recognition for AUB. After that, his travels were in a different style. From Amman, one could drive north via Damascus or take a forty-five minute flight. But with the Beirut Airport still closed and the Damascus-Beirut road in the line of Syrian-Israeli fighting, the only way to Lebanon from Amman was to fly to Cyprus and take the final leg by boat. Knowing that this was the route travelers to Beirut were currently taking and that the quality of ships was unpredictable, we had gone to our local camping store and bought an air mattress for Malcolm the day before he left Los Angeles.

After the flight to Cyprus from Amman, Malcolm found himself a place on the private yacht of an English couple who had decided to earn some extra income by running voyages between Nicosia and Jounieh. In his first letter home he described the voyage:

> We were seventeen passengers and we had a luxurious cruise with a gourmet dinner and video movies (saw a James Bond movie and, the next morning while waiting for the Israeli army

200

to clear us, *The Sound of Music.*) However, there were only a few
bunks and I wound up on the upper deck on my Taiwanese air
mattress, which inflated quite easily but refused to deflate fully
the next morning. It was definitely not a comfortable night's
sleep. Anyhow, the Israeli navy, consisting of two or three
mini-destroyers, held us up for four hours just for the hell of it.
. . . On finally arriving in Jounieh and getting off the boat, I
was surprised to find that there was nobody there to meet me,
so I took a taxi to the U.S. Ambassador's residence [in a suburb
in the hills of East Beirut called Yarzi] for a $40 fee and threw
myself on the mercy of the embassy personnel there. Before long
I had a swim in the Ambassador's private pool and my friends
the Salems came over from their house in Baaba to pick me up,
and I got over my complex about being stranded on the dock.

For the first time in many months, Beirut citizens could drive
back and forth between the east and west sides of the city. But in
those days just after the summer of 1982 Israeli invasion, people
were still gun shy and hesitant to cross the Green Line. Malcolm,
untempered by months of living in fear of sudden shelling or explosion and impatient to get on with his job, seized the earliest
opportunity to go to West Beirut to visit the AUB campus.

For the first three days I stayed away from Ras Beirut since
it was considered somewhat risky to go there, what with the
PLO evacuation going on and the armed groups there feeling
jumpy about Bashir Gemayel being elected president. . . . Yesterday I hitched a ride in a U.S. embassy car, escorted by Lebanese riot police and stayed overnight in Marquand House. This
entailed crossing from east to west Beirut at the Museum
and driving through interminable alleys and small streets through
terrible devastation from the Israeli bombing and shelling; and
today when we returned by a different route I saw even worse
specimens of devastation. . . . The driver took us past the beach
area and the Palestinian camps near the airport, and I almost
vomited. For several miles you see nothing but wrecked buildings. Some are just showing a couple of large gashes where a
shell hit them, wrecking one or two rooms; others look OK
from a distance till you approach and see that the entire interior
has been burned out (phosphorus shells). Others (not so many)
have been hit from the air by blockbusters and the whole apart-

ment house just collapsed all the way down, and you know that dozens of bodies are still in there under the rubble . . .

Here and there were occasional squads of French and Italian soldiers, part of the international peacekeeping force—the U.S. marines are at the harbor, which I haven't seen yet. I would say that the eastern and southern sectors of Beirut which were not shelled by the Israelis, look quite clean and very prosperous, whereas the west Beirut neighborhoods look much worse than anything in the slums of major cities in the U.S., with their caved-in buildings, the rubble, the garbage, and the congestion. The AUB neighborhood has not really been hit, but it is very shabby. Today the final group of the PLO left Beirut, and we heard gunfire continuously from the AUB campus as friends of the PLO emptied their ammunition into the air in salute. Apparently a lot of people have been killed so far by stray bullets from the shots fired in celebration . . .

I came back to the Salems' house in the afternoon but will return to AUB tomorrow to settle in. Life there is very quiet and there is no reason to fear for one's safety. The armed groups that had infested the campus throughout the summer have all left. I do have a local boy walking around with me as a bodyguard, and I only venture out on the streets with a carload of police, but I don't think these precautions will be needed for more than a few weeks. This morning, my first day at the office, I presided over a meeting of the Board of Deans at which we discussed the David Dodge situation—there isn't much we can do—and the question of what date we would announce for the opening of classes in the fall. We decided to postpone classes for a week after the initially scheduled date to give people a chance to get back to some sort of normal existence and for the faculty to return from abroad. So we will begin October 21.

Within a week, Malcolm settled into Marquand House where his life was in sharp contrast to the destruction and death outside.

I've been installed here on campus for ten days now and am getting used to the idea of being the Lord of the Manor, though I do miss having the Lady and all the little Lordlets around as well. I've been playing tennis every two or three days, and have been jogging a couple of times, and am just waiting till the day after tomorrow when the AUB swimming beach is supposed to open up. . . . I have also had numerous friends over to hang around the Marquand House garden with me for lunch, dinner, etc. In the meantime, life here is very tranquil. I am rattling around all by myself among the five bedrooms on the second floor, one of which I'm using for my study, while on the ground floor there is nobody except Muhammad the cook, two of his sons, Hassan the housekeeper and his wife, daughter and new baby, four policemen, a gardener, the gardener's daughter, two gatemen, my bodyguard, and all the friends and relations of all the above . . .

One very curious thing I have learned in my few days here so far is that a great many people in Lebanon were so fed up with the PLO and its antics that they have actually regarded the Israeli army as saviors, even though the Israeli army destroyed half of Beirut in the process. Not that the Israelis are popular per se, but the PLO and their friends are the object of unbelievable hostility, and not only from right wing Christians but also from Muslims. I am getting a new perspective on a number of things in this regard. Most particularly it puts the election of Bashir Gemayel in a different light. He has a background as a thug and a bully, but many people see him as Lebanon's only chance to return to some kind of sanity. Right now it does look as if the situation in Beirut will return to quasi-normalcy, although no one is sure that the same will be the case in the Bekaa or in Tripoli, where large numbers of PLO and Syrians are still entrenched.

With the PLO evacuated from Lebanon, the partial withdrawal of the Israelis to the south, and the Syrians suggesting a willingness to give up the caretaker role in Lebanon they had assumed in 1976, a window of opportunity opened up that brought hope for a breakthrough in the long, troubled history of U.S.–Middle East relations. On September 1, President Reagan gave an address, which became known as the Reagan Plan. In it, he implied an American recognition that the Palestinian question was the central problem of the Arab-Israeli conflict and called for negotiations between the concerned parties. This brought cautious optimism to the Arabs whereas the reaction of the Begin government was to announce a new extended settlements program in the West Bank. The United States did nothing to counteract Begin's action. For all the good intentions of the Reagan speech, there were no tangible efforts to back it up. In Arab eyes the United States was unwilling or unable to curtail Israeli aggression and continued to allow our policy with that country to be a case of the tail wagging the dog.

But the hope engendered by Reagan's rhetoric and a break in the logjam kept optimism alive in Lebanon for the next several months despite turbulent events. It seemed that the good luck our family was accustomed to enjoying continued. Malcolm had arrived at a propitious time when AUB would have an instrumental role to play in the rebuilding of Lebanon. The involvement in his new job brought out greater enthusiasm and commitment to his work than I had ever seen in him, though he treated each challenge with the usual wry humor and occasional irreverence that were his trademark. He recorded each new episode in a continuing flow of family letters with a boyish spirit of adventure reminiscent of letters from his father in Turkey written over forty years earlier when he was working with the Near East Relief.

> Despite all the destruction and everyone's disgust at what the Israelis have done—and what we read every day that Begin or Sharon has just said—it's amazing how upbeat the mood is here now, at least among almost all the people I've met. The departure of the PLO is a great blessing and with them the departure of the armed gangs. The Lebanese Army and police force have at last gotten off their behinds and are progressively taking over more and more of the city. . . . Wherever they go, they plant a Lebanese flag, so when you drive around and see so many flags, there's the appearance of celebration . . .
>
> I went to pay a call on President Sarkis [president of Lebanon] the other day! On Monday I'm going to visit Prime Minister Wazzan. After that I expect to visit Saeb Salam and, finally, President-Elect Bashir Gemayel ("Super Beast," as the foreign journalists call him). He takes office on the 23rd and the country is holding its breath to see how conciliatory to his opponents he's going to be, as well as whether the Israelis decide to give him a chance by getting the hell out of the country. A Syrian plane was shot down near here a few days ago.

On September 11, only seventeen days after they had been deployed, the U.S. Marines were withdrawn from Lebanon, their mission to oversee the safe departure of the PLO accomplished. The withdrawal satisfied those in the United States who had feared a long Vietnam-type engagement in Lebanon with great loss of American lives. It was also a move encouraged by Israel's General Sharon who wanted free rein to clear out any dangerous PLO people Arafat might have left behind. The withdrawal of 800 marines left the U.S. in no position to keep its promise to guarantee the safety of the PLO families remaining in Lebanon. This guarantee had been the key element in obtaining agreement from the PLO to evacuate. Ambassador Habib had demanded assurances for their safety from Prime Minister Begin and President-Elect Bashir Gemayel and then promised U.S. guarantees for the assurances he had received.

During the next few days a number of disastrous events took place. On September 14, Bashir Gemayel was assassinated and within hours, Israeli forces seized the opportunity to move into West Beirut and take control of the city, clearly in violation of the cease-fire agreement, and contrary to assurances given to the United States only days earlier.

Malcolm wrote from Marquand House on September 17:

We've had a couple of exciting days. First I was awakened late at night with a phone call from Radwan Mawlawi, our public relations officer, telling me of Bashir Gemayel's assassination. The bomb had gone off at four that afternoon and it was widely known, but it had been claimed that he had escaped. I had been indoors at a meeting and had heard nothing. The next morning there were fusillades of gunfire all over west Beirut (some of which sounded so close I thought it was coming from Nicely Hall, next door—but it wasn't), as the unreconciled die-hards in this part of town celebrated the news of the murder. Meanwhile the Israeli Air Force buzzed the city for over an hour, announcing that they were in charge. Of course people here hardly need to be told that, after the events of the summer; in fact they are so completely convinced of it that they assume the Israelis organized Bashir's assassination, a theory that even I tend more or less to believe. Then through the day, we began hearing bits of news about the Israeli army moving into the outskirts of west Beirut . . .

At 9 a.m., I looked out the window from David Dodge's

office on the third floor of College Hall and there on Rue Bliss, just outside Uncle Sam's and Faisal's, were a dozen Israeli infantry men armed to the teeth. They carefully peeked around the corner up Jeanne d'Arc to look for snipers and then scampered, one by one, like scared rabbits across the intersection. More soldiers kept coming and doing likewise. Meanwhile an occasional Lebanese civilian would show up and wander casually down the street, oblivious to the war around him, while others watched curiously from balconies. Finally a parade of three or four gigantic tanks rumbled up Rue Bliss. They all proceeded down toward Rue Sadat and up toward the Mayflower Hotel. We heard a great deal of firing, including deafening artillary explosions, all over Ras Beirut, as the Israelis covered themselves before moving in on their targets. Quite a few buildings in Ras Beirut were heavily damaged and the AUB Hospital has treated perhaps 100 casualities . . .

It really is very sad, for until the assassination it was obvious that the country was moving rapidly toward reconciliation and the army and police were progressively taking over the city without a fight. Even after the assassination, if the Israelis had kept their hands off, the Lebanese could have taken care of themselves. Evidently this is not what Begin wants.

In moving into West Beirut, the Israelis became responsible for the safety of the PLO families living in the Sabra and Shateela refugee camps located in that part of the city. The United States, mindful of its promise to Arafat to protect the PLO families and angered by Israel's clear violation of the cease-fire agreement in spite of the assurances received only two days earlier, demanded that they withdraw. It took them ten days to do so. In the interim, General Sharon, as the Israeli Kahane Commission later substantiated, opened the way for the Phalanges to enter the camps and massacre more than a thousand Palestinians.

Public revulsion at the massacre grew in Israel and the United States and around the world. Arab nations put American credibility on the line, saying in the United Nations that "Israel has chosen to lay bare the ability or the credibility of the United States as guarantor of the Beirut agreement."

Malcolm wrote, "I don't know what reports you are getting about the massacre, but here there is no one who doesn't hold

Israel responsible, since they let the Haddad people [South Lebanon Army] into the area in the first place and sat by and watched through binoculars as the massacre took place. In the words of a U.S. Embassy man who had been down to survey the scene there, they supervised the whole thing. They are now trying to pin it on the Phalange, their erstwhile friends."

Along with evil deeds of war, Malcolm regaled us with human stories.

> The country has run out of mazout [cooking and heating fuel] and there is no electricity—except here at AUB where we have our own generator. We too were about to run out of fuel for the generator and had we done so, the hospital would have closed down, pulling the plug on 30 patients on respirators, etc. So guess who we got 30 tons of fuel from this morning? You guessed it. Yesterday Muhammad, my bodyguard, drove Joe Simaan [assistant dean of the medical school] and me around town in his ancient Fiat looking for Israeli military headquarters, which turned out to be in the Riviera Hotel just down on the Corniche. The lobby was full of scruffy looking soldiers lounging around, plus one plump woman of uncertain age and even more uncertain virtue lounging with them. "Does anyone speak English?" I asked. "Yes," said a soldier and "Yes," said Madame. "We have an emergency. We need fuel oil for our hospital," I said. Madame turned to her companion and said, "They have an emergency. They need fuel oil for their hospital." Presently a bearded officer with thick glasses and a cap, looking exactly like Woody Allen in *Bananas,* appeared and introduced himself as Major Spiegal . . .
>
> In any event, this morning they delivered the fuel in two tanker trucks without a hitch and declined to accept payment, nor did they make any effort at publicity. Abu Yaakov [Malcolm's nickname for Major Speigal] said he would return in three days to see what else we needed. (We will probably need more fuel.) It's just as well they didn't charge us because now I don't need to deduct $1500 for the damage to our gate made by the tank the other day; in fact, to make up the $1500, I figure they still owe us a couple of tons of fuel. I asked Abu Yaakov when they would open the crossings to East Beirut. "It'll be another two or three days," he said, "until we finish cleaning the city of terrorists." This seemed a particularly graceless re-

mark since the Shateela-Sabra massacre had just occurred yesterday, in celebration of Jewish New Year, but I smothered my
temptation to say anything, especially since Col. Abu Yaakov
looks pretty mean.

Malcolm gained local popularity by forbidding Israeli military
from visiting the campus in a shouting match where he remained
adamant that no foreign forces would enter the campus. On another occasion too, he refused entry to Israeli military sightseers.

I just went to the Medical Gate to refuse admission to two
Israeli generals and seven or eight soldiers. The top general, Ben
Gal, was apparently Deputy Chief of Staff and a Harvard graduate, and just wanted to tour around. I told him I too had gone
to Harvard and would have liked to escort him on another occasion but that we had strict rules, the situation was sensitive,
and his government had assured mine that they wouldn't touch
us, etc. He was very nice and apologized for bothering us. . . .
    I am enclosing some press interviews that appeared here and
that I liked—especially the one that referred to meeting me in
my 'immense office.' (It really is!) I hear I also made the front
page of the *Herald Tribune* for chasing Israeli soldiers away from
the IC gate [the west gate of the campus facing International
College, the preparatory school adjacent to AUB]. But that's
nothing, compared to getting to pitch in Dodger Stadium [like
Steve], or to be the leader of a whole Boy Scout troop at Catalina [like Andrew].

In the next few days, events reordered themselves in such a
way that there still seemed to be hope for the window of opportunity that had opened up with the exit of the PLO and the recently offered Reagan Plan. Malcolm wrote:

Things are really looking up once more with the election of
Gemayel II [Bashir's brother Amin] and the announcement of
the return of the Marines. Everyone is delighted that the western peacekeeping forces are returning, though people take note
of the difference between the French and the Italians and the
American marines: the former declare that they will fire if fired
upon, while the position of the latter is that if there is any

shooting they will promptly pull out. There's nobody so tough as the marines.

An American presence, however pacifist, still brought a certain confidence to most people in Lebanon that things were going to get better. While on their first tour of duty, the marines were to stay only through the departure of the PLO, their new mission was to stay until all foreign forces were withdrawn. It was anticipated, without any great evidence for thinking so, that the Syrians and Israelis would leave within a matter of months. Hopes were high in Lebanon and at AUB as the semester began in the fall of 1982 that the civil war was at last coming to an end and a period of reconstruction was beginning. Accordingly, Malcolm's work became more and more demanding.

> The office work has become extremely busy now that everyone is back and the school year is getting under way. I love it! There is lots of wheeling and dealing to be done with our $58 million budget, which would be $80 million if we were doing all the things we should be doing. I have also been very busy meeting groups of faculty members to learn what is going on in agriculture, engineering, etc. and how to recruit a few new deans. I am laying plans for a high powered seminar on Thanksgiving Day with fifteen or so AUB alumni and other friends of the university telling us how to shape up and cash in on Lebanon's needs. So far I have recruited Rafik Hariri, his banker, and the head of an insurance company who wants to sell hundreds of millions of dollars worth of bonds for AUB. This Saturday I'm going to Hariri's medical complex and school near Sidon to have a look.

On October 21, the academic year opened and Malcolm gave a convocation address telling of the pride he felt in being the first graduate of AUB to become president: "I therefore feel a natural identity not only with the faculty but also with the students, as a member with you of the same AUB family, and this is the spirit in which I hope to lead the university." He wanted every student to understand the special qualities of AUB and spoke of its liberal arts tradition, its international quality, and its concern for the individual.

Later I teased Malcolm for saying an uncharacteristic "God be with you" at the end of this address and for invoking the name of God occasionally in conversation now that he was the president of AUB. He shrugged and dismissed my suggestion that it was out of character. "The culture calls for it," he said unconvincingly. It seemed apparent to me that his complete embracing of his new job, and the sense of historical responsibility it inspired in him, made this invoking of greater powers more than just a cultural concession. The following year when Andrew and I joined him in Beirut, Malcolm was quite agreeable to attending an Anglican service held in the German Chapel, a five-minute walk from the campus. He even got out his old college textbook on world religions. That was the book that was sitting on his bedside table at the time of his death.

As happy as Malcolm was to be in his new job on the campus where he had grown up, he missed his family very much and told us so in every letter: "I have been missing you more and more as time goes by and it sinks in on me that this life of solitude is going to be the norm for the next nine months. Bachelorhood is for the birds." He wrote to his mother that eating meals alone made him appreciate even more the difficult adjustment she must have had after his father's death. When he learned that the fall board meeting of AUB trustees was to be postponed to December, enabling him to come home for Christmas, his spirits rose remarkably. "One thing's for sure: I am definitely ready to go home. After all, I have to see Hogie—especially now that you have lowered the basketball backboard in the driveway, giving Hogie his chance in a lifetime to make a shot."

Meanwhile we planned for our November reunion when I would travel to Beirut to attend Malcolm's inauguration ceremony during my between-quarter break from my teaching job at USC. We thought hard about having his mother attend too for she wanted very much to come. She and I had been having regular Saturday morning telephone conversations where we compared notes on the letters and phone calls we had received from Malcolm that week and also exchanged the latest news from the Middle East. After long consideration, she wrote Malcolm, "I hope nothing prevents your inauguration Dec. 3rd. How I wish I were 75 and could be there! Instead I can't forget that I'm almost 87, and have to depend on my imagination and pride and love for you. I wish Dad were here in person. Nothing could please him more than to see you made president of AUB which he loved so much and to which he gave his best. . . . I think and pray for you and your safe return every day."

The inauguration would be a large and ceremonial occasion with government officials, AUB trustees, and academics from other universities attending. It was also to be a reunion for Malcolm and me after a three-month separation, voluminous correspondence, and a thousand dollars worth of phone calls. As a surprise for Malcolm, Susie and John were going to attend the inauguration ceremonies, but I would get there a few days ahead so we would have some time by ourselves.

I was met at the Beirut airport by Malcolm, his bodyguard, the director of the airport, Omar the chief of AUB drivers, and Tanios, the special driver of the president—hardly the circumstances one would order for a long awaited reunion. The presence of this barrage of welcomers made it possible to hold back the tears I felt overwhelming me at the relief and delight of being with Malcolm again and of being able to hold on to him. At the front door of Marquand House, out flocked Muhammad the cook, his wife and son who had moved into the servants quarters after their house had been bombed, Hassan the housekeeper and his wife Zeinab the upstairs maid, and their two small children who lived in a house in the back of the garden. After this grand welcome, we were at last free to go upstairs to our bedroom and be alone. An early winter rain was falling and occasional thunderclaps along with the noise of the surf pounding on the rocks along the corniche seemed to insulate us throughout the night from all that was going on in the world, even the sound of distant shelling in mountains far away.

The next day when we finally went downstairs, Tanios the driver, was waiting in his best three-piece suit and freshly polished black shoes to take us on a drive and picnic to the mountains above Jounieh Bay, up the coast road north of Beirut. The bodyguard would not accompany us on this excursion as Malcolm had grown very tired of his company and Tanios could do double duty. From the outset, Tanios, in his painfully shy but fastidiously polite manner, was beside us to meet our every need, except what we wanted most—to be by ourselves. When we reached our destination, he scampered over the rocks in his impractical but very shiny shoes, carrying a heavy picnic basket, thermos jug, and tablecloth which he soon spread out before us for a picnic à trois.

Our official duties began first with an alumni banquet where Malcolm was the guest of honor and gave a winning speech in Arabic. I got to sit next to the prime minister and struggled to converse in my flawed French and Arabic all evening about the difficulties of governing Lebanon under current conditions. Spending the evening with this warm and friendly gentleman helped to make up for my chagrin in realizing that nobody at the banquet seemed particularly aware of the fact that I was giving just as much to AUB as Malcolm by staying home in California, taking care of our children, and letting them have my husband. I would have some catching up to do when I arrived for good to establish the first-lady role I had imagined for myself back in Pacific Palisades.

The arrival of Susie and John a few days before the inauguration worked out as the surprise for Malcolm that we had hoped. On the evening they were due, we came home after a party in the faculty apartments and sat down in front of the fireplace awhile before going to bed. According to plan, and with the cooperation of the drivers Omar and Tanios, Muhammad the cook, and Hassan the housekeeper, the white presidential Buick rolled into the circular driveway of Marquand House to the back of the garden near the kitchen door. Keeping an eye out the window, I saw the lights of the car approaching and began to panic that all this might be too much of a surprise and cause Malcolm to have apoplexy. I tried to prepare him by saying how much I wished our children could be here to witness this momentous occasion in our lives. I was sure that my tone of voice must be a dead giveaway, but Malcolm apparently picked up none of it, for when Susie and John nonchalantly walked into the living room as if nothing out of the ordinary were happening, his expression turned incredulous. He jumped up and hugged them in joy and disbelief—by enveloping them, reassuring himself that they were really there.

Within the next day or two, dignitaries began arriving for the ceremony, among them representatives of Harvard and UCLA, A. J. Meyer and Wilfried Mommaerts, who were old friends, and

12. Malcolm with Susie and John
in Marquand House before investitute, 1982.

former professors at AUB. The president of AUC, Richard Ped
ersen, and his wife, Nelda, our good friends from Cairo, came and
stayed with us in Marquand House where we talked about the
possibilities for cooperative endeavors between the two American
universities in the Middle East.

The day before the inauguration we arranged for an AUB van
to pick us and our guests up to go on a picnic to Beaufort Castle
in south Lebanon. This area had been impossible to visit during
the fighting of the past seven years; in fact, the old crusader castle
perched high on a mountaintop commanding the Litani River Valley below had traded hands between the various factions fighting.
After the Israeli invasion there was a tentative truce and the area
was guarded by Israeli and local Arab soldiers. The drive south
took us along the route of the Israeli invasion from this border
north to Beirut the previous summer: their stated purpose—to
clear the country of the PLO. Evidence of the invasion was every-

13. The Kerr family, before inauguration,
on the steps of Marquand House.
Left to right: Susie, Malcolm, Ann, and John.

where in the form of burned and bombed buildings. It was eerie to
be in the region which had so recently been the scene of terrible
fighting.

The day of the inauguration Malcolm donned his new canary
yellow academic robe with black velvet hood, and he impatiently
demanded that we all be downstairs early to be ready to walk over
to College Hall where the academic procession would congregate.
He grudgingly paused so we could take a family picture on the
front steps of Marquand House and then rushed ahead of us in
characteristic fashion to promptly get to where he was supposed to
be.

As Susie and John and I entered the chapel, we were told that we must sit separately, they with the trustees in a side section and I in the first seat of the front row. It seemed unfair that, on this momentous occasion, anyone could tell me that I couldn't sit with my children. I was ushered to a seat set apart from anyone else's and waited for the ceremony to begin while TV camera men clattered about arranging their equipment and blocked my view of the podium. I wondered with chagrin where the satisfaction was for me in this new public life we were entering.

The huge old pipe organ, which brought back memories of morning chapel in our student days, began to play strains of Brahms, and the academic procession began. Malcolm looked slightly self-conscious but very proud as he held the President's Chalice and walked with other administrators of the university at the end of the procession. He had written his inauguration address with sureness and zest a few weeks earlier and now was ready to present it in the same spirit. "It is impossible for me to describe to you the pride I take in accepting the appointment of President of this great university. No honor could be greater. No responsibility could be heavier. No challenge could be more exciting. No comradeship could be more heartwarming."

After welcoming the many guests assembled, Malcolm spoke of his regret that his mother could not be present and then of the other missing person who should have been among the other deans and vice president sitting behind the podium in the front of the chapel. "There is one other face that is absent from this room, a friend of all of us, a pillar of this university and a personification of its history, a devoted servant of the people of Lebanon and the Arab world, outrageously singled out to be a hostage for decency in a world of violence and hate. Until David Dodge is returned to his family and to us, I can still take pride in becoming President but I cannot feel any joy."

He recalled some of the university leaders he knew by reputation from his childhood and some of the stories he remembered— of Dean Nickoley who enforced the traditional rule against smoking on campus,

> but who, as a man of the new and changing times, was broadminded enough to pass out keys to the gate behind Bliss Hall to the few smoking members of the faculty who found quickly

14. Malcolm at investiture ceremony, November 1982.

enough that if they took a walk and lit their cigarettes just outside the main gate, they had just enough time before finishing their smoke to reach the Bliss Hall gate, which of course acquired the nickname of Smokers' Gate . . .

Smokers' Gate has now been locked for many years, and the smoking is done inside the campus, while new and far worse things have been invented to be done outside, though not we hope by faculty members. AUB has slipped imperceptibly from the austere era of the Protestants to the more tolerant and accommodating era of the Greek Orthodox, much to the relief of all of us who harbor a taste for new and dangerous ideas, good food and drink, fast cars and fast women.

He then made a quick shift to redeem the seriousness of the occasion and talked about "the generation of distinguished research scholars that the new era had brought, Charles Malik, Constantine Zurayk, Nabih Faris, Jibrail Jabbur, Zeine Zeine and Albert Hourani, scholars of Arab origin whose work confirmed the maturation of AUB as a truly international institution." Malcolm went on to describe the influence on AUB of Stephen Penrose, the president from our student days in the fifties who had with great vision moved the university out of its traditional role as a small liberal arts college into a major university with faculties and graduate schools in professional fields and, for better or worse, financial support from the U.S. government. And he described the problems that had beset AUB for the previous decade.

Today we are looking for an end to a decade of declining fortunes, of uncertainty about our cultural mission and despondency about our ability to finance a university worth keeping. Of course the years of anarchy and violence in Lebanon did nothing to help, but let us not forget that AUB's difficulties had already started making themselves felt before 1975 . . . I believe that there are two essential principles we must follow: First, we must build and not tear down. We must grow and not shrink. We must identify the things that we can do better than others, and that this society needs the most from us, and get busy to make the most of these opportunities . . . AUB has had a glorious past, and there is no reason why it cannot have a glorious future, if only we be sufficiently determined to make it so. . . . Let us pledge ourselves today to make that effort, so that a century from now our descendents will remember that the men and women of AUB in the 1970's and '80's not only showed the courage to survive eight years of destruction and turmoil in the country, but the imagination and initiative to bring their university out of the bomb shelter, into the sunlight, and up to the mountaintops of excellence once again.

CHAPTER 16

Hopes and Fears

With Malcolm officially inaugurated as president of AUB and Lebanon in a mood of hope and optimism for the future, we flew to the United States for the Christmas holidays with a stop in New York for the trustees' meeting and a grand promotional luncheon in Washington. Najeeb Halaby, the chairman of the Board of Trustees, invited hundreds of well-placed friends to encourage them to participate in reconstruction projects in Lebanon contracted through the engineering or architecture or medical schools of AUB. The mood was electric with the special enthusiasm of people who were eager to embark on new ventures and ready to sign a deal. Secretary of State George Shultz and Ambassador Philip Habib were the guests of honor. Habib, fresh from his success at negotiating the evacuation of the PLO from Beirut, gave a rousing pep talk on the large potential for moral and financial investment in Lebanon, while alumni passed out badges and balloons with the university's cedar tree logo that said "Support AUB." Reconstruction fever was at a high pitch in the crowded room as Habib brought his speech to a climax, exhorting everyone present to play a part in putting Lebanon back together again.

I went ahead to California to put our own house in order for Christmas, uncertain of what conditions I would find after having left home and car to Steve and Andrew for two-and-a-half weeks. I was so relieved to see both boys well and in one piece that I was not interested in asking questions, not even about the potted ferns in the living room that smelled like beer.

219

. . .

During her visit to Beirut, Susie had asked us if she could bring her friend Hans van de Ven home for Christmas. Hans was a fellow Harvard student recently arrived from Holland and studying for his Ph.D. in Chinese studies. Malcolm and I had hesitated, thinking that, with his mother coming, we would already be a big household and that we would like to have a family Christmas without guests; however, as we realized that Hans might be a candidate to be our son-in-law, we could not say no. So, in succession came Malcolm and his mother, whom he had met in New Jersey, then John, and then Susie and Hans. Elsa Kerr, at almost eighty-seven, had lost some of her mobility but none of her energy and mental quickness. Still a tall and imposing woman, she sat on a high stool in the kitchen to help with the cooking.

We all found Hans engaging, and my parents too gave their voice of approval. Fortunately, along with being interested in Susie and China, Hans also liked basketball, tennis, and the beach. By the end of the holidays, it became evident that he had an irreverent sense of humor and a relaxed manner that made him a hit with everyone in the family. It looked like we might be fitting a wedding into our family schedule during the next year.

Malcolm left for Beirut on New Year's Day, accompanying his mother on her eighty-seventh birthday back to her retirement home at Meadow Lakes near Princeton. Susie wrote him in her usual breezy style to tell him what he was missing out on at home.

> If you think we miss you around here, Pa, well, I've got news for you: You're right! It's not nearly as silly around here. Misbehavin' ain't so much fun without a misbehavin' Daddy to egg you on. . . . We've been having such a blast: making chocolate chip cookies, bugging Microphone Man [Andrew] about his loudspeaker voice, playing basketball, watching TV, enjoying John's musical sneezes, lying on the floor with Hogie (the family dog—You know him?), forcing Mom to get the giggles, laughing at Steve's hysterical jokes and making up names for Hans (Hans McGillicutty), etc. etc.!

John wrote him a few days later. "First things first: did you get to see any of the Rose Bowl when you got to Granny's house? I don't need to tell you that the good guys won. . . . I hope you found the stack of my resumes to give to people in Beirut. I put them there at 4:30 AM New Year's morning after Susie, Hans, Andrew and I stayed up drinking champagne and playing a pretty mild game of Truth-or-Dare. We found out about Andrew's girl-friends in Cairo at age 12. We had loads of fun. Hans and Susie are a pretty good match."

The family togetherness of the last month and our willing optimism for the future of Lebanon and AUB were tonics for us all. Having shared some of Malcolm's new life with him in Beirut and knowing that our long separation was almost half over, I was ready to throw myself back into the basketball and Boy Scout worlds of Steve and Andrew, but I worried that Malcolm would feel bereft in Beirut with no family around.

> I'm thinking of you so much, hoping the interest and exhilara-tion of your job offsets the loneliness of being in Marquand House by yourself. Tonight you should be having your big din-ner party. I can just see the buzzing in the kitchen with Muhammad and Hassan cooking up a storm. . . . It is so com-pletely different now than before I went to Beirut, so much easier to be separated after having had a taste of what our new life will be like and seeing you so happy at AUB in your new job. I feel quite rejuvenated by our five weeks together—no longer the prune I was becoming in the fall.

Mindful of Malcolm's statement the year he was being consid-ered for the AUB presidency that the only thing he'd rather do than watch Steve play basketball was to be AUB president, and knowing that on a given day that statement might be reversed, I tried to keep him well informed.

> You wouldn't have believed Steve's game last night. Palisades High won in the last four seconds of overtime against Hamilton in a series of remarkable plays that I couldn't begin to recount. Steve was the pivot of it all, of course, in an unending number of tight situations. He was 8 for 8 in free throws, the last two of which won the game, but not until Hamilton got the ball away again twice and Pali recovered it twice, all in the last few sec-onds. . . . Steve will explain it all in more detail—if he can get away from the TV this weekend. It's Super Bowl Sunday.

And to remind him of what the battlefront on the homefront was like, I added,

> That may finish me off. Andrew has been sick all week. Naturally—he's always sick after a Boy Scout weekend, particularly a skiing weekend. But this time he was really laid low with a high fever and cold for five days, and he's still not well. He of course prefers the comfort and TV of our bedroom to his own, so that our room is beginning to look like his—gum wrappers on the floor, dishes half filled with jello on the tables, empty glasses around, tangled bed clothes, a bridge of electric wires from my new radio and the dial control of the TV blocking access to my side of the bed because he's moved it all to within easy reaching distance from a prone position. He does move to his room at night, thank goodness, but it takes me half an hour to clean things up enough to go to bed. We'll see whether Steve or Andrew monopolizes the TV this weekend. I think I'll take shelter in the living room . . .
>
> Forgot to tell you a nice story. Steve and I were talking after dinner the other night as we were washing the dishes about how lucky he was to have such a privileged life. A few minutes later he murmured pensively, "No—I don't have my Dad." But then we rationalized that he had been pretty lucky to be under the same roof with you for as long as he had. (And I wanted to add, now to have me staying home with him while he finished high school).

Malcolm was also buoyed by those weeks at home over the Christmas holidays and was ready to get back to work. He moved easily into all the activities that awaited him. Within a few weeks he left on a tour of the Gulf to meet alumni and government officials and to capitalize on the current mood of hope for AUB and Lebanon to appeal for donations. He wrote to Susie from Bahrain.

> Greetings from the midst of my four-country tour. If it's Tuesday this must be Bahrain. Every city has a "Gulf Hotel" with baskets of fruit in the room and Egyptians and Pakistanis waiting on you all over the place. It also has Cadillacs, boulevards, banks, and instant universities—all the latest equipment and nobody using it. We're visiting them all . . .

It was great fun being together at Christmas and very nice getting to know Hans. He is a thoroughly attractive person and you may be sure that "the family approves" (as they used to say in the 17th century). Mom and I are glad to see how well suited to each other you are and how happy and relaxed together. Best of luck—keep your head screwed on straight; I think you have already and will.

Malcolm wrote that letter on January 18, just one year before the day of his death. By the time he got back to Beirut, he found the political situation had taken a turn for the worse, and the causes for hope that had opened in September were perceptibly changing. On February 1, he wrote to his mother.

The situation in Lebanon has not been very good; in fact it has visibly deteriorated during the past week or two: a number of bombings, shellings in the mountains between Druzes and Maronites, etc. Two nights ago the most appalling event took place: General Sharon showed up for dinner in an East Beirut restaurant, escorted by some Lebanese supporters and was actually applauded by a number of the clientele, who then sang Happy Birthday to him. He subsequently visited Pierre Gemayel and openly threatened that President Amin Gemayel might disappear suddenly if he did not give in to Israeli demands. It is harder than before to see how the Lebanese Government can stand up to Israel with this kind of crumbling position in the country. How all this will affect AUB is hard to tell at present, but it is not good: either Lebanon will become a pro-Israeli bastion, in which case all our Arab ties will become unacceptable to the authorities and we will be faced with the prospect of becoming a captive cooperative university, or else Lebanon will degenerate once again into a jungle. I still cling to the belief in miracles, that the Lebanese government will somehow, with American help, get rid of its occupiers and gain full control over the whole country. Without optimism, there is little to be done, so we might as well think positively.

And in a letter to the boys and me written on the same day, he wrote of the demands and satisfactions of his job.

Tomorrow I am to visit the "House of the Future," a Phalangist think tank in Antelias founded by Amin Gemayel years ago.

We must try to improve AUB's relations over on the eastern side. Friday I have to give a speech at a Beirut University College conference on higher education, also to be held over in that region, near Dog River I think. Oh yes, and on Thursday a lecture at the Center for Arab Unity Studies. . . . After all that I will have several days devoted to reviewing the budget proposals of the various deans . . . and talking to our fund raising consultant. Pretty exciting, don't you think? I often wish at odd moments that I could return to the quiet routines of UCLA and Pacific Palisades—certainly from the point of view of home and family, Sunday evening TV, Steve's basketball games, the UCLA swimming pool, walks with Hogie, and hugs with everybody; but not from the Meaning of Life point of view, and I cannot regret making the move.

The miracle that Malcolm hoped for, that the Lebanese government, with the help of the United States, would get rid of its occupiers and gain full control over the country, was not forthcoming. The Syrians and Israelis were not easily gotten rid of; each country had its own agenda. The Syrians had provided a peacekeeping force in Lebanon since 1976 under a mandate from the Arab League and by an invitation from the Lebanese government to provide them protection against the PLO and dissident Muslim factions. They also had their own security concerns with Israel in the Beka'a Valley. The Israelis, as part of their plan for invading Lebanon, wanted to coerce a full peace treaty with Lebanon that would, among other things, guarantee them a twenty-five mile security zone north of their border in South Lebanon. The Syrians were not in favor of a peace treaty because it would give additional recognition to the legitimacy of the State of Israel created in 1948, as had the Camp David accords and the Egyptian-Israeli peace treaty. Arab countries other than Egypt believed that recognition of Israel was the only card they had to play and that it should be held on to until a homeland for the Palestinians was secured. A Lebanese-Israeli peace treaty would also allow Israel rights of intervention and flights over Lebanese territory, which would be denied to other countries, including Syria, who might be hostile to Israel.

In a complex web of actions to achieve a peace treaty, the Israelis prevailed upon the American government to persuade President Amin Gemayel to come up with the kind of treaty they wanted. Secretary of State Shultz, recently appointed to office, was anxious to close the chapter of the Israeli invasion of Lebanon and its unpleasant implications for the United States. He involved himself personally in bringing the authority of the American government to pressure the Gemayel government into conceding control of South Lebanon to Israel in order to secure a peace treaty. In trying to achieve this goal, which was in America and Israel's interest, he neglected consideration of Lebanon's internal problems. We Americans living in Beirut at the time were hopeful that because Shultz had had previous Middle East experience, while working with the Bechtel Corporation in Arab countries, he would see the need to help local governments solve their internal problems in order to bring overall stability to the region. Malcolm kept lamenting, "The United States has got to make Gemayel pay attention to the demands of the opposition groups." Meanwhile, Shultz plowed ahead to get the peace treaty that America and Israel wanted, ignoring the fact that Muslim feelings were strong against granting Israel the special rights it demanded in South Lebanon with a Christian army and leader of their choice, Major Sa'ad Haddad in charge. In his negotiations, Shultz also neglected to confer sufficiently with President Assad and the Syrian government and involve them as partners in the negotiation process. He relied instead on assurances from moderate Arab countries that Syria would withdraw from the Beka'a when Israel withdrew from South Lebanon.

.   .   .

A peace agreement was eventually achieved under American pressure which did nothing to satisfy Syrian and Lebanese Muslim interests. President Gemayel was criticized for being an American stooge and thereby crippled in his attempt to broaden the base of his government. Eventually, Gemayel was forced by opposition factions in Lebanon to renounce the agreement, making America look like the loser and Syria the victor. The various militia groups representing the different Muslim and Christian factions renewed their fighting. The goals of the battles they waged were by their nature unclear, and alliances among the militias shifted according to whim or at the instigation of the powers outside of Lebanon who supported them. In Lebanon, it had become hard to know who was doing what to whom and why. Even in retrospect, it is difficult to glean much perspective.

The glimmer of hope that Amin Gemayel's government might unify the country was lost in part by his own weakness and in part by the lack of attention of the American government to the complexities of Lebanese factionalism and regional entanglements. Any hope was also diminished by America's unquestioning backing of Israel, even when it was not in its own best interests. Internal conditions continued to deteriorate. Malcolm described the latest events in Beirut.

> You have probably heard about the car bomb that exploded in Ras Beirut yesterday afternoon, the equivalent of 570 pounds of TNT. It wrecked two buildings across the street from each other, just a block off Sadat Street and next to Cedric Haddad's house. The 12 year old boy of one of our professors was killed; he was riding a bicycle at the time. I went to the funeral this afternoon and shook hands with the family, who were horribly broken up. The Greek Orthodox church near AUB was overflowing; I think many, like myself, showed up not just out of friendship with the parents (I hardly knew them) but as a gesture of outrage against the mass murder that the perpetrators, whoever they are, have dared to bring back to this city after several months of peace. According to the press, there were 18 dead and something approaching 200 wounded, most of them fairly lightly injured by flying glass. I went after the funeral to inspect the building for myself. Although it looked very bad, it wasn't any worse than a lot of other burned out rubble we have seen around town since last summer, except that there was broken glass all over for 200 yards and everyone in the neighborhood had had their windows (and sometimes doors) broken . . .
>
> It is very discouraging to see this return to violence, which spoils so much optimism and confidence that had been present before Christmas and that seems essential if people are to be persuaded to invest money, behave legally, enroll at AUB, come from Saudi Arabia to our hospital, etc. etc. There have been several bombs lately, and also the artillery duels raging between Aley and Abaih (with Ainab in between) have now spread down to the coastal plain, and all the way over to Broumana on an-

other mountain range. Two days ago shells fell in East Beirut, killing five people, and today I understand the Druze forces in Aley burned down a large part of the town belonging to Christians . . .

Meanwhile the Israeli occupying army sits by idly, that is when they aren't busy stimulating each side to shoot at the other. It appears to many that Sharon's game is to demonstrate to the Lebanese government that it is powerless to negotiate with Israel or to govern the country and that it may as well capitulate to Israel's terms, which are very humiliating and destructive for Lebanon, or else turn the country over to the Phalangist forces whose leaders are foolishly and deliriously enthusiastic about Sharon and Israel. General Sharon himself appeared in an East Beirut restaurant last week (a blatant violation of the agreements of last September) and was actually serenaded by the band and applauded by many of the customers. This is what the Lebanese government has to contend with in trying to bargain with Israel. I have dates to talk with two of these pro-Israelis from the Phalangist forces (both AUB graduates as it happens) later this week, and am apprehensive about the kind of browbeating they might try to indulge in—such as insisting that AUB reorganize its staff and admissions policies to suit their anti-Muslim, anti-Palestinian fanaticism. Apparently I am already being condemned for having appointed a Muslim vice president of AUB [Abdul Hamid Hallab]. The fact that we already have three Christian vice presidents and five Christian deans counts for nothing.

In an uncustomary outpouring of his commitment to his role at AUB, Malcolm wrote: "The Druzes and the Maronites have just about destroyed each other by now, with Israel looking on, and all my brave words here and there about a new era at AUB are sounding a bit hollow, but I am going to keep it up and one day it will become true."

As we had all predicted at Christmas time, Susie and Hans's romance moved along quickly. Susie's letters to Malcolm in Beirut and Andrew, Steve, and me in California kept us informed.

I'm not going to make any decisions about Hans and next year for at least another month since it might make things somewhat clearer if I have a little time to let things settle. Although I am pretty hooked on the man of course. We were listening to this funny song, a folksong called "The Dutchman" which starts out, "The Dutchman's not the kind of man who keeps his thumb jammed in the dam." OH BROTHER! His mother is probably going to visit in early March, so while she's checking me out, I can check her out! . . . no rash decisions for me now! Not for at least a week! Then I'll start making my rash decisions. Seriously Pop, I am, as you say, trying to keep my old head screwed on straight! It's a cinch this time because it's not my first time around, and I really have a good idea about what I want out of life and all that stuff. So don't worry about a thing.

A week later, Malcolm received a letter from Hans. "Dear Mr. Kerr, Too bad that you cannot be here right now because I have some very important news for you which I wanted to tell you personally. If you have read Wednesday's telex already, you will know what I am talking about, and I hope you are as happy as I am." The telex had said essentially what was said in the letter. "Well, Susie and I decided that we like each other so much that we would like to get married (wow), and so can be with each other the rest of our lives. This letter then, asks for your consent (as they would say in the 17th century)."

We would all have a chance to celebrate the engagement in March when Malcolm was due in New York for a board meeting. He was eagerly awaiting that occasion and wrote to me in February:

Imagine, only two weeks till we meet in New York. . . . Your missing letters arrived a day after we talked on the phone. I'm not sure why they came later than other letters, but they did and I loved it all: your two letters plus ones from the boys and all those lovely clippings about Steve and you. Yours was awfully brief, just the photo and a short article about your painting exhibit, but it was well done and I liked the picture, with its wistful expression that implied that there was something unfulfilled about Ann Kerr since she is there and he is elsewhere. We will soon do something about that . . .

It sure will be fun to have Andrew around next year here. He's such an enthusiast. The whole complexion of life is going to be so different, and so totally superior in every way, having you and him on hand all the time and being back to family existence. To think that despite this painful separation I am loving AUB anyway, and then to think that in the future I can have both—and that you will love this place—is a sign that basically things are good for us and there is a lot to be thankful for.

Only a paragraph later, apparently oblivious to the contrast of his words, Malcolm described a situation that was potentially very ominous:

I went to visit the Thabets and had a long talk with Samir about how to mend fences with the Maronites and with the government. This will not be easy, and it seems that they have me tagged as ideologically unfriendly and AUB as a hotbed of what they don't like. Two days ago, the Minister of Education summoned me to his office and gave me a lecture similar to those we previously got from Amin Gemayel: AUB must show its face outside Beirut, get rid of its trouble makers, and stop hiring anyone other than Lebanese or Americans. As we were constantly interrupted by phone calls and men who came in to whisper in his ear, I never had a chance to rebut except very briefly, so I was rather put out. There are so many misconceptions about AUB and, for that matter about me, and it is so hard to counteract them. It is now going to be very difficult for us to hire Arabs other than Lebanese on the faculty, and I don't know what is going to happen to our student body. It's a shame to think of this little country getting so chauvinistic, when its whole past prosperity was built on openness to the surrounding environment.

On my way to meet Malcolm in New York where he was coming for AUB board meetings in March, I stopped in Cambridge to be with Susie, Hans, and his mother, who was visiting from Holland, to celebrate the engagement and talk about wedding plans. Hans and his mother cooked a splendid engagement celebration dinner, which they served in his room in Conant Hall. One of the guests was my ninety-one-year-old uncle, Ralph Wetmore, who had lived in the room down the hall as a student some seventy years earlier and had later been a professor at Harvard for forty years. Susie and Hans were radiant and I wished so much that Malcolm were there to see them. We would have to continue the celebration in New York.

When John, Susie, and Hans arrived in New York to see Malcolm, we proudly introduced our prospective new son-in-law to our AUB friends. After the board meetings were finished, there was a day for the continued celebration we had planned. I remember, as we took pictures of one another over a huge feast in a Chinese restaurant, feeling that Malcolm and I were somehow on a double date with Susie and Hans, and what fun it was to look forward to a lifetime of double dates.

Back in Beirut a few weeks later, Malcolm wrote in a letter to all the family:

> It was great seeing some of you and talking to others on the phone last month, but I feel very badly (a) that I didn't see John again after the first week, (b) that I saw so little of Mother, (c) that I talked so little to Marion and (d) that I didn't talk to Dorothy [his sisters] at all. Everything was too rushed and there were too many things to try to do all at once. The other thing I feel badly about is having had to leave Los Angeles at all, after an idyllic week there. It's funny to have taken the AUB job in a mood of boredom with Los Angeles and now to feel so wistful at having left it, but the reason is obvious, namely the continued presence of certain people there (both two-legged and four-legged). The last day there, Ann and I found out that it was possible to walk all the way from the bedroom to the kitchen while hugging and that made the whole three weeks in the US important! It will be hard to do in Beirut since to get to the kitchen you have to walk downstairs, just as it would have been hard in Los Angeles with the four-legged member of the family. (That really gives one something to think about.) . . . This is the day, I believe that Steve is supposed to start getting responses from colleges. I'm hoping you will summarize all the information in a telex one day soon. I'm anxiously waiting for the news, but I guess just because I'm nervous, wondering how much of a tuition I'm going to get socked for next year and so on, it doesn't mean I can approach your level of nervousness, wondering where you're going to wind up. Just remember that any place you get in and want to go to will be OK with me, especially if I can visit you there once in a while. The first such

occasion is likely to be next November when the AUB Board of Trustees meets in San Francisco. Gonzaga, Santa Barbara, Stanford, Brown, and Amherst are all accessible from San Francisco or from New York on the way. Even Southwestern Tennessee Institute for the Mentally Handicapped is a short ride by dogsled from Nashville, which can be reached by stagecoach, after taking the river paddleboat from Pittsburgh to Cincinnati. However, I HAVE NO IDEA HOW TO GET TO PITTSBURGH . . .

Andrew, how's your poison ivy? Mine is finally clearing up but has left ugly red splotches all over my hands and legs. No more walks on that trail! I hope Hogie doesn't have poison ivy. It's hard to imagine how a dog would look with it!

As the spring of 1983 progressed, American efforts to bolster the Gemayel government continued. The U.S. administration hoped that by providing weapons and military advisors to build up the Lebanese army, President Gemayel would eventually be able to unify his country. But in wholeheartedly backing the Gemayel government while neglecting opposition demands and ignoring long-standing Syrian involvement in Lebanon, the opportunities for compromise among the various factions which had opened up at the end of the Israeli invasion were quickly closing. There was again a rigidifying of all the diverse elements in Lebanon. The Israelis and the Americans gave full support to the Maronite Christian forces, the Syrians aligned with the Shiite and Sunni Muslims, Druzes and any Christian groups that opposed the Israeli-Phalangist coalition.

Although the Lebanese economy had remained remarkably strong to this point in the Civil War, the disparity between rich and poor was growing sharper. While there was no official census, it was considered that the population of Lebanon now numbered about three million people divided approximately as one third Christian (still officially considered the majority), one third Sunni Muslim and one third Shiite Muslim. Impoverished Shiites, rapidly increasing in number by virtue of a high birthrate, were being driven out of their villages in the south by Israeli occupation and by the ill will of the newly powerful, Israeli-backed Christian army led by the local warlord, Major Sa'ad Haddad. The Shiites were also disliked by Palestinian refugees who lived in camps established in the south of Lebanon after 1948. The dislike was partly because of religious differences (most Palestinians were Sunni Muslims) and partly because of too many disadvantaged people trying to occupy too little space. These Palestinians had increased in number by mere birthrate over the decades, but they had gained in number of political activists in 1970 after King Hussein's expulsion of hundreds of Palestinians. Though not economically well off, the Palestinians had financial support from established agencies for refugee aid such as UNRWA, the U.N. Refugee Welfare Agency, and from successful Palestinians outside Lebanon.

The Shiites, the most beleaguered of all the minorities in Lebanon, were pouring into the area south of Beirut near the airport, finding shelter wherever they could and creating a new quarter of the city which assumed the name of "Southern Suburbs." The cabins of St. Michel Beach where Malcolm and I used to have picnic lunches when Susie was a baby were becoming homes for these new refugees, but with corrugated tin or cardboard boxes thrown up between the cabins to provide shelter for more people. The Lebanese Shiites attracted the influence of Khomeini Shiites in Iran, a close ally of Syria, and a number of Iranians came to proselytize in Lebanon. Their stronghold was in the Beka'a Valley which was under Syrian control. The shadowy Islamic Jihad organization was thought to have its headquarters in this region where the snowcapped Lebanon range and the Temple of Baalbek dominated the landscape and where fields of poppies fed a flourishing narcotics trade. No one was very certain about the size or extent of the Islamic Jihad. Was it a group of the most extreme of Islamic fundamentalists who wanted to wage a holy war, as the literal translation of the name implies, against whomever they considered infidels? Some conjectured that if it existed at all, it might be only a telephone organization. Whatever its tangible form, it seemed to be an idea that magnetized people who were underprivileged or disenchanted with the elements of Western culture that conflicted with Islamic values. The infusion of Khomeini influence inspired increasingly radical activities in the name of Islamic Jihad.

The deterioration of internal conditions over the previous two or three months was accentuated in late April when a suicide truck full of explosives slammed into the American Embassy on the Corniche Road just below the AUB campus. The front side of the building instantly became a hollow shell and 63 people were killed, some blown up, some buried alive. The American ambassador, Robert Dillon, who had been at a meeting on an upper floor in the back of the building, survived, shaken and dusty but unharmed. This event signaled a major downward shift in the mood of many Muslim and Christian Lebanese, for regardless of our misguided policies, a strong American presence was a symbol of hope. There was a reserve of respect in Lebanon for the United States as a nation of principle that could help bring peace, and its superpower presence was tangible evidence that the world had not forgotten this country of tragedy.

On May 17, the U.S. government finally succeeded in achieving the peace treaty that Israel wanted, signed by Lebanon, the United States, and Israel. This act further weakened the position of America and of Gemayel. Just before that, I was to visit Malcolm for the third of our much planned and anticipated reunions of our year apart. I wrote to him before leaving.

> I had a wonderful afternoon with the Simonians today, a champagne brunch at the Bonaventure followed by a Brahms concert at the Music Center. I missed you especially all the way through the 4th symphony because I know you like it so much. . . . It helped to alleviate my depression only a little over the tragedy of the embassy explosion and the continuing lack of stability in Lebanon. It's like going through last summer and fall all over again, not knowing what's happening to you and just waiting, hoping that the worst doesn't happen. I look forward so much to being with you, though of course consider that the boys will have both parents in the danger zone.

Malcolm, leaving the serious worrying to me, wrote to all our children. At the time I was en route to Amman via Holland to help make wedding plans with Hans's family.

> Dear Kiddies, Since your mother is currently a wayward woman I think the least I can do is write to reassure you and check up on you. Mom should still be in Amsterdam tonight (unless she's in Hong Kong) and tomorrow morning I am supposed to leave Beirut for Amman to meet her for a hot Jordanian weekend. We'll spend one night in Amman and then go to Aqaba for a

weekend of snorkeling. The only thing is that today there was shelling from the mountains—over 100 shells allegedly fell in various parts of Beirut and suburbs, though none anywhere near this part of town—and everyone is trying to figure out who did it and why. Probably a combination of the Syrians and the Druzes explaining in their own tactful way to the Lebanese government why they should think twice about signing any agreements with Israel. So I am hoping that there won't be more shelling in the morning that might close down the airport or make it difficult to get there. This kind of nonsense is quite new, in that while there has been plenty of it between rival groups in the mountains for months now, Beirut has been safe. The explosion at the U.S. Embassy seems to have touched off a wave of incidents. We don't feel in any danger at AUB and we have half the Lebanese army guarding us—tanks outside the gates, etc.—but it would be nice to feel that life was really normal once again . . .

I had a very nice letter from Mom written at Anza Barrego in the desert telling how she and Andrew danced all night. Andrew, you really ought to give the Old Lady a break. At her age all that exercise can be dangerous. But I hope you had fun. Mom has more spirit than ninety-nine percent of the women her age. That's why I decided to meet her in Amman. She has strict instructions to bring the snorkels, the flippers and the frisbee. We will have to be careful not to venture across the frontier into Israeli waters, if we don't want to be drafted into the Israeli navy. Andrew, I think you are going to get a great kick out of living in Lebanon: ACS [the American Community School], with only six or seven students per class and seventy-five percent of the teachers able to read and write and the chance to visit three occupying armies on any Sunday afternoon.

During our weekend in Aqaba, Malcolm for the first time told me in other than a joking or offhand manner that he believed he was being personally singled out by the Gemayel government as an enemy. He had been told by trusted friends, that one, if not more administrators and former administrators within AUB were involved in whispering in the ear of the president and his supporters to plant or reinforce the idea that Malcolm was against the Phalangist regime. Malcolm had already written us that AUB, and he as well, were not terribly popular with the present government.

AUB stood for free and open exchange of ideas among all religious and political groups and for pan-Arabism, with the concern for a just solution to the Palestinian problem which that entailed. Malcolm, in his writing and teaching throughout his career, and now in the AUB presidency, personified those ideas.

Malcolm was also unpopular with the government for his official stand against a recently established branch school of AUB, known as the Off-Campus Program. This was a small extension of the university opened by the trustees in a building in East Beirut to accommodate Christian students who felt unsafe going to West Beirut. The intention of the trustees was to keep the program very small with the understanding that it was a temporary expediency and would be closed as soon as political conditions permitted. The idea of a separate branch of AUB for a single religious group went against the principles on which the university was founded, which proclaimed that AUB was an institution where people of all religious faiths could come together and exchange ideas.

The tangible form of the government's displeasure with Malcolm and AUB was a policy of harassment in refusing to renew residence and work permits of American and Palestinian-born employees. This radical action threatened to uproot families of several professors who had spent their entire career and sometimes student days as well at AUB. It was unlikely that these individuals posed a security problem to Lebanon.

Malcolm's description of these sinister problems terrified me and, though I usually managed to control myself, I occasionally poured out my fears for his safety. But it could be no more than an outburst of pent-up emotions, for I knew I could not ask him to turn his back on AUB now. I also wanted my crack at being the president's wife and at teaching there, but if he were to decide for himself to leave, though I would feel let down, I would rejoice. I couldn't implore him to leave, but to impress upon him how dangerous I considered the security risks, I told him of my plan if anything should happen to him: I would go to Cairo and try to get a job teaching at AUC and let Andrew return to Cairo American College. I was not asking for any particular response on Malcolm's part, and he did not reply, for there was really none to give.

From Aqaba, Malcolm and I went to Beirut and were soon caught up in the whirl of AUB life. I wrote to Susie and Hans:

I am sitting in Dad's office on this Saturday afternoon while he writes a speech to give on Monday at the opening of the Bonfils collection of 19th century photos of Lebanon that we saw at the Semitic Museum at Harvard in March. Just as I predicted in our last phone conversation, Susie, it is much easier to feel relaxed now that I am in Beirut. It is quite difficult in this beautiful campus setting with birds singing and the perpetual ping of tennis balls from the courts below (which starts at 5:30 AM and never stops till sundown) to keep reminding oneself that danger lurks in many forms in this country. Add to this of course, the wonderful time Dad and I are having being together, the hundreds of old friends we are seeing and the fact that we really don't know what's going on outside the campus as much as I do when I'm home listening to every scrap of news ten times a day on the television and car radio, and you see why we are having such a nice time. It's hard to remember now what an irrational wreck I was when I left home.

In the letter I went on to describe my stop in Holland en route to the Middle East and discussions with Hans's family about wedding plans and the conclusion that it was really best to have the wedding in the bride's home.

Here in Beirut this past week we have been thinking what an ideal place for a wedding the AUB chapel and Marquand House garden would be, and every day we try to imagine how the political situation might improve to the point by August that we could safely have it here, but being quite realistic, we realize it's too chancy to make such plans. . . . So we are coming to the idea—Dad and I—that our choice for your wedding would be California in mid-July. Obviously you are the ones to make the final decision. Remembering what a wonderful time we all had together there at Christmas, I think it could be a relaxed and lovely setting for your wedding and a chance for our two families to become better acquainted. I believe Vahe Simonian [a family friend and former minister of Pacific Palisades Presbyterian Church] would be available to marry you and we could have the wedding in our patio.

Malcolm wrote to Susie and Hans a few weeks later:

It's too bad we couldn't consider having the wedding in Beirut, but I think there wasn't really any choice. Not only could something happen at the last minute to derail everything, but even now we are having some troubles with the Lebanese Army which guards our campus, supposedly for our protection but with such overenthusiasm that it seems as if we were under military occupation. They have no hesitancy in declaring that we have to cancel such-and-such an activity because they have decided it's a security risk—most recently, the Miss AUB contest. There had been two rival student groups each wanting to organize its own Miss AUB contest, a Miss Left-Wing AUB and a Miss Right-Wing AUB, and after heroic efforts the Dean of Students finally got them together on one wave length, only to have the army move in and scrap the whole thing! . . .

In any event, Los Angeles will be a great place for the wedding and you will be glad to have Vahe Simonian officiate. We can have a terrific party afterward in the patio. And you could go camping in the Sierras for your honeymoon. Besides, how else could Hogie attend the ceremony? But I am sorry you won't be able to come to Beirut. There will be other chances; I am planning to stay in this job for a long time, provided my newfound enemies don't manage to get rid of me.

I left Beirut for California in late May with less than two weeks to get started on wedding plans before it was time to leave with my parents for John's graduation from Swarthmore and then to Susie's graduation from Harvard. With all these pending activities to think about, it was easier not to dwell on all I had learned about problems at AUB. Malcolm wrote the day after I left:

Now that the Pan Am flight has left, I no longer have to feel so bad that you didn't stay longer. After all, you'd be gone by now anyway. The first result of your departure was that I woke up at 3:30 a.m. You are my sleeping pill and I missed you. I thought of you periodically during the day imagining where you were— taking off for Amman; waiting at Amman airport; then for an interminable time still en route to New York. Now it is 8:15 in the morning there and I suppose you are sitting over a late breakfast with the Overtons [friends in New York]. I hope the trip onward to LA is OK and that the boys will be shipshape . . .

I got Susie's one word telex about their plans for next year:

Taiwan! That's pretty exciting. Now all we need is a one word telex from Steve: Colorado. (Or anything) . . .

You will be relieved to know that the matter of residence permit renewals for AUB has been alleviated. Last night I went to a meeting cooked up by Bob Dillon with him, the head of security who issued all the denials in the first place, and the presidential adviser on national security. It was all friendly and low key, and Bustani [the head of security] ended up by offering to extend the residences till July 31 during which time he would "study the cases," which I take him to mean reverse the decisions in a veiled way that doesn't leave him looking too ridiculous. Tom Sutherland [Dean of Agriculture and later to be held hostage for six years] will have to wait another week and then I think he will get his visa. The whole point of the hold-ups was that the head of security wants us to hire more Lebanese at AUB! . . .

I then stayed another hour with the president's adviser on national security and talked about why the President doesn't like me, and it sounds to me as if this will turn out all right in time but maybe quite a lot of time.

Ten days later, as the graduation dates approached, Malcolm wrote us:

I will be thinking of Susie and Ann and the Zwickers tomorrow on the Big Occasion, wishing very much that I could have made it too. It's fantastic to think of Susie as a Harvard M.A., and John as a Swarthmore B.A. I think they must have inherited all their talent from their mother, for I know that if I had to go through school at this point I would never make it . . .

While Susie is graduating, I will be delivering the main speech at a ceremony at the Amiliya Technical School in my best Arabic, with either the President of the Republic or the Prime Minister or both, plus the Speaker of the Parliament, looking on. I have already practiced my text ten times and will try it out at least another ten so they will all think that I know Arabic better than I really do. The Amiliya is a very highly respected philanthropic institution founded by a wealthy Shiite family, mainly for Shiite students, none of whom has to pay any tuition. It was wrecked last summer in the Israeli bombardment and the ceremony tomorrow is to re-lay the cornerstone of the main classroom building . . .

Steve and Andrew, I hope you (and Hogie) are taking good care of the house in Mom's absence . . . I realize another graduation is coming up one of these days, Steve, which I am also very sorry to miss, and after that a birthday on July 9th which I won't be there for either. I guess I'm not much use these days. But I won't forget to come to the wedding!

Although not likely to forget, Malcolm was detained to the last minute by commencement and a meeting of the board of trustees, which was so heated over the issue of how to solve AUB's problems with the Lebanese government that at one point he said he felt ready to quit. He did not, however, and on July 13, three days before the wedding, Susie and I went to the airport to meet Malcolm and his mother, whom he had stopped to pick up in New Jersey. He looked exhausted as he came down the ramp toward me with arms outstretched, and, referring to our long year apart, he said, "It's over."

CHAPTER 17

No One Wants to Shell AUB

*T*wo weeks after Susie and Hans's wedding on July 16, 1983, and a week after a short camping trip Malcolm and I took to the Sierras with John and Andrew, we left for our new life in Beirut. Another milestone event of those past two weeks had been a telephone call to Steve from Coach Lute Olson at the University of Arizona, offering him a full basketball scholarship. It was a tangible reward for the time Steve and I had spent together going through his senior year with all the hopes and disappointments of a high school basketball star being courted and dismissed by suitors in the form of college coaches looking for just the kind of player they needed. Steve had three weeks before he had to be at Tucson, so there was time for him to go with Malcolm, Andrew, and me to Beirut to see what our new life was going to be like.

Before our departure we rented our house, dog included as usual, to a family with two small children, who agreed to relinquish it to us each summer for two months so that our family could all gather there. Experienced packers that we were by now, we got our belongings organized in a day or two ready for an air freight company to pick up and ship to Beirut. The biggest challenge was what to do with the vast collection of Malcolm's books that he had had to empty from his office at UCLA after submitting his resignation and giving up his job and office of twenty years. The burden of what to do with that rich array of books, which Malcolm had collected over his adult lifetime, now piled in boxes on our garage floor, struck me as symbolic of the tremendous transition we were about to make. The bookshelves in our house were full and the basement room below the guest house was too damp for storing books. "Ship them to Beirut," Malcolm declared in his characteristic decisive manner.

Susie and Hans were to spend the coming academic year in Taiwan on a research grant for Hans. Before leaving for Taiwan, they would stay on in Pacific Palisades for a few weeks housesitting in the home of our friends, the Adams. John, who planned to find a job in Lebanon and be with us for a year, had to finish his summer job doing research for a UCLA economics professor. He, too, went to stay at the Adams' house with Susie and Hans, making it possible for him to claim that he was spending their honeymoon with them.

Once again my parents had to gamely accept our leaving for the Middle East, but this time their fears were more justifiable. Throughout the previous year, my father had made frequent comments about the danger of going to Lebanon—to which I made lame responses about the newspapers making things look worse than they really were. Now they were seeing us off at the airport again. They drove one car, Susie and Hans another, barely enough space to transport Steve, Andrew, Malcolm, and me and all our luggage. In the commotion at the airport, there was no time for lingering farewells. Malcolm would be home again in November for an AUB board meeting and faculty recruitment trip around the country. He would see my parents and Steve and his mother, but this was the last time Susie and Hans would see Malcolm.

On our way to Beirut, we stopped to see Elsa Kerr in New Jersey who was resting up after giving us all the help at the wedding she could muster with the health problems of her eighty-seven years, first in the kitchen sitting on a high stool to prepare food and then standing with difficulty to read a passage from the Lebanese poet, Khalil Gibran, during the ceremony. During our visit with her, she asked me to check on the womens' dorms at AUB to find out if new furnishings or decor were needed—a task she had tended to for many years when she was advisor to women students.

We had received the good news a few weeks earlier that David Dodge had been released by his kidnappers, just a year after his abduction. He had gone home to Princeton with his family, and we were able to see him while we were there. Malcolm's mother was delighted to see David whom she had watched grow up in Beirut and whose mother and father had been her close friends. David's return seemed to bestow a blessing on our family as we departed for Beirut to begin our new life. But he warned us during his visit that our situation would be dangerous. He knew from experience that Khomeini groups were highly organized and professional.

When the four of us arrived in Beirut on August 4, we were met by airport and AUB officials with much acclaim and attention to all our needs. We were now public figures. At Marquand House, Hassan, now the chief cook and housekeeper since Muhammad's departure, rushed to meet us at the front door and effusively kissed Steve and Andrew on both cheeks. His ebullient Egyptian wife, Zeinab, welcomed us in Egyptian Arabic, a loving reminder of my special fondness for that country. Their beautiful little daughter, Dalia, with the dark skin and fine features of her Sudanese father, hung shyly behind her mother's skirts, awed by the sight of the new occupants of the house, particularly the two tall, blond boys who towered over her. Her baby brother Muhammad was asleep. Inside we were welcomed by Dr. Hamilton Southworth, an AUB trustee who had suffered a mild heart attack while attending the June board meeting on campus and was restricted from traveling. He and his wife had been staying in Marquand House for the past four weeks and would be there for two more.

Though it was almost midnight, it was still hot and sticky, even in the large rooms of that beautiful old house—which now seemed barnlike in comparison with our own house and garden that had been so full of life with the activity and celebration of the wedding. We went to bed to the sound of distant shelling and images of the eerily silent pockmarked city we had just driven through and of the strange color cast by yellow streetlights on blackened, gouged buildings.

Shortly after our arrival I wrote to John, Susie and Hans, still at home in California.

> Hope you have not been alarmed by news from Beirut. Life has been predictably tranquil and pleasant here at AUB and we only hear occasional booms off in the distance. Hassan gives us reports from the morning news of what's happening and we see

the headlines as we eat breakfast. Then we concern ourselves with our own day's activities, Dad at his office, but only for summer hours, me seizing the reins of power at Marquand House and organizing our lives here, Andrew and Steve [ages 15 and 17] lounging in their air-conditioned rooms reading, rough housing, pretending our birki [small Arab pool and fountain] is a swimming pool, attending social events with us and impressing all our friends with their good looks and charm.

I'm writing this hastily as Steve may have to go early tomorrow because of the latest troubles. We were not aware of the shelling of the airport today, though heard quite a few booms in the distance on a picnic with the Dodds in Beit Meri and Bikfaya [mountain villages considered to be in a safe area]. When we returned home we heard the news that the airport had closed and later that three ministers had been kidnapped. So we've decided to send Steve a day early if the airport opens.

Risks aside (and often I wonder what we're doing here), this is an amazing time and place to be living in. Andrew laps it up—everything, life in Marquand House, social life, observing the Marines, visiting the US ships by helicopter last Sunday, etc. I have been quite homesick from time to time, but there's not much time to think about it. Was the wedding really such a short time ago and was it really so perfect? It's hard to believe so much has happened. Susie and Hans—hope all goes well with your departure for Taiwan. I hate not being there while you are. Your wedding book has now been viewed on three continents and everyone agrees that it was the perfect wedding and you are the perfect couple.

John, on the job front, Peter Dodd says he believes the ECWA [Economic Commission for West Asia] job in Baghdad might still be yours. If that doesn't come through there are plenty of interesting experiences and things to learn here.

Along with all the letters Malcolm and I wrote from Beirut, I also kept a daily journal of our activities. I had not regularly kept a journal before, but it seemed that we were living in the midst of an historic period that should be recorded. Malcolm occasionally teased me about my journalistic efforts with a comment such as, "Well, have you written down what we had for breakfast yet?" But on another occasion he proffered, "Do you think I should be keeping a journal too?"

The next morning we were told the airport might reopen. Haj Omar, AUB's crack driver, would take Steve and me and help us through departure procedures. Inside the airport, Omar moved with skillful and cocky self-assurance from one official to another, introducing us when it was helpful in gathering information. All planes had remained in Amman overnight for security purposes, but presumably two were en route to Beirut, one extra for yesterday's stranded passengers. Steve was supposed to get a seat on the extra plane, if it came. We waited half an hour, sitting on the baggage scales together, Steve reading *Catch-22* and I writing letters for him to mail in the United States. Suddenly a medium-sized boom sounded outside. People looked up quickly (like deer who have just smelled danger, Steve later remarked) and soon after went back to their business of trying to depart. I jumped and grabbed Steve's arm. Omar admonished us in his slightly broken English, "Don't be fraid." Then with a certain sense of showing us something only he could show us, he called us to the window to see where it had struck—just beside a Czechoslovakian Airlines plane that was full of passengers waiting to take off. He took us back to our seats on the scales. "This the safest place. No glass here. You wait." Another shell landed ten minutes later, this one further away and somehow less scary. "We'd better go now," I said hopefully. "Wait five minutes," he told us. Omar was right; the airport soon closed, and we scampered through the parking lot in great haste to our car and back to the soothing tranquillity of the campus.

The next day Malcolm wrote to John, Susie, and Hans:

Poor Steve! He's already been to the airport two times expecting to leave, only to be sent home again. This afternoon, Mom phoned me to say that he was going on Senator Kasten's military plane to Cairo. Was I ever surprised to see them piling out of the car back at the house two hours later, Steve having been bumped at the last moment. We have considered all sorts of other wild schemes: a helicopter ride to Tel Aviv with Ambassador MacFarlane; a cruise ship to Lattika and Cyprus; a public bus to Tel Aviv from Tyre (illegal but commonplace): and now, as our ace in the hole, an automobile ride with an AUB group to Tripoli, Homs, and Damascus, where the others would catch planes and he would be taken on to the Jordan border by the driver so he could still pick up his Alia flight in Amman. If we are lucky, of course, the airport will be open tomorrow morning and he can fly out as planned, 24 hours later . . .

I'm fearful that all this uncertainty and inconvenience, not to mention even a sense of physical danger, has not done Steve's image of Beirut much good, and in his present mood he wonders what any of us are doing here. It's too bad, because until yesterday we were having a really good time and I think he was coming to appreciate the value of our being here . . .

John, if the Baghdad job [with ECWA] doesn't work out, you could have a pretty interesting time in Beirut and I sense that we could help you find some sort of job if you were not overly particular about what it was. We could have a lot of fun together and you could always take some courses at AUB. You are more able-bodied than I was when I came to AUB on crutches the year after I graduated from college, and that would make a difference in your morale. We're ready for you if you're ready for us.

Steve got off the next day in a car for Damascus and Amman and reached Arizona in time to register for the fall semester and begin his basketball training. After our special closeness of the last year, I found it very hard to have him leave for college, as did Malcolm who was just beginning to catch up with Steve again after being apart for a year. Andrew was left to his own devices, of which he found plenty. He missed Steve and he missed California and summed it all up in a letter to Susie and Hans: "Maybe I should describe this place as very exciting, shattered by dullness."

With Steve gone, I set about arranging tennis and piano lessons for Andrew in an attempt to divert his war buff enthusiasm in the working laboratory around us. The American Community School would not start for another six weeks and, since there were few people of his age around, we were concerned about how he would spend his time. He was becoming far too interested in going out to inspect the latest shrapnel marks in the neighborhood and in picking up spent bullets he found on the ground. Perhaps we would even have to consider buying a video machine to keep him at home. The tennis and piano lessons helped, as well as a budding friendship with other third generation Beirutis, Danny and Skander Dodd, the sons of Malcolm's childhood friends Peter

Dodd and Erica Cruikshank Dodd who both taught at AUB. Besides needing entertainment to keep Andrew off the streets, we also needed it to watch videos of Steve's basketball games that he had promised to send us.

On August 18, Malcolm and I celebrated our twenty-seventh wedding anniversary on an overnight trip to the Hotel Bzummar in the mountains of Keserwan. Our room had a pristine view down mountains spotted with pine woods toward Jounieh and the sea but was marred by a monstrous pile of litter and garbage dumped just beside the hotel. It was a hotel with a distinctly working class air and was filled with families who seemed to have settled in for a long vacation while the elite had gone to Paris. Laundry hung from the balconies and children rode their tricycles on the terrace, while three generations of family members sat around tables sipping Turkish coffee and eating pistachios under huge umbrella pines, enjoying the cool mountain air. This was exactly the atmosphere we were looking for, minus the garbage, and we happily found our own table and ordered Turkish coffee and pistachios.

Later in the afternoon after a long nap, we set out on a sunset walk to an Armenian monastery further up into the mountains from our hotel. The peaceful walk of the kind we remembered in the same mountains long ago was now made less bucolic by refuse strewn alongside the road and by cars whizzing around the sharp mountain turns. Amidst pine trees and traditional old stone buildings were unfinished cement blocks with wires left sticking out of the top to add more floors one day when the owner could raise additional money. Heaps of construction rubble were carelessly piled beside them.

It was a relief to reach the monastery gate and the tranquillity and relative cleanliness inside. We were greeted by an old Armenian gentleman, also visiting from Beirut, who wanted to show us around. We listened to his stories of the history of the monastery and accepted his offer of some local wine as he spun more tales, and then he proceeded to ask us which of his relatives in California we knew.

Walking back to the hotel we reflected on how little the war had directly affected the village of Bzummar, but reasoned that the refuse and rubbish we saw everywhere and the ill planned, unfinished cement buildings must surely be related to the wartime conditions in the country.

We wished we could stay longer and have a little more time to ourselves, but we had to leave the next day in order for Malcolm to be back at work and for me to be on hand to distract Andrew from overexercising his war buff tendencies. We drove through the prosperous, overbuilt villages of Maronite Mt. Lebanon, supported in part by many of their citizens who had emigrated and sent money back home to relatives. Below, the sunlight sparkling on Jounieh Bay, and the familiar view of Beirut shimmering in shades of soft white to the south belied the evil that was now so much a part of this jewel-like country.

Back at Marquand House we found Andrew in the kitchen sitting with Hassan practicing his Arab-accented English, overseeing the cooking of lunch and taking apart a short-wave radio he had found. He reported that he had spent the morning playing basketball with some U.S. Marines on the courts below our house. After lunch, Tanios drove us up to Hamra Street to buy the television and video sets we had been thinking about. We made our purchase for much less money than we had anticipated, for electronic devices in Beirut, like whiskey and French perfume, were sold at black market prices. In the state of near-anarchy that existed in Lebanon, there was no enforcement of government taxes or tariff regulations.

On the way home Tanios took us for a bit of sightseeing in the downtown area which was formerly the scene of intense fighting and was now a blackened no-man's land. There were a few landmarks still recognizable that reminded me of the great fun I used to have shopping in the souks of Beirut when they were full of flowers, tempting fruits and vegetables, brilliant gold jewelry, and French fashions. I tried to describe the way it used to be to Andrew, but he was too busy conjuring up his own images of the battle and smoke that had gone on here more recently, brought to him in vivid color by television in California. He was not interested in my romantic images.

I recognized the Bab Idris intersection where I had gotten off the tram my first day in Beirut almost thirty years earlier on my junior year abroad when I had met an AUB medical student who showed me all around town. The sign above the ABC variety store

hung by a few wires from the skeleton of the building that used to
sell almost anything one could buy at a Woolworth store at home.
Further down the tramline was the half-standing dome of the Central Mosque, and nearby some Greco-Roman ruins that had weathered another turbulent epic in the history of Lebanon.

Tanios turned our white Buick into a street of old arcaded
buildings that was in sharp contrast to the other areas we had just
come through. I recognized it as the street where I had shopped
for fabrics to make clothes for Susie and me when she was a baby,
an atmospheric street in the Middle Eastern tradition of one small,
dimly lighted shop after another selling the same goods. Now it
had been transformed to almost Disneyland cleanliness and untar-
nished beauty with old stone buildings restored, copies of original
street lights installed and cobblestone streets laid down.

All this was the work of a magnanimous and imaginative Lebanese billionaire [later prime minister] named Rafik Hariri who
wanted to demonstrate the possibilities for reconstruction to his
countrymen. He had also engaged in a project to clean up the
garbage in West Beirut after the Israeli invasion and to repair
streetlights around the city. His beautifully restored street was a
symbol of the resilience and creativity of the Lebanese that was an
intrinsic part of their character. Hariri well knew that this reconstruction could become a war zone again at any time, demolishing
the results of this tremendous endeavor.

We, like our adoptive hosts, embarked upon some reconstruction of our house. I had been looking forward to changing Marquand House from a residence into a home since my first visit to
Malcolm there the previous November. I eagerly began selecting
materials for the redecoration with the help of my friend, Rima
Shehadi. Rima, who personified Lebanese feminine charm and
beauty, was a talented decorator and very generous in sharing her
ideas and access to beautiful fabrics available in Beirut despite
years of war. Malcolm was happy to at last have his house turned
into a home and applauded our progress while making sardonic
comments likening Rima's and my efforts to those of the Romans
on the eve of the fall of the Roman Empire.

I decided that to ward off possible criticism of my endeavors at
a time of university impecuniosity and national crisis, I would pay
for the redecoration with the teaching salary I would soon be earning when the school year opened. We chose Laura Ashley fabrics

in warm gold and beige and wine red that would bring life to the drab rooms. We would remove the unsightly insulation tiles carelessly installed some years ago in the dining and living rooms to reduce noise level, but in the process hiding the stately high ceilings that were part of the intrinsic atmosphere of the house. And to control the acoustics we selected soft coral beige wall-to-wall carpeting.

As workmen pulled down the ugly insulation tiles in the dining room, we had a glimpse of the history of Marquand House. The original high ceiling had once been pale yellow and at another time pale green. I wondered if Teddy Roosevelt had visited when it was yellow or green and if Mark Twain had really dined under this ceiling and presented the signed photograph Malcolm had found in an upstairs closet to one of the early Blisses. I was having the autographed photographs of both of these men framed to hang in the dining room, along with a few of the watercolors I had done in Beirut some time after the Twain and Roosevelt visits.

As a souvenir of my forty-ninth birthday (August 24) and as an addition to our new home, I indulged myself in purchasing a genuine Euphrates fertility goddess, whose age made my advanced years look quite insignificant. She reminded me of a similar statue that had captivated me in the Los Angeles County Museum of Art. I went with an AUB biology professor friend to his favorite antiquities dealer, a grocer who obtained old objects brought by Syrian soldiers from the Euphrates Valley Dam construction site, and displayed them on the shelves of his shop between Brillo pads and small bags of Turkish coffee.

When we got back to the campus, I took my new acquisition straight to Leila Badre, the AUB museum curator, to see if I had bought a genuine antiquity or not. By a simple water test, she determined that it was three original parts of different statues pieced together—well reconstructed and not of great value. I was delighted; it was not the monetary value I was interested in but rather in the actual possession of an object that provided a tangible link with a Middle Eastern civilization that had flourished thousands of years earlier. There was reassurance in holding in one's hand the creation of an artist who had lived so long ago and who surely had within him or her the potential for all the same good and evil and joys and sorrows that we had.

The next day the news was not good. The Israeli army was

expected to get out of the Chouf mountains south of Beirut, where they were receiving too many casualities, and to regroup further south. This had a destabilizing effect on the configuration of elements involved because the Israelis had a talent for setting different factions in Lebanon against each other, especially when they were about to withdraw from a certain region. People were hoping for a settlement between the Christians and the Druzes in the Chouf region before the departure of the Israelis. There was a lot of shelling going on in many mountain regions, and we learned that an AUB student had been killed when a shell exploded close to her car in the Keserwan area, near the mountains where we had been ten days earlier.

.   .   .

That night we went to a dinner party at the American ambassador's residence. The former foreign minister, who was one of the guests, sounded gloomy about the future of Lebanon, whether by disposition or by some information he was privy to. The American ambassador sounded rather optimistic, for perhaps similar reasons. In any case, he had a right to feel optimistic about the world when he had, only four months earlier, survived the bombing of the U.S. Embassy.

Much to Andrew's delight, the American Navy fleet commanders came to our home for lunch on Sunday afternoon, August 27, along with several AUB families. They arrived in two jeeps with an escort car full of Marine guards. Our naval guests looked around incredulously as they walked into the Eden-like setting of the Marquand House garden. One of the commanders came into the house, saw the piano, and asked if we would mind if he played. The other commander wanted to do some bird-watching and photography. I hoped that Andrew was taking note of the fact that U.S. Navy officers could be interested in things other than war and weapons.

A new round of political problems started while we were having lunch. At about 2:30, Lebanese army checkpoint soldiers near the Shiite area around the airport shot at two people who went through their barrier without stopping. By evening, fighting was spreading. U.S. Marines and Shiites were fighting at the airport, which closed at 7:30, while we were at a movie theater near the campus with the Dodd family seeing *The French Lieutenant's Woman*. We returned to the Dodd's apartment in the AUB faculty building for supper where we listened to the news and spent the evening sitting on their balcony, conjecturing on what might be about to happen. Meanwhile, Lebanese leaders were at the same time having talks in Paris with Ambassador McFarlane, head of the American negotiation team, unable to have a peaceful discussion in Lebanon—but able to do so in Paris while indulging in fine wine and cuisine.

There was widespread shelling that night and intermittently throughout the next morning. We heard that the Shiites and the Lebanese Army were fighting, rather than the Druze and the Christians (the battle that many had been anticipating), but nobody knew for sure what was happening. It was hard to believe that we had been traveling around the country so freely in the first two weeks after our arrival. Now we could not even go swimming or play tennis because of the danger of stray bullets.

Malcolm kept on working in his office, absorbed in getting through a huge pile of papers and, therefore, distracted from thinking about the fighting. Andrew's natural interest in weapons gave him a certain detachment about the shelling going on around us as he analyzed who was firing shells from where by listening for the length of time between firing and landing noises. Unable to maintain the cool of my husband and my son, I jumped every time a shell fell. No longer was the shelling noise like distant thunder; rather, it seemed to be getting closer and closer. By late afternoon the buildup of tension and the inability to concentrate on anything except the shelling left me in a state of unaccustomed jitters. In desperation, when a period of quiet came, I went out to the deserted campus to run as hard as I could through the hot, sticky dusk.

Later that evening, Mahmoud, the son of the former Marquand House cook Muhammad, dropped by. When Muhammad's family home was bombed, he had brought his wife and children to live in the servants' room of Marquand House. At the time, David Dodge was acting president and not living in the president's residence, so Muhammad's family tended to spill over into the rest of the house, experiencing freedom and luxury which they quickly grew used to. When I was visiting Malcolm the year before, I had observed that the phone rang as often for them as it did for Malcolm, and we would often encounter Mahmoud and his girlfriend on the front porch as they and we were coming into our house.

Mahmoud was an AUB student and, from what we had heard, a so-called Shiite Christian Fundamentalist. In Lebanon, all sorts of religious and political combinations were possible, but this one was particularly unusual. Mahmoud, by nature a bit obsequious, or perhaps believing he had perpetual rights of access, stopped by to gratuitously let us in on what was happening in the battle going on around us. "Some Amal students have taken over the TV station," he told us in a voice of authority. Amal was a Shiite faction, so we didn't know if Mahmoud was pleased or disappointed. He went on to advise us not to let Andrew go on campus by himself. "Many Shiites have Khomeini antennae," he explained mysteriously. This brought to mind the fact that there had been rumors of student involvement in the kidnapping of David Dodge.

. . .

More evidence of student political involvement came that evening when Peter Dodd phoned us to say he had been walking their dog on the campus and observed students putting up political posters in a "calculated and organized manner that was quick and efficient." Later, when Malcolm and I walked over to his office to make phone calls home to the United States, it was hard to resist the temptation to pull them down. Not only did they give an unsightly appearance to the campus but they were politically inflammatory and, therefore, against the rules of the university, which Malcolm was trying so hard to enforce. The security guards advised us that it would be best to leave them for a few days, and then they would take them down.

That night was quiet, and the BBC confirmed the next morning that fighting had subsided. There was no ping of tennis balls the next morning when we awoke at 6:00, so we seized the opportunity to run down and get a court. The silence was eerie—no planes coming in, no noise in the city, and no one on campus except for a couple of joggers on the green field. Hassan served Malcolm and me breakfast on the terrace outside the dining room, torn up from the reconstruction work which was now at a standstill because the workmen couldn't come through the fighting from their homes to work. Pungent white flowers of the big frangipani tree shading us dropped occasionally onto the table, looking delicate and waxlike and perfectly formed. The Mediterranean sparkled bright aqua-blue in the morning sunlight through the big umbrella pines at the edge of our garden. No sound broke the strange silence.

By afternoon shelling started again, as if all the fighters had awakened at once to renew battle after a respite for eating and sleeping. While Andrew settled down to watch videos, Malcolm and I spent the afternoon reading and napping as if there were a bad storm outside. In an odd way, it was rather cozy.

We were surprised that evening when a guest we had invited for a drink, Mr. al-Haj, arrived at our door as if nothing unusual had been happening all day. He said he had been stopped at many different checkpoints on the way and asked to show his identification. As a Druze, he was controversial, but as the banker and financial adviser of Rafik Hariri, his name carried much weight. Like his boss, he was interested in seeing AUB survive and thrive and had come to talk about plans for financing a new faculty apartment building. We could not sit out on the terrace for fear of falling bullets, so we sat in the living room and looked out the window at the lights twinkling on the other side of the bay in East Beirut, wondering if someone over there was deliberately aiming shells at us. As we sipped our gin and tonics, there were a couple of loud booms that sounded very close. I jumped involuntarily and almost spilled my drink. "Don't worry," Mr. al-Haj said to me. "No one wants to shell AUB. This place is always safe. You'll get used to the explosions. My wife used to be afraid of them too, but she got used to them." I tried to find reassurance in these thoughts, but I wasn't sure of the logic behind them, regardless of how well intended they were.

During the night, the shelling got worse. Andrew came into our room with his mattress to be away from the vulnerable side of the house. We turned on the air conditioner to block out the noise outside, still too new to these conditions to know that we should not stay on a top floor when shelling was going on.

When something seemed to explode directly over the campus around 10:00 P.M., we had a call from security to ask where the keys to the shelters for the dorm women were. Malcolm, who had been plagued by an irritating rash, was taking a medicated bath which the doctor had told him would be ineffective if interrupted. When I called to him to come to the phone, he asked me to tell the security officers that he didn't know where the keys were kept and to look for them at the dorms, and if they didn't find them to call back in fifteen minutes. This struck me as out of character on Malcolm's part, and I couldn't understand that any health problems should prevent him from coming to the phone and meeting the responsibilities of his office in these particular circumstances. Is this what happens to people when they've been living through a war for a long time, I wondered? If it was, then that was all the more reason for us to get out of Beirut while we still could. I said to him with irritation, "You're the president of this university. Would you please close your book and get out of the bath and come to the phone." Andrew, who was thoughtfully tape recording the explosions as they were going on, caught this historic conversation as well.

As the night went on with crashing noises outside keeping us awake, Andrew came and got into our bed just like old times when he was younger. At one point during the night he observed, "This isn't a real night; it's just like passing the time waiting for it to be morning." I replied, "What makes you think the day will be any different?"

At breakfast, Hassan said he had taken his wife and children to a friend's building that had a basement used for a shelter. On the way back, he had bought vegetables and fruits from a vendor cart. For the past eight years these vendors and their carts had been the first signs of life to reappear after intense fighting. We learned that several shells and pieces of shrapnel had fallen on the campus during the night. So much for the words of our guest the night before.

True to the common pattern, after the morning lull when fighters took a nap and citizens bought supplies for the day, the shooting started again. Andrew and I sat downstairs in Marquand House and listened to the tape he had made of the previous night's explosions, as if the present noises weren't horrible enough. I resorted to writing in my journal to let off steam.

> All of us—Malcolm, Andrew and me—completely in character
> in Andrew's tape. Huge shell just exploded nearby, maybe on

the campus. Then whizzing of rockets or shells going overhead. We saw the white spray of one that landed in the water. Now quiet again—so eerie. Like hitting your head against a wall because it feels so good when you stop. Thank goodness for a temporary lull. Can't believe I sounded so cool and calm in the tape when I felt/feel so agitated inside. I jump every time a shell explodes. Andrew is genuinely fascinated. Shells are falling every minute—very close. I am terribly frightened, but Andrew isn't. Malcolm is in his office. All this brings out his impatience. Can't tell if he is hiding his fears or genuinely less afraid than I am . . .

We don't know who is shelling us. Nobody knows for sure. We hear the army is gaining control of Beirut, but what good will that do if the Syrians are shelling from the mountains. Their fire is so high and can cover so much area. I hear Hassan's radio from the kitchen playing a John Philip Sousa march. Hassan has been through the whole civil war in this house. Now he is singing. He and Andrew are at the front door seeing where things are landing.

All I could think of was how much I wanted to be anywhere else but where I was at that moment: I would like to be evacuated if it were possible, but Malcolm would never leave and I'm not sure if I should stay with him or follow my instincts for survival. These are very strong, as are those for protecting my child.

That afternoon while Malcolm was out inspecting shell damage on the tennis courts near the women's dorm, a call came from his secretary to say that John was on the telex from Athens asking whether or not he should try to come to Beirut by boat now that the airport had closed again. Andrew and I dashed from Marquand House across the short distance to Malcolm's office where we had a telex conversation with John. We agreed that, unless the situation changed miraculously in the next few days, he would go to Cairo where we had many friends he could stay with while he looked for a job. Then we would commute for visits whenever possible.

.   .   .

Malcolm was home when Andrew and I returned. The shelling seemed to have stopped for awhile so we sat in our living room instead of the inside hallways where Andrew and I had taken refuge earlier. Hassan served us tea, which I drank with shaky hands.

The tea and the blessed quiet after the shattering noise of the last few hours brought relief. The three of us sat there not saying much. The only noise was the rattling of my cup and saucer as I lifted them. Andrew and Malcolm held theirs quite steady.

Suddenly the hour-long lull was broken by two thundering crashes. I jumped and ran back to the interior hallway; Andrew and Malcolm followed. "Those must be from Syrian-backed parties in the mountains," Malcolm assessed, and Andrew added, "Seems as if they are aiming for AUB or the American offices in the British Embassy." (After the bombing of the American Embassy the staff moved some of their operations to the British Embassy down the street.) Suddenly there were three more explosions closer than the first two. Andrew blurted out that he wished Malcolm were teaching at UCLA and that we were living in Pacific Palisades. I felt the same way at that moment but was glad Andrew had said it instead of me. I was Malcolm's partner in this job, which we had decided to do together, but at that moment it was hard to remember the commitment. Malcolm, no doubt, had his uncertainties too, but this was not the time to discuss them. He went to the phone to call the security guards at the main gate of the university to find out where the damage had occurred. "Two of the shells landed on Rue Artois [just behind Rue Bliss, a block from AUB]. The Greek Orthodox church was hit and the family in the house next door was killed."

I recorded the rest of those events of August 29 in my diary the next day:

> Finally got Malcolm to talk about what we should look ahead to, i.e. whether or not Andrew and I should leave and go to Cairo if it were possible—that I should not look reproachfully at him every time a shell explodes, as if to say why did he get us into this—whether or not this is a viable job anymore—the fact that all that has happened in the last three days was completely out of the realm of what we would have predicted. . . .
>
> We slept in our own rooms last night after things calmed down in the late afternoon and evening with the idea of moving downstairs immediately if shelling started again. Left air conditioner off because of electricity shortage and to be able to hear what was happening. I felt like I was on guard duty, so slept lightly. I almost wanted to stay awake to savor the wonderful

relief of not being shelled and to be able to waken Malcolm and Andrew if it started again. The protective instincts returned when basic survival was not at stake. Yesterday I would have forsaken my desire to be with Malcolm and grabbed Andrew to run for the first helicopter, had there been one.

The war in Lebanon was like the weather in normal places. When it was bright, people went out and had a good time; when it wasn't they stayed in. As the Lebanese Army asserted more control over West Beirut in the next day or two, the weather improved. Workmen returned to complete the renovation of our house, shoppers poured into the streets, and at the AUB beach, water-skiers whizzed by with their usual abandon. I paid the visit to the women's dorms which I had promised my mother-in-law I would make to check up on their needs. She would have been surprised at the great difference in the present day atmosphere, but knowing her she would have applauded the sight of girls sitting in the lounge with their male guests watching TV and signs on the walls announcing coed sports and social events. I visited briefly with the two head residents who were saying good-bye to students going home at the end of the summer session, and made plans for regular meetings throughout the school year to air dorm needs and problems.

At home Andrew continued his normal summer habit of sleeping until 10:00 A.M., and then having a leisurely breakfast, chatting with Hassan and Dalia, fooling around on the piano, playing with his collection of shrapnel and spent bullets, checking with the Dodd boys about the latest round of horrors in their respective neighborhoods. Then when it was time for lunch, he claimed to have been bored all morning.

Malcolm and I again discussed the possibility of Andrew and me going to Cairo for a couple of weeks to have a break from the war. We could be with John while he was getting settled, see all our friends there, and perhaps have Andrew attend Cairo American College until the American Community School in Beirut opened. With the Dodd boys about to leave for school in England, Andrew would have no friends to visit and might pay even more attention to matters of war than he already was.

It was thought that the fighting might get worse again after the Israeli withdrawal from the Chouf in the next few days and that conditions were good at present for anyone who wanted to drive out through the mountains to leave. We talked to Haj Omar who agreed, "If you're going to go, better go today than tomorrow, tomorrow better than the day after. I take you this afternoon." The Dodds were pleased at the prospect of having a way to get their boys to the airport in Amman where they could get a plane to England and on to their respective schools. We agreed with Haj Omar that he would pick us up after lunch and drive us to Damascus through the mountains north of Jounieh. From there we would hire a taxi to Amman.

It had been little more than a year since Malcolm had left us to go to Lebanon in August 1982, and now it somehow seemed that the tables were turned. He was the one to stay behind and we were going off on an adventure. I did not like leaving him, but I was thrilled at the prospect of going to Egypt and seeing John, and of getting away from the shelling.

CHAPTER 18

The School Year Opens

*I*n Cairo, we stayed first with AUC friends and then in the
unoccupied house of an absent professor for a few weeks, visited
our friends, and saw John find a good job and an apartment. Andrew had a brief stint at his former school, Cairo American College, and we all went on a snorkeling-diving trip to the Red Sea at
the tip of the Sinai Penninsula. It was the kind of trip to Egypt we
had been looking forward to as a perquisite to living in Beirut,
but preferably at a time of our choice and with all of us together.

Malcolm was able to join us for a long weekend by traveling
by boat to Cyprus and then flying to Cairo. He was proud to see
that John had settled himself so well and happy to be in contact
with the outside world. He wrote to Susie and Hans:

> I had a lovely visit to Cairo last weekend to see Mom and the
> boys, and found a stack of letters from you that John had carried
> to Cairo a month before. But it's discouraging to be so out of
> touch! All depends on Beirut Airport remaining open. Life is
> better here now than it was when Mom and Andrew left, and
> will improve greatly when they return tomorrow, but it's been
> pretty discouraging and there still is an atmosphere of gloom
> and apprehension. People are fed up and appalled to realize that
> after a year of relative quiet they are now in for it all over again.
> And the country is crawling with refugees from bombed out
> villages, Druzes escaping from Maronites and vice versa. No one
> gives the country more than cautious odds now to pull itself out
> of the mess.

There have been several times when the US navy fired its

259

five inch guns, but the USS New Jersey, a World War II battleship that Reagan sent here, has not fired its celebrated 16 inch
shells, each of which weighs as much as a Volkswagen and can
travel 27 miles. . . . I have tried to picture hundreds of Volks-
wagens raining down on our tennis court in Ainab.

Everything is quiet now and normal life has sort of resumed.
I went to a fancy lunch in Ashrafieh today, and met the former
foreign minister who generally predicted collapse and failure.
We are trying to open AUB Oct. 24 and collect a greatly increased tuition fee from our students whose families have been
devastated by depression and destruction. I don't know if it will
work. At least we can blame everything on Syria and Israel, so I
guess it's OK. If somebody will just fix up the tennis courts
below Marquand House, including some major remodeling. It
reminds me of the dictum in Parkinson's Law to the effect that
institutions tend to invest heavily in physical improvements and
expansions just on the eve of their collapse.

On October 5, Andrew and I returned to Beirut, secure in the
knowledge that the airport had finally reopened and the American
Community School and AUB had set a time to begin the fall
semester. On the crowded Middle East Airlines flight, while Andrew was extolling each new battleship that had arrived in the
harbor in our absence, I looked at the passengers around us and
wondered what compelling reasons they had for going to Lebanon
in these precarious times. We squeeeezed onto the airport bus with
all the other returning refugees, but were soon whisked off by an
official and ushered into a waiting limousine for the two-minute
ride to the terminal where we were met by a beaming Malcolm,
the airport director, and the usual contingent of AUB drivers and
officials.

The tranquillity of the AUB campus and the ease of our life
there presented an ironic contrast to the daily battles we had fought
in Cairo against dust, dirt, traffic, crowds, and noise. I relished
walking on clean floors in bare feet, having a washing machine to
throw our clothes into, and our maid Zeinab to iron them—and
strolling through the lush green of the campus with Malcolm to
the tennis courts or down to the beach to swim. With the help
of our friend Rima, Malcolm had continued our redecorating project. The original high dining room ceiling was now restored, and

soft wall-to-wall carpet covered the cold tile floors. The newly framed, autographed photographs of Teddy Roosevelt and Mark Twain hung on either side of a large mother-of-pearl inlaid mirror from Damascus which Rima had loaned to the house from her collection. We would have to begin soon to redecorate the living room.

On our second night home, we went to a farewell party at the home of the American ambassador who was being transferred. The rumor was that the Gemayel government perceived him to be unnecessarily sympathetic to the Palestinians and the cause of pan-Arabism. The war seemed remote or somehow make-believe as we sipped our drinks and chatted with the players in the Lebanese drama whom I had been reading about in *Time* magazine during the past weeks in Cairo: Ambassador Robert McFarlane, the new chief negotiator who had replaced Philip Habib; Colonel Tim Garrity, commander of the Marine contingent in Lebanon; Pierre Gemayel, the head of the Gemayel clan and father of the president; the U.S. fleet commanders who had come to lunch at Marquand House a few days before Andrew and I left for Cairo; members of the Lebanese cabinet; and assorted ambassadors, U.N. representatives, and AUB officials.

There was a general mood of discouragement, though McFarlane and his team made optimistic statements which did not ring true. Ambassador Dillon stated frankly that he thought another round of fighting was likely. The newspaper photos of him emerging dust-covered and shaken from the embassy explosion six months earlier came to mind, and I presumed that he could not be too unhappy at the prospect of leaving his post. Many of the guests asked Malcolm and AUB Vice President Samir Thabet how the university could be planning to open on October 24 with such political division in the country. "Aren't you going to have student clashes?" asked a man with cold green eyes and a sinister expression which gave the impression that he was planning to instigate the troubles himself. I learned later that he was the representative of the Lebanese forces in the United States, though I could not imagine exactly what the job entailed. It was easy to wonder whether some people in Lebanon had perhaps learned to thrive on war for their livelihood and as a way of life.

On Susie's advice in a recent letter, Malcolm wrote a letter to my parents to explain the political situation in Lebanon to them so they would know what they should and should not worry about.

> Of course I know how concerned you are about our having taken the plunge to move here, after the deterioration in the past six weeks. I have to admit that I didn't anticipate it, for ever since the Israeli invasion a year ago, it looked as if Israel had done a thorough job of cleaning out the illegal gangs and had turned over the city of Beirut to the central government once and for all. But it has turned out that they [Israel] had their own reasons for failing to disarm the private armies in the mountains, one Christian and one Druze Muslim, and even went so far as to encourage the two of them to fight each other, thereby paving the way for Israel and Syria to stay on in parts of the country at the expense of the Lebanese government.
>
> If we see during the next year or so that there's no chance of doing more than just limping along, and that Lebanon can't accommodate a real university anymore, then we'll call it quits and come back to the States. Ann and I have talked about this many times, of course. She has been understandably nervous these past few months—so have I—and sometimes wonders out loud what the hell we're doing here; I wonder the same thing silently. But allowing for variations of mood and perception between us, I think she and I both see it basically the same way. We're not here to be heroes or foolish romantics and we are not interested in getting ourselves killed, but simply to do something extremely challenging and exciting that we have always looked forward to, as long as it remains possible. We don't want to turn and run at the first sign of trouble, especially since part of the job for both of us is that other people depend on us to give a lead and set a good example. But if the job can't be done effectively, that will be that, and we'll not hesitate to leave, with due notice and in a decorous way. So far, despite everything, I'd say we are far from about to reach that conclusion. A great deal will depend on the events of the next two months, as we find out whether it's possible for the Lebanese (or anyone else) to govern this country. It looks like their last chance.

On October 8, still in a mood of celebration after Andrew's and my return from Cairo, we celebrated Malcolm's fifty-second birthday. Had we known it would be his last, we would have done nothing differently. We filled the day with all his favorite activities, a rousing tennis game and then off to the mountains of Faraya north of Beirut with our good friends Ralph and Laure Crow who had taught at AUB for many years. In a simple restaurant by a spring in a canyon of apple and poplar trees, we ate our favorite Lebanese food, shish kebab, tabouleh, humus, and baba ganoush washed down with arak. Andrew was, as always, a lively addition to the day. After lunch the three of us walked to one of Malcolm's favorite childhood sites, a huge natural bridge in a canyon of dramatic rock formation. We climbed up to the top of the bridge and sat there awhile; Malcolm was clearly in a mood of total satisfaction as he enjoyed the country of his childhood with close friends and at least part of his family, situated in the job of AUB president for which he was so ideally suited.

The next few weeks were filled with preparing for the opening of classes at AUB, continuing with the remodeling and decorating of Marquand House and Malcolm's office, and getting Andrew started in ninth grade at the American Community School. There was not time to worry about the political situation, though it was an inescapable backdrop to all that went on and always a major topic at luncheon or dinner parties. I wrote in my journal: "Cease-fire continues precariously while all sorts of shooting and shelling go on around the country and participants of all parties haggle over how and when to hold reconciliation talks. No matter what plan is devised it will be knocked down by the Syrians who seem to have all the cards at the moment."

On October 19 there was terrible shelling off and on all night that kept us and everyone awake. We guessed that it was probably caused by the Syrians trying to show displeasure over the choice of a location for a reconciliation meeting. "They would show displeasure over any location," Malcolm quipped. The next day, despite the heavy shelling of the previous night, students flocked to register for the new semester. As I helped with registration in the English Department, I was impressed with how attractive and well behaved the students were. My thoughts turned back twenty-nine years to the fall of 1954 when I had registered at AUB and found my new classmates to be extremely helpful and polite. Still bearing the same good manners, these students of the eighties were dressed in blue jeans rather than the chic fashions of the fifties and resembled American college kids. It was hard to realize that they came from families representing dozens of different political factions who had been fighting one another for the past eight years. Most of them were from the silent majority of Lebanese who were caught in the middle of factional fighting, but some students were very politicized.

In order to avoid some of the political problems that had been a part of campus life in previous years, the administration requested that, because of the present conditions of civil war, students sign a pledge at the time of registration promising not to become involved in any political activities on campus. A few students began protesting this mandatory pledge. About twenty-five students went on strike in West Hall, the student social center just behind the wall of the back garden of Marquand House. They held up registration procedures by trying to interfere with picture taking for identity cards. Registration continued anyway, but it was considerably slowed down. "It's the same old students who usually spearhead these strikes with instigation from outsiders," Malcolm observed. "One of them has been a student at AUB for seven years. Now he's working on his second M.A. It's hard to keep these dissidents out." At one point during the discussions we invited the strike leaders to our house for tea. They came wearing their best clothes and carried a bouquet of roses for me. The polite but hackneyed quality of the conversation reflected the traditional good manners and respect toward elders of the Lebanese as well as the overused rhetoric of veteran protesters. I vainly hoped that they could be swayed by the warmth of our home and by Malcolm's disarming humor. After their departure, he remarked half seriously, "They're probably back reporting to their militia leaders right now on the contents of our living room."

Campus life went on as usual during the week of the strike. We went to an afternoon lecture series on the history of Arab geographers by one of the leading authorities on the subject of Arab science, our old friend Ted Kennedy. Ted and his wife Mary Helen had come to AUB to teach shortly after World War II and had raised their children and built their careers there much as Elsa and Stanley Kerr had done a generation earlier. They had bought the Kerr family house in Ainab when Elsa and Stanley retired in

1961 and hoped to eventually retire there along with our friends Ralph and Laure Crow who had bought one of the other Ainab houses. Now the Ainab hilltop was a less inviting place, having been occupied by various militia groups at different times and in the line of fire of Israeli planes and American navy ships. The Crows and the Kennedys, along with other expatriate families, had remained at AUB throughout the civil war and planned to continue to do so. They would ultimately be forced to leave a few years hence when the spate of kidnappings of Westerners occurred.

On the morning of October 23, Malcolm went to his office at 6:00 A.M. to try and catch up on desk work after being preoccupied for so long with student strike negotiations. At about 6:20 I heard an all too familiar loud explosion noise. It could have been a small explosion close by or a big one further away. Anywhere else, it might have been a sonic boom, but not in Lebanon. It sounded too much like the boom we heard the day an assassination attempt occurred against Walid Jumblat the previous December. I called Malcolm to see if he was all right. He said he would finish what he was doing and come home. A short time later, Radwan Mawlawi, AUB's security officer, phoned to say there had been two explosions, one on the French base of the peace-keeping force and one on the American Marines near the airport. No one knew yet how many casualties there were. Malcolm came home for breakfast, but we were stunned and could hardly eat. The numbing effects of the news continued as we listened to the radio and heard the casualty list grow. These were the boys with young, innocent, clean-cut faces who jogged on the campus and played basketball with Andrew and said, "Yes Ma'am" at the end of every sentence. They were military men, but they were the same ages as our boys and had parents who were our contemporaries who loved their sons as we loved ours. Our numbness grew into paralysis. Casualty figures kept rising and finally when several phone calls came asking if we were still having our faculty garden party, we realized we had to get ourselves together to start the wheels in motion to cancel it.

When Andrew awoke at his lordly hour of ten and came down for breakfast, we told him what had happened. His reactions to the explosions and deaths of so many Marines was unemotional but stunned. He said, "Oh God," and then started to ask very matter-of-fact questions about what had happened. I wondered if this monstrous deed would dampen his enthusiastic interest in weapons and war. We continued the day in our paralyzed state, broken occasionally by phone calls and visits from other administrators and later several professors who dropped by to discuss the student strike and negotiations. There were no new words that one could think of to communicate with each other at length about the explosions and the death rate that was climbing into the hundreds; people just agreed on how horrible and tragic and unbelievable it was and left it at that.

The thought struck me often that day of how many times I had heard people in Lebanon say, "You learn to get used to these things," and of how ludicrous that seemed. Why should anyone ever get used to or want to get used to the shooting, shelling, terrorist attacks, or wanton violence?

Finally, in midafternoon, Malcolm and I started to unpack cartons of our books which had been stacked up in the study for weeks. It was an odd, defiant act, unpacking at a moment when circumstances would seem to dictate packing up.

Later Andrew and I went to visit the Marines who had been brought to the AUB hospital. In the emergency room we were met by the same nurse who had worked in the newborn nursery when Susie, John, and Steve were born and brought them to me to be fed. I had not seen her since. I did not know then that I would see her once more three months later when I went to the emergency room to find out if Malcolm was alive or not.

· · ·

Our visit was more for our sakes than for the injured Marines—an attempt to do something healing when there was really nothing that we could do. The chocolate chip cookies I had made could not possibly be appreciated by unconscious men whose heads were bulging and eyes popping from the horrendous explosion they had been through that morning. Many were swathed in bandages and still dazed from anesthetic. We met other people also visiting; a tall, attractive doctor from the battleship *Iwo Jima,* who spoke to each Marine caringly and reassuringly. Probably the most helpful visitors were several young women from AUB and the American Community School who sat for long periods of time at the bedsides of the Marines, holding their hands and talking softly.

The bombings did nothing to deter the dissident students from keeping up their protests against the new student pledge of no political involvement they were being required to sign at registration. They occupied West Hall just behind our house and played loud music all night long. Malcolm had appointed a negotiating team of the appropriate religious mix: the Muslim Dean of Students; a Shiite professor of business management; and a Greek Orthodox professor of political science. They did the direct negotiating with the students and then reported back to Malcolm. He held a meeting with the faculty to explain the progress of the negotiations. Finally a compromise was reached to make a change in the wording of the pledge which did not fundamentally alter its meaning. Registration would resume the next day; classes would begin the day after. The successful negotiations were a victory of principle for Malcolm, and we hoped, though without much optimism, that the mandatory pledge would prove effective.

Perhaps what lay behind the words of our well-wishing friends when they assured me that one learned to get used to the atrocities of the civil war was that the ongoing demands of daily life prevented one from dwelling continually on the fears and dangers of war. Each day that passed after the bombing of the French and U S bases, our attention was drawn increasingly to the needs and activities of our family and the university. An AUC friend, George Scanlon, was coming to lecture at AUB on Islamic art and would bring us mail from John in Cairo. (Mail services in both countries were unreliable so travelers often became mail couriers.) There was George's schedule to arrange, and date bread to bake for John, and letters to write for George to take back to Cairo. I had my sophomore English class to prepare for, our dispirited new cook to coax and train, the faculty reception to reschedule, and French homework to struggle over with Andrew. And Malcolm was busy being the president.

On October 26, the fall term began and I met the students in the class I was to teach that semester, the second level of four English classes AUB students were required to take covering communication skills and literature. There were twenty-five students in the class with a mixture of Christian and Muslim names. From the autobiographies they wrote that first day, I learned that some had to travel from the east side of Beirut every day across the Green Line, which separated the mostly Christian east from the mostly Muslim western portions of the city. These divisions had become more pronounced in the years of civil war when Christians or Muslims, who had lived together in the same neighborhoods, felt pressured by the power of local militia groups to move to areas where their own religion predominated. Some of the Christian students in my classes had grown up in West Beirut near AUB and now lived in the eastern part of the city.

I had been told by my fellow teachers that the previous high quality English of entry level students at AUB had suffered as a result of high school education being disrupted by the war and the depletion of good English teachers. Perhaps it had been better before, but I found their written language to be quite good and their spoken language very good. All their autobiographies contained an expression of their feelings of good fortune at being able to attend AUB, which they considered their best guarantee of success for the future. As for my feelings at being their teacher, I wrote in my journal that evening, "Strange to realize that a goal of twenty-nine years is being fulfilled—I'm teaching at AUB!"

In the next few weeks, I had a chance to see how students at AUB had been surviving for the last eight years. Just as I had learned how daily life went on in our family and in others' in spite of war, I watched my students carry on their studies in the midst of sporadic fighting. They often had to study without electricity, and there was always the uncertainty of when shelling would begin again and they would have to move to an interior corridor or basement shelter. The most difficult problem for them was determining when it was unsafe to commute to the AUB campus. There were different ways in which people's antennae told them how the fighting would be going on a given day—the radio, the taxi driver news network, rumors passed around by neighbors, and a kind of sixth sense about whose turn it was to begin fighting whom. There was a similarity to weather forecasting in trying to predict what the war was going to be like on a given day. My students were experts in this art, having had eight years of training during their childhood.

As the torrential rains and thunderstorms of the Beirut winter began, people took comfort in the fact that militia fighters preferred not to go out and fight in the rain. But this was never certain. I described in my journal a rainy Saturday in late October: "We tried out our new video machine this afternoon. Andrew, Malcolm, and I curled up on the couch watching *Chariots of Fire,* feeling cozy and falsely secure after the last few days of no nearby shelling. Thunder and lightning started up outside, and we had to turn the sound down to listen to make sure it wasn't shelling. Thought we heard distant shelling, maybe in the mountains but impossible to be sure with so much thunder. The difference seems to be that thunder rolls and booms while shells just boom."

The next day, the rains continued intermittently, but we went ahead with our plans for a picnic to the ancient seaside town of Byblos with our friends Leila Badre and Don Schanche, a correspondent for the *Los Angeles Times* who had come from Rome to cover the Marine bombing and the reconciliation talks. Byblos and the route up the coast from Ras Beirut was not currently an area of conflict, and we had fallen into the local habit of hoping that a rainy day meant less fighting. The rain stopped long enough for us to have our picnic on the stage of the Roman amphitheater, sitting on sarcophagi and long fallen Aswan granite pillars. Because of the climatic and political conditions, there were few sightseers around, but some of the local inhabitants came out for a walk over the remnants of this city of their ancestors. The colors of the sky and sea rewarded our intrepidness in a dramatic display of dark blues changing to light greens with the sharp contrasts of whitecaps in a raging sea. As Don spoke of his pessimistic views of the political situation in Lebanon, the turbulent beauty of the scene behind him seemed a fitting backdrop to his assessment of the future for this troubled land.

In November, Malcolm began preparing for his trip to America to attend the AUB Board of Trustees meeting in New York. He would also visit our respective parents and Steve on a swing around the United States to interview prospective AUB faculty and administrators. I regarded his trip with a mixture of relief that he would be outside the war zone for a while and anxiety at the thought of our being separated again.

I wrote in my journal on November 7:

Still feeling pangs of Malcolm's pending departure, even after all these years of his frequent traveling. So many things for both of us to do before he leaves. He is speedy and efficient—manages to keep his mind on everything that needs to be done without getting distracted. Ted and Mary Helen Kennedy have come to stay with us, refugees from the fighting in Ainab and general war in the Chouf [mountains southeast of Beirut]. Lovely to have them and good company for Malcolm's absence. Finished wrapping Christmas gifts and writing letters to all the family for Malcolm to deliver.

Malcolm's departure the next day meant I could start looking forward to his return rather than feeling depressed at the thought of his leaving. I knew my students and Andrew, plus the usual round of social activities, would be good distractions. I described them in my journal:

Had very good class discussion today on story by a Mexican author—quite symbolic, but students understood it and had lively discussion. Student conferences all morning to go over comps. Becoming very attached to these kids—all bright and most of them very hard working.

[And on another day] Played tennis with Mr. Mubarak, head of building maintenance who helped me look for antique furniture for Marquand House. Quite different from playing with Malcolm. "Lovely shot Madame." "Thank you Mr. Mubarak." "Hard luck Mrs. Kerr." "Thank you, Mr. Mubarak" . . .

Had dinner with Regiers and Heinekens this evening in the faculty apartments. [Frank Regier was kidnapped two years later and released after several months of captivity.] From the balcony, we looked down on the Corniche to the state of siege below. Marine posts, U.S. tanks, barbed wire, huge anti-truck barriers—all eerie in yellow street lights. Barriers being constructed around British Embassy against suicide attacks. No wonder faculty apartment residents are getting tense. It's raining and thundering hard now. Difficult to distinguish from U.S. jets flying around awhile ago—part of frequent night-time flights to show authority. Makes me angry. Wish Malcolm were here.

Malcolm had phoned me earlier that day from Texas on the account of a generous AUB alumnus who was his host. It was so good to hear his voice. He was full of news about his visit with

Steve at the University of Arizona and the fun they had had together. He had stayed in Steve's room and gone to watch his basketball practice and gotten acquainted with his coach, Lute Olson.
As I had suspected from my experience the previous year, he worried about our safety from the distance of the U.S. and all the
media coverage of the Middle East.

In mid-November fighting intensified in several areas. There
was heavy shelling in East Beirut which local analysts (that meant
everyone) said was probably intended to express displeasure over
recent talks between Syrian foreign minister Khaddam and President Gemayel. The Druzes don't like not being included in
the talks, it was stated, and many factions were concerned about
Syria's influence in Lebanon. The shelling was so loud one morning that it was hard to carry on classes, but my students were
remarkably attentive in spite of the noise. The classroom atmosphere gave some stability and civility to their lives in the midst of
turmoil.

The night before, bombs had been set off in front of three
Christian-owned shops. I recorded in my journal: "One of the
shops bombed last night was Wardi where our new living room
carpet (already paid for) awaits delivery. I wonder if it was burned.
The frequent shelling and now terrorist bombs get me down.
Sometimes I just want to take Andrew and get out of here—such
barbaric actions behind the polite and religious veneer of this society. It makes me angry and depressed."

The most serious fighting was now taking place in Tripoli,
Lebanon's second largest city to the north. Reports said that it was
worse than the fighting the previous summer when Arafat took
Beirut hostage. It was expected that the Syrian-backed Abu Musa
faction of the PLO would probably defeat the Arafat faction eventually, flattening the city of Tripoli in the process. Meanwhile, in
the southern part of Lebanon, the Israelis cut off the country at the
Awali River, requiring people living there to have Israeli-issued
residence permits to enter, but only on foot. Cars had to be left
outside. This was an insulting condition for the local residents.

The Chouf had been emptied of many inhabitants through the
months of shelling and Druze-Christian fighting. There was now
strong anti-American feeling among those who remained who believed it was American shelling that had killed their relatives.

Shiite groups in the southern suburbs continued to clash with the Lebanese army and were a likely source of some of the terrorist activities. In the Beka'a Valley Syrians had moved in SAM missiles and fighting persisted there.

.   .   .

Without Malcolm at home to talk to, I grew more and more pessimistic about all that was happening. I wrote in my journal:

> Beirut is choking itself on security which doesn't seem to guarantee protection from terrorist attacks anyway. The multinational peacekeeping force is being pulled further and further into the local morass. The embassies all look like fortresses. AUB is an indefensible place. Anyone can get a fake ID card to show to the guards or throw a bomb over the wall if they want to. Our local AUB guards who have been here forty years sit with a few Lebanese Army soldiers and some local police at the three entry gates but could be wiped out in a terrorist attack . . .
>
> I don't want Malcolm to come back here. He could be a target for anyone who wants to give vent to anti-American feelings. Why should he endanger his life for an institution that is no longer serving the purpose it used to? If anything were to happen to him, most people would accept it as God's will, and of necessity harden themselves to the fact as they must do to every other atrocity that goes on around here and continue with their daily affairs.

As had happened in late August when fighting had intensified, I thought of escaping to Egypt. I wrote:

> In state of nervousness and indecision about whether or not to take Andrew and go to Cairo for the upcoming four-day weekend. Would be so good to get out of here for awhile and to see John. Phoned Malcolm in New York to ask his advice and confess my nervousness. He had been up to New Hamphire to look at the Proctor School for Andrew as a possible place for him next year. Strange to think of Malcolm in a normal and predictable environment. Poured out all my fears and indecision about whether or not to go to Cairo. He said he had been worrying about us a lot. American newspapers gave a black picture of conditions in Lebanon. Said he had even entertained the thought

of quitting, but then rejected it of course, saying we couldn't quit in midstream. The same applies to my job. We must finish the year and then leave if we want to. Malcolm said his colleagues at UCLA want him back and have invited him as of July 1 if he wants to come. He advised against going to Cairo for fear of not being able to get back if the airport closed and then missing too many classes. Then half an hour later, he phoned back to say he wished we would go to Cairo and get away from all our worries here. I told him I had already decided not to go. Very disappointing not to see John.

A few days later I had a chance to talk over my concerns with some of my former AUB classmates when we were invited to tea at the home of Alice Fakhry whose husband Majid had been my philosophy professor. My roommate, Naziha Hamza Kineo, now a successful artist and mother of two AUB students was there and also Lillian Naaman, a classmate who had lived down the hall from us in the women's hostel. They all had children at AUB. There was lots of talk about our student days together and the good fortune of being able to see each other again—and about why we were all in Beirut in the midst of war. My friends represented some of the families that refused to leave their life in Beirut to become refugees in a new land. They relished the warmth and sociability of life there and were hesitant to move to the U.S. or Canada where people were more isolated from each other. They also wanted their children to study at AUB. They talked about ways they've devised of staying sane during the war. Naziha painted vivid and wrenching paintings of war, which I had seen at a recent exhibition, and many of them practiced meditation.

I confided to Lillian that I had been full of fears for our family's safety recently. She advised that I keep them to myself and not speak of them on campus. "Give the impression that nothing is bothering you. If you're afraid, don't sleep in Marquand House. It's unwise to reveal too much of one's feelings in Beirut." This would be easier advice to follow after Malcolm came home and I could pour out my fears to him.

Monday, November 21, was the Lebanese National Day. Students were released from classes in order to participate in orderly observances of the occasion, but it became a time of political outbursts which I described in my journal:

A horrible Lebanese Flag Day today. Shortly before 11:00 I was in a meeting with my colleagues in the English Department office when deafening noise of continuous rounds of shooting began just outside our building, closer than any I have ever experienced. My stomach felt like it was dropping out of my body. Some ran to windows to see what was happening. Others cautioned them, shouting that bullets could come through the windows. We moved to interior halls to wait and see what was happening—but of course no way of knowing for sure. That's the difficult thing about these "events," as people refer to them. You hear lots of noise but have no idea what's going on till it's all over and people begin to piece together what happened. Those who had been around a long time said it was probably the army shooting in the air to disperse demonstrating students. Later learned that a group of Phalangist students, perhaps from the Off Campus Program in East Beirut, had come to the campus to insist on having their own Flag Day ceremony after the one sanctioned by the university had been successfully completed. The first ceremony had presumably been a neutral one, but many claimed it was Muslim, thus causing some Christian students to think they should have their own ceremony . . .

Finished our meeting in the hallway. Shooting had stopped so we looked out the windows. Saw army forcing students out of the campus—then got word that entire campus was to be evacuated. Rumors flew about how many students were injured. As it turned out only one was hit by shrapnel, an innocent bystander whom I went to visit at the AUB hospital later in the day. His relatives filled the hospital room, a Druze family from Shwayfat who had moved to a hotel in Beirut because of the war. A moving sight to see all those people sitting there saying El Hamdulilah (Praise God) that their son was not harmed any more seriously than he had been. Interesting to observe the Middle Eastern cultural assumption that no one wants to be alone when he is ill. Brought back recollections of when I had had Steve in that hospital. People came and went, talking and smoking, some sitting awhile, some only saying hello and then leaving. Chocolates were immediately offered to each new visitor.

[Wednesday, November 23] No classes yesterday. [after the disturbances of the previous day] Sky was brilliant and air crisp. Complete quiet. Felt that soothing anesthetic effect after a time of violence, as if one's body provided a balm to counteract this abnormal, insane life in Beirut. Rima dropped by to discuss the progress of our redecorating—sat with Andrew and me while we had our breakfast. Reported that her children [students at AUB] and her friends were surprised that Flag Day had been sanctioned in the first place. She asked who was making decisions in Malcolm's absence. Was it widely known that Malcolm wasn't here so he would not be blamed for wrong decisions? Many people questioned why the army used guns instead of tear gas. Others reply that the army has not been trained in such techniques. Andrew's answer to Rima when she suggested that if Malcolm had been here it might not have happened, was that he would have decided to hold classes on Flag Day . . .

Al Reynolds [President of International College, the preparatory school adjacent to the AUB campus] and his wife Nancy came for dinner. He says that as head of IC, he is afraid for his own safety for the first time in ten years here—worries about the vulnerability of AUB to a terrorist attack as a secondary target now that all the embassies are so well protected. . . .

Students returned to campus today as if nothing had happened. Only notable difference was the presence of riot squad cars and police officers on campus. Walked into town to have my hair cut. A pleasure to be in the streets with normal hubbub of activity, colorful vegetable carts, ladies shopping—cool brisk air and bright sun. Even the piles of garbage didn't matter too much when the sky was so beautiful. Swam at the AUB beach at lunchtime. Weather has stayed warm enough for swimming all the time Malcolm has been gone.

[Saturday, November 26] Went to women's dorm open house in Van Dyke Hall with Fawzi and Yvonne al-Haj [AUB Dean of Students and wife]. Strange to see students living in what used to be Stanley Kerr's lab. Visited all the rooms on two floors—a party going on in each room with elaborate food, stereos playing American and European music, and friends, male and female gathered. Lebanese very good at socializing. Hard to believe that some of these students had been at each other's throats a few days earlier. Fawzi confirmed that they were.

[Sunday, November 27] Still feeling anxious and depressed, maybe because Malcolm is coming home today and I don't want him back in the danger zone. Distant bombing and shelling throughout the night. I keep worrying about College Hall or Marquand House being blown up—or maybe even the faculty apartments. Andrew loves to brag about his ability not to worry because it won't do any good—true enough.

[Later] Went to airport with Tanios and another AUB official to meet Malcolm. Roads were choked with security. Scary to drive through southern suburbs where there's so much discontent and concentration of Shiites and Muslim refugees from the south. Tanios shot through that quarter at about seventy miles per hour. Many roads blocked. Took us an hour to reach airport because of traffic. Malcolm already there waiting for us, looking wonderful. Instant feeling of relief to see him back—someone to share the worries and talk over everything with. He'll tell jokes about it all. He'll make good decisions based on clear thinking, maybe taking a little more time to think about all the angles than he did last year.

CHAPTER 19

Dreams and Goals Still Hoped For

M alcolm was in a mood of hopefulness after some success in the U.S. in recruiting good prospective candidates for jobs that badly needed filling at AUB. He was heartened to know that the attraction of joining a unique institution like AUB still held its old magic in spite of the war. Several interested candidates would be coming to visit the campus in the next few weeks. One was Vahe Simonian, the former minister of the Presbyterian Church in Pacific Palisades, who had officiated at Susie and Hans's wedding. His wife, Ani, and I had been classmates at AUB. Vahe and Ani had met in Beirut when he came from his home in Boston to study at the Near East School of Theology. Now he was interested in being the Director of Development for AUB. Other candidates would be coming to consider and be interviewed for the positions of dean of engineering and administrative vice president. With these positive events and the pleasure of returning to the tranquil beauty of Marquand House with its gardens, view of the Mediterranean, and Andrew and me still safely there, Malcolm was relaxed and happy—and so was I. Our life together resumed with a mixture of work, social activities, and intermittent intrusions of the civil war. We were learning what the Lebanese and, I suppose, people in any country at war learn: to carry on our daily life regardless of those intrusions.

I recorded in my journal on November 30:

6:00 A.M. tennis with Malcolm on indoor court—a fast game with new graphite racket he brought me. Malcolm relaxed and

277

well after his trip. So good to have him back—even though he's safer when he's out of here. He has so much work to catch up on . . .

My students quite a handful lately. We're getting to know each other very well. They are charming, attractive, responsive, energetic, and good humored, but also manipulative and opportunistic. Maybe this is the way all students are. Teaching them effectively requires organization of every minute of class time, keeping a fast and varied pace, constant checking to see if they have done their homework, and keeping up pressure of tests—also a sense of humor and being quick to respond to them. Challenging to teach and very hard work but extremely satisfying . . .

Declined lunch invitation to U.S. ambassador's—occasional shelling there lately, but a more constant problem is the terrible traffic due to strangling security conditions. Can't afford the time away from our work. Took sandwiches to AUB beach instead. Had to leave early when shelling started at the port. Sweet Mr. Basila [an AUB accountant who put his four children through AUB and two through medical school], a daily swimmer for the past thirty years, just lay there sunbathing as if nothing had happened. Said nobody wanted to shell AUB beach and if a random shot came, it was because his time was up."

[Thursday, December 1] President Gemayel in Washington, but not much hope of his achieving anything that will help the situation here. Even if the U.S. could persuade the Syrians to be more cooperative, the internal problems of Lebanon grow worse. Tripoli is a battle zone with Arafat holding out there. Several thousand Palestinian prisoners from the Ansari Camp in South Lebanon were exchanged for six Israeli prisoners in Tripoli. Students brought red roses to every classroom today in celebration . . .

The refugee problem in Lebanon grows worse with many residents fleeing from Tripoli. Southern suburbs of Beirut are full of impoverished Shiites seething with discontent and religious fervor. The U.S. government is reaffirming its alliance with Israel in a very loud voice—probably discouraged with trying to get the Arab countries to work together. Syria and Israel and the Multinational Forces occupy Lebanon—the Marines, Lebanese Army and local police occupy the AUB campus.

The results of the Reagan-Gemayel talks were not encouraging. Reagan made some remarks about wanting to restore Lebanon to the jewel it was but gave no indication that he would pressure Israel for concessions. While we had no reason for optimism on the political front, we continued to feel encouraged about conditions at AUB. The visit of Vahe Simonian, the first of several visitors to consider and to be considered for administrative positions, was a visible positive event for the university community.

The second evening of his visit, a dinner party was given in Vahe's honor by the university development officer, Nazieh Zeidan, and his wife who lived in the faculty apartments at the bottom of the campus. As Malcolm, Vahe, and I walked there through the campus on the road that leads down to the sea gate, we suddenly came upon a very tense American Marine, positioned behind a newly constructed cement block, anti-terrorist attack device. He was pointing his rifle right at us. When we challenged his being inside the campus, he said a sniper had fired one shot at them at their post on the edge of the campus ten minutes earlier from the College Hall clock tower. Malcolm told the Marine that he was the president of the university and no one had told him about it. The poor Marine, already scared stiff, became very polite and answered all his questions. Malcolm wanted to run right up to the Marine position that had been fired at to find out what was happening, which Vahe and I thought was a very foolhardy thing to do. We convinced him to go into the Zeidans' apartment and start phoning. He conceded and many phone calls back and forth to the embassy ensued. Malcolm was irate that the Marines had moved from the Corniche Road outside the lower campus wall near the sea into the campus without permission from the university. The presence of Marines on campus could be a great provocation for someone to attack. It was finally agreed that they would leave.

This episode was not the best way to begin a dinner party, especially one that was planned in order to convince Vahe that he should come to work for AUB. Discussion remained on the subject of the Marines for quite a while. Their bases should be moved further away from the campus, as should the offices of the American and British embassies whose close proximity to AUB, International College, and the American Community School endangered all those institutions. Even without the sniper incident the atmosphere of this social gathering would have been tense. Among the guests were the wives of the Minister of Health and the Minister of Foreign Affairs who were feeling the strain of having their husbands in public office in time of war and the threats to their safety which that involved. Conversation was filled with words and thoughts that were often in my mind—"sinister," "evil," "the impossible task of trying to accomplish anything," "people seeking hopeful news but unable to find any."

Shortly after we had finished dinner, a phone call came from the Marine Command saying that they believed the sniper shots had not come from the clock tower but from some point further away off campus. Once again, I and others felt the balm of relief that comes when immediate danger has passed, no matter how short-lived that calm is likely to be. The warmth of our hosts' hospitality, the bountiful dinner, and the good Lebanese wine had also had their calming effects. The durable capacity of the Lebanese to enjoy themselves came forth, and for the rest of the evening people slipped back into a mood of relaxed sociability.

These swings of mood when any reason for hope came along were characteristic of war-torn Lebanon and of AUB, both institutions that so many people wanted to see survive. There were plenty of vital signs of life that gave us good reason to be hopeful, which our visitor Vahe also saw. On Sunday morning after our adventurous evening of the night before, we took him to the Anglican service in the old German Chapel near the campus, known for the German missionaries who had built it. After the service, we went to the Goethe Institute for an art exhibit of local German painters, our favorite of whom was a professor in the AUB School of Architecture, Martin Geisen, whose work depicted Lebanon in war with a striking blend of realism and nostalgia.

Later in the day at a Sunday afternoon volleyball game with faculty in the Marquand House garden, friends brought a copy of the newly republished *Daily Star,* which had been out of print for several years. The English-language daily, known for honesty and even-handedness, had been a mainstay of life in West Beirut in pre-war days until the political assassination of its editor in the early years of the civil war. Now his son, Jamil Mruweh and his American wife had decided to reestablish the newspaper. This was a vital lifesign that brought confidence and hope to the community. The next day we said farewell to Vahe who was to leave by boat for Cyprus as the airport was currently closed. In his ten days with us, he had caught the AUB spirit, in spite of everything, and wanted to take the job as vice president for development. His decision buoyed everyone at AUB.

A few days later, the mood of hope was again shattered when news came of a massive car bomb explosion at a large apartment building in West Beirut, which killed many civilians. As usual, no one had any explanation for who was responsible. The television news showed vivid pictures of human mutilation. In the same news report we heard that U.S. planes had bombed Syrian positions in the mountains of Eastern Lebanon. One of them had been shot down. It was frightening to think that this might cause retaliation against Americans or American institutions, perhaps AUB. Not much else was left of American interests in Lebanon except the Embassy and the Marines.

Some students went on strike in protest against the car bombing. When I went to my class I found the main entrance to Nicely Hall blocked by student members of the Amal Party, a conservative Muslim Shiite group, most probably aided by outside party members. Near the entrance to the building I met some of my students who complained about the strike and wanted to hold class anyway, so we sat on the large oval lawn behind Nicely Hall and went over their compositions.

A women's dorm open house planned for that afternoon in Bustani Hall went on as scheduled in spite of the strike against classes. Malcolm was feeling the pressure of desk work piled up in his office, so I went for both of us. The students always enjoyed these events, which were one of the few occasions when men could come into dorm rooms. I was getting to know many of the students by now and was having such a good time that I forgot to look at my watch. Malcolm was waiting at home, entertaining a guest I had invited for dinner, a Lebanese businessman who traveled regularly to Taiwan and was going to deliver Christmas gifts to Susie and Hans for us.

When I got home I found that Malcolm had been entertaining the guest for half an hour and was feeling tired and impatient for my return. Later that evening we had a rare and penetrating argument boiling down to my lack of awareness of time and his impatience. I remember, in the tension of arguing, pulling at the necklace I was wearing so hard that it broke and the beads went rolling across our bedroom floor. I worried that Andrew would be awakened in the next room by our loud voices. We both felt terrible and didn't sleep well. It was a horrible feeling to have one's most secure relationship threatened and stung, especially when everything seemed to be collapsing around us. After a few hours of fitful sleep, we awoke early and began to talk about the concerns we were both having, how much more war pressure we could tolerate, the uncertainty of when it would ever end, the difficulty of living in a gilded cage in the middle of the campus with very little privacy and unable to move around the city or the country without worrying about security. We were also concerned about Andrew, whose habit of going out and collecting souvenir shrapnel and bullets after every battle made us worry about his continuing to live in a war zone. And we did not like being so far away from the rest of our family and knowing that they were worrying about us. When we got up and started dressing, Malcolm said, "This just makes me want to pick you and Andrew up and take you back to California."

When Andrew came home for lunch, we continued our conversation of the early morning with him. He had heard our argument of the night before and seemed to be sympathetic in a fifteen year-old way to the tensions we were feeling as we discussed them with him. Malcolm had had a meeting that morning with Abdul Hamid Hallab to discuss the possibility of hiring a group of security men who would be with us around the clock. The thought of living with armed guards in our house was not appealing. We wondered aloud if it would really add enough security to warrant further loss of privacy? Andrew thought it sounded very interesting to have some soldiers around with effective weapons whose names and descriptions he started reciting to us with ease, thanks to his nightly reading of war and weapons magazines which he kept stashed under his bed because he knew we didn't like them. He became even more interested when Malcolm mentioned that a bullet-proof car might be sent up from Jordan for our use.

On Saturday, December 10, I wrote in my journal:

A new cease-fire was announced today. [Foreign Minister] Eli Salem is going to Damascus for talks with President Assad who pulls the strings for so much of what goes on in this country, particularly with Amal [a Muslim Shiite group], so once again people feel hopeful. We haven't heard any shelling for several days. It's really the horrible terrorist attacks that threaten us most, but shelling noise is unnerving and wears people down day after day, night after night—even when it's far away in the mountains. So when we go for four or five days without shelling and there are no car bombs, we get involved with all our activities and forget about the war—such a relief.

That afternoon Malcolm and I received a visit from Fahmy Abu Hassan, the student who had been wounded by a stray bullet on Flag Day a few weeks earlier. He and his mother came to thank us for our interest in his welfare and brought me a knitted white shawl which she had made, something very lovely. We sat and had tea and listened to the story of how the war had affected their lives. They had moved to Beirut to stay with relatives when the fighting between Christians and Muslims forced them to leave their village in the Chouf mountains. They were gentle people and seemed not to be embittered by what had happened to them, only thankful that Fahmy had not been more seriously hurt and that he was able to study at AUB.

The continuing vitality of AUB could be felt in the breadth of activities that went on there initiated by many different segments of the population. I was asked to be a part of the President's Club, a group of dynamic alumnae women who kept an eye on student needs and raised money for improvement projects such as buying washing machines for all the dorms. They were well off and very attractive and chic in a manner exclusive to Lebanese women. Following a meeting with them in the Senate room of Marquand House on a Monday afternoon, I went over to the West Hall common room to meet Malcolm for a meeting of the Cultural Club of the South, a group of mostly Muslim students, probably predominantly Shiite and some Palestinians, from modest income families in the south. They were celebrating the release of a group of Israeli-held prisoners from Ansari Prison, some of whom were their friends and relatives. Malcolm gave a rousing speech of congratulations in Arabic as they passed around flowers and candy. These students were pleased to have an American president who spoke

Arabic and understood the problems of the south, where Israeli incursions into Lebanon in an effort to secure their northern border had caused fifteen years of suffering.

From this gathering we went upstairs to the West Hall theater to see the Drama Club's presentation, *Freezing A Mother-in-Law.* This was a very different group of students from those in the Cultural Club of the South. These were affluent, smartly dressed, mostly Maronite Christians from East Beirut or Mt. Lebanon. In the audience were many people from the Ras Beirut community, happy to be able to go out and enjoy some good entertainment in a relatively safe place.

I was becoming acquainted with the various student clubs at AUB, which Malcolm had told me were sometimes politicized. We had held an open house a few weeks earlier for the presidents and advisors of campus organizations. As we sipped punch on the Marquand House terrace, the noise of the judo and karate clubs playing loud music came over the high garden wall from West Hall behind our house. I was glad the guests could hear this noise and realize how close we lived to student activities, though I didn't have any illusions of the noise level being reduced. The variety of clubs represented was impressive—International, Debate, Meditation, Student Welfare, Music, Fight Pollution. "That club," Malcolm told me later, "fights much more than pollution. One of the militias has planted some of its members there, but the dean of students is trying to keep them from coming on campus."

The wide variety of students at AUB, representing all the different religious and cultural groups of Lebanon, had always been one of its greatest assets and made the university a microcosm of the country. Now in time of war it continued to be an asset in some ways and a liability in others. Members of all the militias wanted to have their children study at AUB, which remained the best path to success in the future. There seemed to be a tacit policy among them to leave AUB alone as a safe haven for their children, but this premise could not always be counted on, for war brought atrocious and irrational deeds. For Malcolm, too, there were dangers. If he were perceived by the Maronite Gemayel government as being too sympathetic to Muslim or Palestinian interests, problems might arise for him or for the university. It was known that, in their eyes, Malcolm and many members of the AUB community were considered too broadminded in their attitudes toward Muslim rights in Lebanon and toward the Palestinians, both threats to the security of the Gemayel government. And the same could be said of the ultraconservative Muslim parties who might have seen Malcolm and AUB as representatives of the West that threatened them. All we could do was try to be as evenhanded as possible and fend off the image of being allied with one side or another. But images were formed in the eye of the beholder, especially in Lebanon.

Christmas was coming soon, a holiday usually celebrated extravagantly by the Lebanese Christians, but with the increasing presence of Shiite conservatism in West Beirut, the decorations, bright lights, displays of fine gifts, food, and liquor were considerably less than in former years. The popular Smith's Grocery Store (run by a Lebanese Armenian woman who had at one time been married to an Englishman) had already been bombed several times, ostensibly by Shiite extremist groups who objected to the sale of liquor, so shopkeepers had to be cautious, particularly at the time of a Christian holiday. On the AUB campus, a few events were being planned: the Christmas party of the AUB Hospital Auxiliary, to be held in the newly decorated living room and dining room of Marquand House, and the annual Orpheus Choir Christmas concert in the AUB chapel. We were planning a party on Christmas Eve with a few close friends. John would be coming from Cairo as well as a friend of Andrew's from Boy Scout days in Pacific Palisades, Bill Emaluth. Bill had been diagnosed as having terminal lung cancer and wanted very much to come visit Andrew in Lebanon. The two boys had been corresponding since we had moved to Beirut. His parents, eager for Bill to enjoy himself, allowed him to make the journey.

The week before all these events were to take place, we had a visit from a man and his wife interested in the job of vice president for university administration. The Smiths immediately showed their adaptability by fitting right into AUB life and our schedule, which was currently a bit hectic because of our house being redecorated, a new dog, and the social activities of Christmas.

On December 15 I wrote in my journal:

Smiths arrived today. Lovely people and seem very interested in the job. Began feeling in Christmas spirit yesterday after Hospital Auxiliary party in our newly painted but uncarpeted and unfurnished living room. They filled the room with potted poinsettias and made it look festive. Horrible entertainment. A Baptist minister who came ostensibly to sing Christmas carols, sneaked in a fundamentalist message before he sang his songs. Very offensive. I wondered how the Muslim guests found it . . .

Had a desperate call from Hassan in my office after class today to please come home right away. Carpet people, curtain people, carpenters and painters all waiting to complete living room but depending on me to give them directions. Vickie Smith was waiting at home to help me. The house was full of workmen. We horrified them by washing windows just ahead of the curtain hangers, an activity which in their eyes was beneath our "lady of the manor" status. Hassan inaugurated the new carpet by tripping over a can of rubber cement which the car-petlayers hastily tried to clean up but not completely success-fully. Then the new dog further initiated it by peeing in the dining room. Workmen brought furniture back from the study and Rima came with huge bouquets of chrysanthemums. We added the finishing touches, and the room was transformed in time for our 1:00 luncheon for the Smiths . . .

In the late afternoon we went to the long-awaited Orpheus Choir Christmas concert in the Chapel. Everyone a bit uneasy after recent bomb explosions outside two churches in Ras Bei-rut, but we all liked to believe that no one would do such a thing on the AUB campus. Choir extremely accomplished—an hour and a half of exquisite singing of classical music and Christmas carols. People were becoming more relaxed in the second half, but during Handel's "Hallelujah" chorus the guns of the New Jersey started firing up into the mountains where the U.S. was trying to stop the current round of Christian-Muslim fighting in their inimitable way. An unmistakable noise, different from the usual shelling or bomb explosions. Deep continuous concussions. The audience remained in place, stirring only slightly, and continued listening, trying to remain absorbed by the music which was so enchanting that it seemed it might have the power to protect us. The choir kept on sing-ing almost as if nothing else were happening . . .

Champagne reception afterwards in our living room for dig-nitaries and lead singers. Everyone buoyed by the music and in a holiday spirit. Just as the last guest, the acting British ambas-sador was leaving, his guards came in and said, "Better not go yet, Sir. A sniper has been reported by the Marines in the lower campus." This came just after we had said to Ambassador Palmer that since he lived so close, he should come and have dinner with us soon. And so he did—while reports from the Marines flew in to his guards on their walkie-talkies and escalated. "A sniper perhaps on the campus" and "Several snipers on top of an AUB building." Then, "An armed gang on campus exchanging fire with the Marines." Hassan, still dressed in his white jacket and bow tie, served us dinner in our elegant new dining room while Ambassador Palmer's six bodyguards in tweedy sports jackets and machine guns roamed around the house . . .

I called the Slade family in the faculty apartments to check on Andrew and the ACS kids having a party there and Landry Slade reported everything was OK. They had heard three shots, but our kids were all staying inside in the apartment of another AUB family. Fifteen minutes later, Andrew phoned to say only somewhat sheepishly that he and his friends were the cause of the whole incident. They had moved their party to the roof of the faculty apartment building where nervous Marines spotted them and assumed they were snipers—immediately sent up flares and tracer bullets. How close the whizzing sound of the tracer bullets came depended on who was telling the story. Andrew thought it was ten feet.

[Saturday, December 17] Said good-bye to the Smiths today. Tanios and a security guard drove them to the airport which has reopened once again. I hope they decide to take the job—they would be excellent. If they are as adventuresome as they seem to be, they will . . .

The remarkable things that go on in this country in the midst of war and the resilience of the Lebanese constantly amaze us. Students sponsored a joint Christian-Muslim holiday event today, a Christmas/Prophet's Birthday track and field tournament on the Green Field. Malcolm and I were invited to preside in the grandstand and oversee passing teams as they paraded by below, tossing carnations into the stands, all led by Miss Lebanon, a blond, blue-eyed beauty. Malcolm, wearing his scruffiest old working-at-home professor clothes, was called upon to greet and shake hands with each team captain. Later we had dinner at the home of my old AUB classmate and now fellow English teacher, Rafika Abdul Futuh. They had been without electricity all day but had prepared a feast for us anyway. They were concerned because we had to walk up seven flights of stairs in the dark. As Muslims, they were forced out of their home in a

15. Malcolm and Ann at the American University of Beirut
Track and Field presentations, December 1983.

Christian neighborhood several years ago by the local militia,
although none of their Christian neighbors had wanted them to
leave.

[Monday, December 19] [Andrew's friend Bill] arrived last
night looking wan and tired from his chemotherapy and long
trip. Hope that spending Christmas with us will give him a
boost. Students in the midst of mid-terms so I spent the morning working with the secretaries in the president's office to send
out our three thousand Christmas cards to all AUB employees
and friends. Just as we were finishing, John walked in the door,
five days earlier than expected. So good to see him and so much
fun from the first moment. I need frequent doses of all my
children. Malcolm was busy with an official luncheon to honor
the local bankers who were helping to sponsor the new Banking
Institute at AUB, Andrew still in school, so John, Bill and I
went out to buy a Christmas tree. Found them imported from
Italy and very expensive but bought a big one anyway for our
first Christmas in Marquand House . . .

Abdul Hamid Hallab stopped by before dinner to talk to Malcolm about the AUB trustees' insistence on immediately initiating a plan for a security team to guard him twenty-four hours a day. I felt irritated with Malcolm for responding sardonically to Abdul Hamid, almost treating the matter as a joke. He has been procrastinating on this matter—naturally has no wish to be bothered with constant bodyguards even in our house, nor do I, but we have to do something. Abdul Hamid is going to hire a highly respected retired general from the Lebanese Army to organize a round-the-clock team of expert guards. The situation has been relatively calm for the past few days, except for fighting in the mountains, which always brings a deceptive sense of security, but Abdul Hamid says that people anticipate trouble over the holidays.

[Wednesday, December 21] Went to Bustani Hall Christmas party today. Malcolm terrific as always in making a little speech to the students which was full of humor—another reminder of how well suited he is to his role as President and what a good job he is doing. I love to see him thriving in it. Everything is so uncertain, but I somehow believe this university is going to hold together. It may be the only thing in Lebanon that does.

[Saturday, December 24] Malcolm and the boys went out to buy our family Christmas gift, a new stereo for the living room, while I worked with Hassan, Zeinab and Dalia to prepare food and decorations for our house warming/Christmas Eve party. The boys came home and set up the stereo—Malcolm fell asleep on the couch listening to Mozart. All turned out well for the party. The evening was magical till shelling started in East Beirut. The bastards, whoever they are.

[Sunday, Christmas Day] Sound of distant guns intermittent during the night. Hard to tell if it's the Christian militias just showing off for the holidays or what. In the good old days, they just rang their church bells louder and longer on Christian holidays. I woke up feeling a little depressed not to be home with all our family for a traditional Christmas. Everyone rather quiet and sullen at breakfast. I wondered if sixteen-year-old Bill was contemplating that this would be his last Christmas and I wondered what Andrew was thinking about his good friend being so seriously ill. The day improved as we talked by phone to the various members of our family around the world, opened our presents under the tree, played some afternoon volleyball and tennis and in the evening had a big Christmas dinner in our new dining room with the Dodds, a UPI correspondent friend of theirs and Randy Harshbarger, our new friend from Catholic Relief Services. So a nice Christmas after a bad beginning.

[December 27] Set off for Faraya [considered to be an area relatively free of fighting] yesterday with the Dodds on our long debated Christmas trip. Had wanted to go to Bisharri, but Malcolm finally acquiesced to advice not to go to Syrian-held territory. Worried a bit about taking Bill to cold climate, but he is anxious to see the country. Snowy picnic on route at Roman temple at Fakra. Climbed all over rocks of temple and tried to ignore the inevitable litter. Found our hotel in Faraya, the Coin Vert, modest but cozy. Malcolm and I immediately settled down for a long winter's nap while the boys went out for a snowball fight. Later an evening of talking, eating delectable Lebanese mountain food and card playing. Good company and very relaxing. Had hotel to ourselves due to "the situation", as the Lebanese frequently refer to their war. Few people travel around the country, contributing further to the bad economy.

[December 29] Last night went to a Christmas party at the Regiers. Many old AUB families there and lots of warm feelings. Holiday atmosphere was interrupted by a series of bombs, one huge one which turned out to be Smith's Grocery Store a few blocks up the street from the campus—their third time in eight years and the biggest to date. People who went up on the roof said smoke came all the way to the Corniche. Fire increased, we heard later because of popping liquor bottles and aerosol cans. Was it the Islamic Jihad—or Phalangists trying to make people think it was? Smith's will very likely begin rebuilding within a week and reopen as soon as possible, just as they have done before.

Today had all dorm students who hadn't gone home for vacation for a Christmas open house, about two hundred in all. Lovely kids, polite and well dressed—many non-Lebanese, Bangladeshis, Maldivians, Jordanians, and a couple of Europeans finishing up Master's degrees. They enjoyed being in Marquand House and wanted to take pictures with us. Some interesting conversations and frank questions. How could my students have a normal class when the president's wife teaches them? I told them they would have to ask my students but that I thought it was not much different from classes I had taught in other universities. In the evening we went to the International Students

Club Christmas party in the lounge of the new men's dorm. Lovely kids again—many the same who had come to our house. Malcolm and I danced and then we danced with some of the students. All the young women wanted to dance with John.

[January 2] We saw the new year in quietly with the noises of the peculiarly Lebanese way of celebrating in the background—guns being fired into the air at the stroke of midnight and off and on for the next half hour. Good to return to classes and routine today, but many students were absent—still away on European holidays with their families. Went home after class to meet Malcolm and see John off to the airport. Hard to have him leave, but gratifying for us to know he has found a job and career interest in economic development that he likes so much—and I am glad to have a Kerr in my favorite country of Egypt. Lots of parallels to what his Grandfather Kerr did at the same age in Turkey.

Ramsey Zeine [a bright young architect and the son of our old Ottoman history professor from the fifties, Zeine Zeine] came for a drink in the late afternoon to discuss long range campus planning with Malcolm. He has sound ideas and imagination—believes that we have to be a bit impatient to get things accomplished. Malcolm emphasized need for better athletic and social facilities for students to channel their energies away from politics. The President's Club is willing to help out financially.

The next day Malcolm came home with the news that students were agitating again about holding student body elections for second semester. A small group of professors representing different religious communities was meeting with representatives of all the different religious/political groups on campus, but the Phalangists refused to attend. They countered by holding a separate meeting at the time the other student groups had their first meeting and will present their own list of demands. These kids have learned so much from their fathers! At night, new batches of political posters go up, blighting the landscape and defacing the beautiful old stone walls of AUB buildings. Malcolm had been working very hard to limit posters to bulletin boards only and got frustrated when the deans couldn't enforce this rule. We were tempted to remove them surreptitiously when we took evening walks on the campus but decided that might invite trouble. The dean of students, Fawzi al-Haj, recommended that they be left up for a few days, and then he would have workmen make a thorough clean-up after dark.

Malcolm had been searching for a candidate to be the dean of engineering and had met several interested people on his trip to the United States in November. He learned that one of them, Dr. Battenberg, would be bringing his wife and coming out for a visit in early January. At about the same time, we learned that our prize new head librarian, Sam Fustukjian, and his wife had decided they could no longer continue raising their small children in a war zone. Sam was torn because he loved his job as library director, which he had aspired to since his student days at AUB. Two other faculty wives also decided to take their young children and return to the United States. This was discouraging news, but at least we had hopes of recruiting a dean of engineering.

> [January 3] Tanios brought the Battenbergs from the airport and then drove Andrew, Bill and the Dodd boys up to Faraya to go skiing. They returned early because Bill was very tired and had had to stay in the car. Beginning to worry about him. His cough grows worse. He is so quiet anyway—hard to know what he's thinking and feeling.
>
> [January 4] Invited engineering professors for dinner to meet the Battenbergs. First time for me to meet some of them. This is a department that has a lot of dissension and is badly in need of a new dean, preferably an outsider who will not be encumbered with old feuds and problems. Later learned that I seated two people next to each other who hadn't spoken in years.
>
> [January 5] Bill coughed all night. He is visibly more wan and lacking in energy. We are terribly worried about him. He won't say much about how he feels except that his back hurts from tension. Rubbing it makes him feel better—also me. Took him to Doctor Caesar Chediac right after my class to get advice. He reported that Bill's tumor was the size of two footballs pressing against his back, filling one lung and part of another, constricting his windpipe and thus limiting his oxygen intake—threat of pneumonia now the problem. It's questionable whether Bill can survive the trip back to Los Angeles, but he's got to be with his family. By good coincidence, Caesar has medical meetings in L.A. and will accompany Bill home.

Had lunch with Bill in upstairs study as he was too weak to go downstairs. Andrew back in school. Malcolm and I tried to keep up normal conversation but felt completely shaken, having become very close to Bill. This is the first time we have ever seen anyone so seriously ill, really close to death. It's hard to imagine how his parents let him leave home, except that he wanted so badly to visit Andrew and have the adventure of seeing Lebanon. We will phone them and Bill's doctor to confer on his travel plans.

[January 6] Stayed with Bill most of the day. Malcolm came home at noon to see him. He is good at talking with Bill and making things seem natural. Bill prefers sleeping on Andrew's bed, so Andrew took a sleeping bag to the guest bedroom.

[January 8] Up very early yesterday to see Bill off—extremely worried about his comfort. We were afraid that he would be completely miserable throughout the flight. Thank goodness for Caesar. We said goodbye, knowing that we might not see Bill again. Andrew showed no outward signs of recognition that his friend might not be alive by summer when we got home to California. He didn't like it when I talked about the seriousness of Bill's illness. Malcolm was more successful. He gently explained that "Mom and I need to express our feelings about Bill even if you don't want to" . . .

We phoned Bill's family this morning and learned that Dr. Chediac had delivered him right to them at the L.A. airport and he was now resting and eating a bit. That gave us a huge sense of relief.

With Bill safely home, we turned our thoughts back to AUB matters. Malcolm wanted to make a concerted effort to be attentive to all the various political and religious groups on campus, which wasn't something that he necessarily had to initiate. The president of the Student Cultural Club of the South visited Malcolm in his office to say that his mother would be coming to Beirut and would like to call on us. This was significant because she was the sister of a Shiite martyr, Musa Sadr, who had vanished in Libya several years earlier. She had become politically active in South Lebanon and commanded a large following. When she arrived for tea at Marquand House with her son, she was covered from head to toe in the style of conservative Muslim dress that was becoming very popular in those circles. Her handsome face was not covered and radiated a spiritual quality which explained the attraction of her followers. I hadn't thought about my own mode of dress in advance and simply put on what I was going to wear out to dinner that evening, a rather tight-fitting, low-necked red dress. Later I wondered what discredit this might have brought to the Kerr name.

Malcolm spoke Arabic with them and I served tea and joined in the discussion when I could understand. Conversation was about the important role of AUB in helping to hold Lebanon together and the inevitable polarizing of students into their own political groups. Our guest also spoke of the difficult living conditions of the refugees from Israeli-occupied southern Lebanon crowding into the southern suburbs of Beirut.

After they left, Malcolm said, "That visit was worth a thousand bodyguards." The news would no doubt travel all over campus very quickly that this distinctive personality in her conservative garb had been to see us. I absentmindedly wondered if we should be arranging equal time for members of other political groups, but they soon came anyway.

The heads of various student organizations asked if they could come and speak to Malcolm about resuming the old AUB tradition of holding student elections that had been discontinued after the outbreak of the civil war. He invited them to Marquand House, and they arrived in their best clothes carrying flowers for me. We knew that some of these students were highly politicized and probably had links with militias and interest groups outside the campus. Over tea and cookies, they made their demands for student elections, which faculty and administrators believed would turn the campus into a microcosm of Lebanese politics outside the campus. Malcolm spoke warmly but firmly to them and reiterated the arguments against having student elections in these tense times and of his hope of resuming them as soon as the political situation made it possible. He described the long history of AUB and its evolving role in Lebanon over a hundred and twenty years, hoping to persuade them that we all had to work together to make sure the university continued in its mission.

They seemed to acquiesce, perhaps out of respect to the person of the president of the university, or perhaps because something of what Malcolm had said had penetrated their thinking. Their Lebanese upbringing demanded politeness and decorum in a social encounter with a professor or university administrator. We would see soon enough whether or not they were convinced of the wisdom of Malcolm's words and would be willing to put their loyalty to AUB ahead of other interests. Our sense of hopefulness after this meeting rose to a mood of elation when a telex arrived from the Smiths in Colorado saying they had decided to accept the job as vice president for university administration.

In the scant six months since Malcolm, Andrew, and I had arrived in early August and established ourselves as a family at AUB, our hopes for a secure future for the university and for ourselves had risen and waned many times. Now we thought we had more reason to be hopeful than at any time in the past, at least from the perspective within the university. We knew, of course, that the political situation in Lebanon was a long way from becoming stable, but our desire for AUB to survive and thrive and our own personal investment in that cause made us concentrate on the positive developments that we had been working hard to achieve. It seemed as if we could dare to hope that the worth of the institution and the commitment of so many people for so many decades might ultimately make AUB victorious over all the evil that threatened it. The entries in my journal reflect that hope and the satisfaction and pleasure of settling into our home and jobs as the new year of 1984 got underway.

[January 11] Went to Malcolm's office to supervise the hanging of the antique clock I found hanging in a back office and took to Tawfik Nasrawi in the engineering lab to repair. Faithful Ilyas Khuri did the hanging. Both have been employees of AUB for thirty years or more, as their fathers were before them. Malcolm's office is looking smashing now with new curtains, newly upholstered furniture, Daniel Bliss's desk refinished and an old portrait I found of Daniel Bliss hanging over it. Richard Mishalani made two beautiful oak book shelves for either side of the desk where Malcolm was at last able to put a portion of his collection of political science books the other day. Two portraits which I unearthed of early trustees look very handsome on the opposite wall and are a good contrast to my Ain Mreisseh watercolors. Hope the chiming of the antique clock behind Malcolm's desk doesn't drive him crazy.

Stopped at faculty apartment basement to watch Jackie

Azouri and Walid Dajani train cheerleaders—an innovation for AUB and something rather daring to do in these days of growing Islamic conservatism. Walid is a medical student and also an accomplished ballet dancer, so the routines he and Jackie have worked out have a ballet flavor to them. There has been great debate as to how to carry this off without offending the fundamentalists. They will try unprovocative dance routines and modest costumes. How they can be cheerleaders and keep their legs and arms covered remains to be seen.

[Thursday, January 12] We went with Fawzi al-Haj to the West Hall theater to see the much acclaimed play, *Ayaam el Ayaam,* [Days after Days] about villagers in the South and the effect of war on their lives—a three hour production in Arabic which Malcolm understood most of but I could understand only part of; but it was completely captivating. Produced and acted by Lebanese professionals who won the Carthage Prize for this a couple of years ago. Lots of students from the South in the audience of course, but also many people of all ages from the Ras Beirut community.

[Friday, January 13] I visited Samir Khalaf [professor of sociology] to discuss his letter to Malcolm about establishing career counseling at the university. Hard to keep on the subject because we kept talking about the way things were when he, his twin brother Nadim [now an AUB economics professor], Malcolm and I were students together at AUB. We agreed we would start some inquiries about establishing a career counseling program. . . .

Held first Art Committee meeting here. Hope to extend decoration of Marquand House little by little to sprucing up the rest of the campus. Invited local artists, Martin Geisen, David Kurani, Zahi Khuri, Rima Shehadi, Richard Mishalani, and Suha Tuqan to help. We'll have a student art competition to begin a collection of AUB art in College Hall corridor outside the president's office and eventually West Hall and Dodge Hall too. We will ask the Photography Club and local artists to donate some of their work. Whenever Malcolm sees me getting enthusiastic about another improvement project at AUB, he makes another joking reference to the Roman Empire embarking on major building projects on the eve of their collapse . . .

Stopped to chat with Elie Nseir in his antiquities shop across the street from the campus. He is now being bothered again, at least weekly, by militia bribers and protection money rings—

everything from "newspaper sellers" who come with their party
news sheets asking a fee of their liking, to outright extortionists
demanding fifty or a hundred pounds for the service of their
continued "protection." He says he would like to move to the
States but can't abandon his old parents who refuse to leave
Lebanon . . .

Went to a surprise party this evening for Ted Kennedy's
seventy-second birthday at the Dodds and a celebration of the
long career he and Mary Helen have had at AUB. Many of the
guests were from off campus and had to leave in time to get
home by the 8:00 curfew. They have so many more problems
than we do with electricity and water cuts. The campus is a
haven for those of us lucky enough to live here with its own
generators and water reservoirs. It also serves as a park for people who like to walk or sit on the benches and look at the sea.

[Sunday, January 15] Yesterday had all of the Said-Shehadi
family for a shish kebab and tabbouleh lunch, another house-
warming to show the Saids the results of their daughter's and
my decorating. A remarkable family. Salwa will always be remembered for her courage in guiding the university as the only
resident trustee during the summer of the Israeli invasion between the time of David Dodge's kidnapping and Malcolm's
arrival. They took very good care of Malcolm last year in my
absence. Spent a long, restful afternoon in our new living room
listening to music and relaxing. Malcolm in fine form telling
one joke after another . . .

Today another relaxing day as guests of Pierre al-Khouri
[son of the first president of Lebanon and an international banker
and businessman] in his two hundred-year-old restored farm
house in a small village in Keserwan. An exquisite restoration,
very simple with a few pieces of modern and antique furniture—ancient artifacts in old nooks, arched windows in the patio looking out to terraced hillsides and a small convent. Sunken
bathtubs in his and her bathrooms looking out to the valley
below.

Home for our Sunday nap, work at our desks, supper in the
living room with Andrew, the new dog and the new stereo.

[Monday, January 16] Students all in class in spite of shelling last night in East Beirut. Amazing kids coming from war
filled childhoods and carrying on every day as energetic, responsive students—sometimes a bit rambunctious, sometimes lazy
and opportunistic, but always lively and interesting. I don't rec-

ognize signs of their political persuasions, but I haven't lived here long enough yet perhaps. I can generally tell Christians from Muslims by their names and style, but I can't distinguish the breakdown of Maronites, Greek Orthodox, Protestants, Shiites and Sunnis the way my Lebanese colleagues can. In any case, we avoid discussion related to politics, perhaps because I am the president's wife.

[Tuesday, January 17] Visited Suha Tuqan and Zaki Khuri at the AUB Press after my class to talk about getting photographs of old campus scenes to decorate West Hall and doing an article on President's Club for AUB Bulletin. Malcolm busy with appointments and desk work in his office. We met in late afternoon to walk down to the Goethe Institute to hear Leila Badre's lecture on her excavations in Yemen.

Home for a kibbeh dinner, one of Malcolm's favorites—the three of us and the dog. Still not sure how we like this dog, but he is fun to roughhouse with on the new carpet after dinner. Andrew and I did our respective homework in the living room and listened to his music which I am trying to learn how to like. Wish Andrew weren't so resistant to his homework. Malcolm went out to play tennis with Martin Geisen. Came home elated to have beaten him in three straight sets. We discussed whether or not it was safe to go to the ambassador's for lunch in Yarzi the next day because of shelling there recently. Decided we would go.

[Wednesday, January 18] It all came to an end today—all the goals achieved and the dreams and goals still hoped for. I can't imagine how I can live without Malcolm. Somehow we never really thought this would happen—lots of troubles and problems maybe, but never really this. We were so happy to be here doing what we were doing.

Right now I think I hear Malcolm coming up the stairs. People are swarming into the house. Have been all day—so many interruptions. Can't write anymore."

Epilogue

I have discovered my plot in the relation that exists between my present and past. But the present is always changing, and the search for order and understanding must be made again and again, in a manner that alters with an altering and yet constant self" (1960, 4). Those words from James McConkey's *Court of Memory,* which I read in the summer after Malcolm's death, provided a focus to the task of reordering my life which his death had dictated.

The task was made easier by the love of my children and parents, by the warmth of friends around the world and by absorption in my work. While "acquaintance with grief" was never far away, I discovered that the demands of daily life forced me to live in the present and propelled me into the future. I was rooted in the past, in my life with Malcolm, but new forms of life could grow up around the old, just as the chaparral in our mountains had sent up new green shoots that intertwined with the stately burned branches which remained after the fire that had devastated everything in its path.

From Beirut, after memorial services at Princeton and UCLA, Andrew, John, and I went to Cairo where we initially lived in the home of the AUC president, Richard Pedersen, who graciously offered us one wing of his penthouse overlooking the Nile. I returned to my former teaching job at AUC, John to his work with Catholic Relief Services, and Andrew to ninth grade in Cairo American College. Eventually, John returned to his downtown apartment, and Andrew and I moved to a faculty apartment in the suburb of Maadi near his school where I lived for the next five years. Our old cook Ali came back to work for us, providing loving care and continuity in our lives and freedom from household chores. Those were years full of satisfying teaching at AUC and travels and adventures with my children and our friends—camping and snorkeling at the Red Sea, trips to desert oases and monasteries, boat trips on the Nile, and holidays with friends living in other parts of the Middle East.

In the summers we all returned to our Pacific Palisades mountaintop. It was there in that beautiful home, where the children had grown up, that we missed Malcolm the most acutely, and at each reunion we seemed to have to grieve together all over again for a few days as we readjusted to each other and were reminded of the ways things should have been.

It took a long time before I felt I could come home and live in our house without Malcolm, but finally the signs all seemed to point to that decision. I was anxious to live and work in my own country again and at last to gather together scattered possessions from Beirut, Cairo, and our garage to create a new home in the old one. In February 1989 I returned to California to begin a new life, once again discovering a "plot in the relation that exists between my present and my past," and well aware that "the present is always changing, and the search for order and understanding must be made again and again in a manner that alters with an altering yet constant self."

My ties to the Middle East are kept strong through my work as a trustee of AUB and an escort for the Malcolm Kerr Scholars Program of the National Council on U.S.-Arab Relations, which sends high school students to the Middle East every summer. I also lecture for community and university groups and give classes on the Middle East.

Malcolm would be proud of his children. Susie completed her Doctorate in Education at Harvard, and she and Hans, now the parents of twin boys, are living in Cambridge, England, where Hans teaches at the university. John earned a Ph.D. in agricultural economics at Stanford and is presently working in Hyderbad, India. Steve graduated from the University of Arizona and plays basketball in the NBA. He and his wife Margot recently brought another baby boy into the Kerr family. Andrew also graduated from the University of Arizona and is currently working for the

16. The Kerr family at home in Pacific Palisades, summer 1984.
Left to right: Steve, Ann, John, Susie, and Andrew.

National Security Council in Washington. I have to hope that somehow Malcolm knows that all this has happened and that he is now a grandfather!

I also hope he knows that AUB has survived the civil war in Lebanon and is evolving to fit new educational needs in the area. And I hope he knows that dramatic progress has been made toward Arab-Israeli peace, the problem which lay behind so many of the political issues that affected our lives.

Bibliographic Essay
Index

Bibliographic Essay

W hile this is not intended to be an academic book, I have consulted both academic and nonacademic books in the process of writing it.

In the first months after Malcolm's death, I was not able to read much, for sustained concentration was very difficult. Then I was given James McConkey's *Court of Memory* by a UCLA professor of history who knew of my interest in writing. That began a spate of reading of personal histories and diaries which recollected the past in ways that sparked ideas for how I might write. From McConkey I recognized a need to discover a personal order in the interweaving of memory and current happening. In Anne Morrow Lindbergh's diaries I saw her desire to create a written record of a close marriage and family life with a similar intrusion of tragedy. May Sarton's books revealed the glory of life surrounded by nature and tangible links with the past in the furnishings of her home. In Gerald Durrell's *My Family and Other Animals* there was merriment and occasional zaniness that reminded me of my family.

As I began writing, trying to interweave political and historical events with the travels and development of our family, I read academic books on the Middle East to verify my recollection of those events. Many of the books were written by friends or by Malcolm.

Wherever I have referred to ideas of other authors, I have included their names and titles in the narrative. These books are also listed below, along with titles and authors of books used for general reference.

Ball, George W. *Error and Betrayal in Lebanon: An Analysis of Israel's Invasion of Lebanon and the Implications for U.S.-Israeli Relations.* Foundation for Middle East Peace, 1984.

Bliss, Daniel. *The Reminiscences of Daniel Bliss.* New York: Revell, 1920.

Friedman, Thomas L.. *From Beirut to Jerusalem.* New York: Farrar, Straus and Giroux, 1989.

Gordon, David C.. *Lebanon: The Fragmented Nation.* London: Croom Helm, 1980.

Hanna, Faith M.. *An American Mission: The Role of the American University of Beirut.* Boston: Alphabet Press, 1979.

Hourani, Albert. *A History of the Arab Peoples.* Cambridge: Harvard Univ. Press, 1991.

Kerr, Malcolm H. *The Arab Cold War: Gamal Abd al-Nasir and His Rivals, 1958–1970.* 3d ed. Oxford: Oxford University Press, 1981.

————. *Islamic Reform.* Berkeley: Univ. of California Press, 1966.

————. "Lebanese Views on the 1958 Crisis." *Middle East Journal* 15(1961):211–17.

————. *Lebanon in the Last Years of Feudalism, 1840–1868: A Contemporary Account by Antun Dahir Al-Aqiqi and Other Documents.* Beirut, 1959.

————, ed. *The Elusive Peace in the Middle East.* Albany: State Univ. of New York Press, 1975.

———— and El Sayad Yassin, eds. *Rich and Poor States in the Middle East: Egypt and the New Arab Order.* Boulder, Colo.: Westview, 1982.

Kerr, Stanley. *The Lions of Marash.* Albany: State Univ. of New York Press, 1973.

McConkey, James. *Court of Memory.* New York: Dutton, 1960.

Munro, John M. *A Mutual Concern: The Story of the American University of Beirut.* Delmar, N. Y.: Caravan, 1977.

Penrose, Stephen B. L., Jr. *That They May Have Life: The Story of the American University of Beirut. 1866–1941.* New York: Trustees of the American Univ. of Beirut, 1941.

Salibi, Kamal. *A House of Many Mansions: The History of Lebanon Reconsidered.* Berkeley: Univ. of California Press, 1988.

Seale, Patrick, ed. *The Shaping of an Arab Statesman: Abd al-Hamid Sharaf and the Modern Arab World.* London: Quartet, 1983.

Index

Names of Kerr family members appearing in subheadings are abbreviated as follows: ANK (Andrew); AZK (Ann); JK (John); MK (Malcolm); SK (Stephen); SV (Susie). Page references in italics denote illustrations.

Abaih, 226
ABC Variety Store (Beirut), 51
Abdu (cook), 158–59, 176
Abduh, Muhammad, 105
Abdul Futuh, Rafika, 287–88
Abu Ali, 121–22
Abu Hassan, Fahmy, 274, 283
Abu Musa faction, 271
Abu Nidal, 194
Abu Yaakov, 207–8
Adams family, 241
Adeebe (seamstress), 113–15
Agence France Presse, 3
al-Ahram Center for Political and
   Strategic Studies, 160, 168
Ainab, xiv, 149; in civil war, 226,
   264–65; European route to,
   150–51; Malcolm Kerr family
   in, 120, 121–22, 131, 133,
   135, 143; Stanley Kerr family
   in, 29–30, 68–74
Ain Mreisseh (Beirut), 82, 143,
   144, 146, 295
Aix-en-Provence, 151–52
Alexandria, 161

Aley (Lebanese town), 52, 59–60,
   68, 85, 226, 227
Aley (Saudi prince), 83
Ali (cook), 176, 300
Ali, Um, 121–22
Amal Party, 252, 281, 283
American Board of Foreign Missions, 54
American Community School (Beirut), 260, 266–67, 279; ANK
   at, 257, 263; MK at, 33, 34,
   234; SK at, 245
American Research Center in
   Egypt, 140
American School for Girls, 124
American University of Beirut, xv,
   36–37, 40–100, 162–63; Arafat
   and, 178–79; Beirut cultural life
   and, 145–46; early years, xiv,
   27–28, 31; under MK, ii, 3–
   20, 201–98; MK teaches at,
   108–35; presidents of, 189–90;
   students of (See Students); World
   War II era, 32–33
—Alumni Club, 9, 11–13

American University of Beirut
  (*continued*)
—Art Committee, 296
—AUB beach, 99, 278
—Banking Institute, 288
—Board of Deans, 202
—Board of Trustees, 210, 231,
  239, 241, 300; Beirut meeting
  of, 169–70; New York meetings
  of, 189, 191, 196, 219, 230;
  presidential recruitment by, 185,
  191; security plan of, 289
—Bustani Hall, 281, 289
—Chapel, 14, 17–18, 214–15
—College Hall, 45, 67–68, 214,
  296
—College of Arts and Sciences, 27
—Dodge Hall, 296
—Drama Club, 284
—English Department, 263, 274
—Hospital: electrical power for,
  207; MK's death in, 6; SK's
  birth in, 143–44; SV's birth in,
  112; war casualties in, 195, 206,
  266, 274
—Hospital Auxiliary, 285
—International Students Club,
  290–91
—Library, 67–68
—Marquand House. *See* Marquand
  House (AUB)
—Medical School, 27
—Milk Bar, 62, 64
—New York Office, 196, 199
—Nicely Hall, 281
—Off-Campus Program, 235, 274
—Orpheus Choir, 285, 286
—Photography Club, 296
—President's Club, 283, 291, 298
—School of Agriculture, 124–25
—Smokers' Gate, 217
—Van Dyke Hall, 275
—West Hall, 96, 264, 267, 296,
  298
—Women's Hostel, *44*
American University in Cairo, xvi,

  175, 181; AZK at, 164, 175,
  299, 300; JK at, 180; MK at,
  157–60
Amiliya Technical School, 238
Amman, 244, 258; AZK in, 161,
  233, 234; MK in, 200, 233,
  234; SK in, 245
Amsterdam, 233
Anglican services, 28, 210
Ansari Prison Camp, 278, 283
Antelias, 223
Anti-Lebanon mountains, 73, 87–
  88
Aqaba, 233–34, 235
Arab American Oil Company, 93
Arab Cold War, The (Kerr), 141–
  42, 152–53
Arabic language, 63, 171
Arab-Israeli conflict, xv, 116–17,
  167, 181. *See also* Palestinian
  question; Suez War
Arab-Israeli War (1948), 79, 91,
  95, 141
Arab-Israeli War (1967), 116, 147–
  48, 151, 153
Arab-Israeli War (1973), 160, 186
Arab Jerusalem, 79, 147
Arab League, 224
Arab unity movement, 95–96,
  108, 122, 132, 141–42
Arafat, Yasser, 178–79, 187, 194,
  205, 271, 278
ARAMCO (Arab American Oil
  Company), 93
al-Arish, 180
Armenian children, 27, 54–58, 84,
  86, 91, 124
Armenian jewelers, 96–97
Armenian maids, 63
Armenian monastery (Keserwan),
  246
Ashrafieh, 260
al-Assad, Hafez, 188, 225, 282–83
Aswan Dam, 103
Ataturk, Kemal, 122
Avenue de Paris (Beirut), 51

Awali River, 271
Ayaam el Ayaam, 296
Azzam, Katie, 46, 58, 78, 79, 93, 125

Baabda, 170
Baalbek, 87–88, 89, 124; drug traffic in, 145, 157, 232; Iranian Shiites in, 88, 187, 232
Baalbek Summer Festival, 88, 122, 195
Bab-Idris (Beirut), 51, 247
Badre, Leila, 5, 249, 269, 298
Baghdad, 47
Baghdad Pact, 95
Baha'i religion, 42
Bahrain, 222
Bantam (freighter), 37, 40
Bartholomew, Reginald, 12
Basila (accountant), 278
Battenberg, Dr., 292
Baysoor, 74, 121
BBC (British Broadcasting Corporation), 252
Beaufort Castle, 213
Bechtel Corporation, 225
Bedouins, 180
Begin, Menachem, 194, 204, 206; at Camp David, 176; in Egypt, 166, 168; Habib and, 205; Haig and, 189; U.S. aircraft and, 188–89; West Bank and, 203
Beirut, xiv, 49–52, 80–81, 191; bombing of, 189, 195, 199, 201–2, 234; economic conditions in, 247; intellectual climate of, 157; nightlife of, 61, 120; 1958 civil war and, 109–10, 111; 1975 civil war and, xv–xvi, 162, 272; prosperity of, 133, 145; religious elements of, 47–48, 50; World War II era, 32. *See also* East Beirut; West Beirut
Beirut Airport, 119, 151, 161, 200, 243–45, 250

Beirut College for Women (Beirut University College), 37, 41, 224
Beirut Evangelical School, 124
Beirut Franciscan School, 144
Beirut localities: Ain Mreisseh, 82, 143, 144, 146, 295; Avenue de Paris, 51; Bab-Idris, 51, 247; Green Line, 268; lighthouse, 123; Martyr's Square, 41; Pigeon Rock, 92; Rue Abdul Aziz, 110; Rue Artois, 256; Rue Bliss, 44; Rue Hamra, 145; souks, 51, 96–97, 247; southern suburbs, 232, 272, 276, 278. *See also* Ras Beirut
Beirut University College. *See* Beirut College for Women
Beit Meri, 243
Beka'a Valley, 87–88, 162; Iranian Shiites in, 187, 232; model farm in, 124, 125; Syrian occupation of, 203, 224, 225, 272
Berber culture, 153
Bethlehem, 77, 78, 161
Bhamdoun, 42
Bikfaya, 243
Bisharri, 98, 118–19, 127–30, 290
Bisharri Palace (hotel), 128
Bizr, 90
Black September, 151, 187
Bliss, Daniel, 28, 45, 189; administration of, 27; cypresses planted by, 171; furniture of, 20, 295; statue of, 68
Bliss, David, 28
Bliss, Howard, 27, 28, 189–90
Bliss, Mary, 28
Bliss family, 249
Bonfils photograph collection, 236
Boydon, Frank, 33
Britain, 139, 257, 258; Arabic language school of, 69; Baghdad Pact and, 95; Beirut embassy of, 256, 270, 279; military forces of, 32, 108; Suez War and, 103

Broumana, 226
Bustani (security officer), 238
Byblos, 98, 269
Bzummar, 246–47

Cairo, 80–81, 163, 169; business trip to, 168; Christmas holiday in, 77, 79–80; Kerr family in, 140–43, 159, 164, 175–82, 259–60, 267; as possible refuge, 235, 272–73; postassassination return to, 17, 176, 235, 299–300
Cairo American College, 17, 175, 235, 257, 259, 299
California, 39, 172–74
Camp David talks, 168, 176, 179, 224
Carter, Jimmy, 167
Carthaginians, 153
Casablanca, 38–39
Catholic Relief Services, 17, 290, 299
Cedars, 74, 98, 99, 118, 127
Center for Arab Unity Studies, 224
Central Mosque (Beirut), 248
Chamoun, Camile, 95, 108, 111
Chediac, Caesar, 292, 293
Chouf mountains, 69–70, 249–50, 258, 270, 271, 283
Christian Lebanese, 47, 251; in Aley, 227; in Beirut, 268; at Christmastime, 285; Crusaders and, 92; at Eastertime, 130; Israel and, 187, 231; political equilibrium and, 132, 156, 187; Reagan administration and, 188; relative prosperity of, 69, 146; Sarkis and, 170; in Shouf, 69–70, 250. See also Maronites
Christian-Muslim civil war. See Lebanese civil war (1975—   )
Christian Phalangist Party, 194, 227, 234–35, 290; Israel and,

187, 231; Sabra-Shateela massacre and, 206, 207; Shihab and, 111
Christian students, 96, 235, 274
Chtoura, 88
Citadel of Salah-ad-Din (Cairo), 160
Cold War, 95, 108, 188
Coptic churches, 160
Crow, Laure and Ralph, 131, 263, 265
Crusaders, 91–92
Cultural Club of the South, 283, 284, 293
Cyprus, 120, 196, 200, 281

Daily Star (Beirut newspaper), 280
Dajani, Walid, 296
Damascus, 86, 161, 195, 245, 258
Damascus Road, 88
Damour, 89
Damour River, 74, 89, 122
Davanian, Ani, 54–56
Deerfield Academy, 33–34
Dillon, Robert, 198, 233, 238, 250, 261
Dodd, Erica, 6
Dodd, Peter, 243, 252
Dodd family: airport fighting and, 251; ANK and, 245–46; at Christmas 1983, 290; English schools and, 257, 258; in Faraya, 292; T. Kennedy and, 297
Dodge, Bayard, 28, 31, 189
Dodge, David, 199, 202, 215, 251; as AUB presidential candidate, 189, 190; Israeli invasion and, 195; kidnapping of, 9, 197, 252, 297; release of, 241–42
Dodge Hall (AUB), 296
Drug traffic, 145, 157, 232
Druzes, 72–73, 85, 251, 259; in Aley, 227; Beirut bombed by, 234; A. Gemayel-Khaddam talks

and, 271; in Shouf region, 250; Syrians and, 231

Dulles, John Foster, 103

East Beirut, 207, 227, 235, 271, 284, 289

Economic Commission for West Asia, 243, 245

Egypt, 141, 186–87; Begin in, 166; business visit to, 168; Christmas holiday in, 78, 79–80; Druzes and, 72; granite from, 88; Israeli accord with, 176, 224; Israeli border with, 151, 179, 186; Kerr family in, 140–43, 159, 164, 175–82, 259–60, 267; in 1973 Arab-Israeli War, 160; as possible refuge, 235, 272–73; post-assassination return to, 17, 176, 235, 299–300; religious minorities of, 154; in Six-Day War, 147; in Suez War, 103; Syrian-Iraqi union with, 140, 142; U.S. employees in, 167, 168, 171; World War II era, 31

Eisenhower, Dwight and Milton, 107

Elusive Peace in the Middle East, The (Kerr), 116–17

Emaluth, Bill, 285, 288, 290, 292, 293

England. *See* Britain

English language: at AUB, 63; in Beirut, 48–49; instruction in, 54–58, 84–85, 124, 191, 267–68; in Mieh Mieh, 91

Euphrates Valley Dam, 249

Europe, xvi, 39, 95, 100, 150–51

Faisal II (King of Iraq), 108

Faisal's Restaurant (Beirut), 81, 133

Fakhry, Alice, 273

Fakhry, Majid, 86, 273

Fakra, 290

Fa'our, Omar (Haj Omar), 195–96, 211, 212, 244, 258

Faraya, 263, 290, 292

Faris, Nabih, 217

Farouk I (King of Egypt), 141

Farr, Elsa, 124

Flag Day. *See* Lebanese National Day

France, 151–52; culture of, 38, 47, 51–52, 81, 152, 153; military forces of, 32, 202, 208, 265, 267; Suez War and, 103

Free French Forces, 32

Freezing A Mother-in-Law, 284

French Mandate, xiv, xv, 30

Fustukjian, Sam, 292

Gal, Ben, 208

Garrity, Tim, 261

Gaza Strip, 167, 180

Geisen, Martin, 280, 296, 298

Gemayel, Amin, 208, 226, 278; administration of, 229, 231, 233, 234–35, 261, 284–85; Khaddam and, 271; MK and, 229, 234–35, 238; Sharon and, 223; Shultz and, 224–25

Gemayel, Bashir, 194, 203, 204, 205, 206

Gemayel, Pierre, 223, 261

Gemayel (Amin) administration, 229, 231, 233, 234–35, 261, 284–85

Geneva peace talks, 167, 177

Gerard Institute (Sidon), 89

Germany, 30, 32, 38, 58, 81

Gibb, Hamilton, 105, 106

Giza pyramids, 80, *142,* 160

Goethe Institute (Beirut), 280, 298

Golan Heights, 147, 160

Gordon, David, 194

Greco-Roman ruins, 164, 248, 269, 290
Greek Orthodox Church (Ras Beirut), 226, 256

Habib, Philip: at AUB trustee meeting, 219; Israeli invasion and, 197; Israeli-PLO ceasefire and, 189, 194; PLO departure and, 198, 200, 205; replacement of, 261
Haddad, Sa'ad, 207, 225, 231
Haifa, 42
Haig, Alexander, 189, 194
al-Haj (Druze banker), 253
al-Haj, Fawzi, 275, 292, 296
al-Haj, Yvonne, 275
Haj Omar (Omar Fa'our), 195–96, 211, 212, 244, 258
Halaby, Najeeb, 197, 219
Hallab, Abdul Hamid, 5, 6, 13, 19, 227, 289
Hamza, Naziha. See Knio, Naziha (Hamza)
Hariri, Rafik, 209, 248, 253
Harvard University: Middle Eastern Center, 106; MK at, 105–7; Semitic Museum, 236; SV at, 185, 229–30, 237, 238, 300
Hasroon, 98, 127, 129
Hassan (housekeeper), 9, 203, 221, 242, 252; ANK and, 247, 255, 257; AUB inauguration and, 211, 212; AUB shelling and, 254; at Christmas 1983: 286, 287, 289; MK's death and, 7, 14, 15–16, 19
Hawkins, Susan. See Zwicker, John and Susan
Hebrew University, 188
Heineken family, 270
Herald Tribune, 208
Hitti, Philip, 119–20
Holland, 38, 58, 101, 233, 236

Holy War. See Jihad
Hotel Bzummar (Keserwan), 246
Hourani, Albert, 135, 139–40, 217
Hourani, Odille, 139
House of the Future (think tank), 223
Hussein (king of Jordan), 108, 151, 187, 200, 232

Immaculate Conception School for Girls (Beirut), 54–58, 84, 86, 91, 124
Infitah policy, 176
International College (Beirut), 208, 275, 279
Intra Bank, 147
Iran, 42, 95
Irani, Roshan, 41–43, 58, 78; Azzam and, 46; on hostel meals, 44; at St. Michel beach, 79; on swimming, 93; teaching career of, 125; on William's Fairy Saloon, 81
Irani, Widad, 77, 78, 79, 161
Iranian Shiites, 88, 187, 232, 242. See also Shiite Lebanese
Iraq, 46, 47, 94; Baghdad Pact and, 95; Egyptian-Syrian union with, 140, 142; 1958 insurrection in, 108, 133; nuclear plant in, 181, 188
Islam, 39, 72, 122. See also Muslim Lebanese; Shiite Lebanese; Sunnis
Islamic fundamentalism, 122, 186
Islamic Jihad. See Jahid
Ismailia, 179
Israel: Begin-Sadat talks and, 167; Egyptian accord with, 176, 224; Egyptian border with, 151, 179, 186; Jerusalem and, 79; Lebanese border with, 91, 187, 224, 225, 284; Palestinian refugees from, 58, 94; South Lebanon and, 225;

U.S.-Lebanese treaty with, 233, 234; U.S. support of, 226, 278, 279; mentioned, 260. *See also* Arab-Israeli conflict

Israeli air power: Ainab, 265; Baalbek, 88; Beirut, 189, 195, 199, 201–2, 205; Iraq, 181, 188–89; Lebanon, 194

Israeli military forces, 227; Amiliya Technical School and, 238; at Awali River, 271; in Beirut, 151, 195, 205, 206, 207; in Chouf mountains, 249–50, 258; in Lebanon, xvi, 191, 194, 213–14, 231, 262; PLO vs., 189, 191, 194, 198, 205, 206; in Six-Day War, 147–48; in Suez War, 103; Syria vs., 200; withdrawn from Lebanon, 203, 209

Israeli Navy, 201

Israeli prisoners, 278

Italian military forces, 202, 208

Italian policemen, 109

Iwo Jima (battleship), 266

Jabbur, Jibrail, 217

Japanese military forces, 25, 26, 30

Jayoussi, Salma, 75–76, 94

Jerba, 165

Jerusalem: AZK in, 78–79; Cairo route to, 179–80; MK in, 181, 188; Sadat in, 160, 166–67; Six-Day War and, 147, 148; SV in, 178, 179, 180, 181

Jewish Defense League, 167

Jews, 26, 42, 148, 181

Jibran, Khalil, 98, 127

Jihad (Holy War), 3, 197, 232, 290

Johns Hopkins School of Advanced International Studies, 96, 102, 104–5, 107

Jordan, 77, 94, 108, 151, 187, 232

Jounieh, 196, 200, 201, 211, 246

Jumblat, Walid, 265

June War (1967), 116, 147–48, 151, 153

Kadisha Gorge, 127

Kahane Commission, 206

Kasten, Robert W., Jr., 244

Kawar, Widad (Irani), 77, 78, 79, 161

Kelibia, Tunisia, 164, 165

Kennedy, John, 131–32, 140

Kennedy, Mary Helen and Ted, 131, 264–65, 270, 297

Kerr, Andrew: Ali and, 176; AUB residency of, 210, 228–29, 260, 269, 277, 282; Beirut shelling and, 253, 254–55, 256, 257, 271; birth of, 148–49; Boy Scouting and, 208, 285; brush fire and, 172; in Cairo, 17, 159, 175, 235, 259, 299; on Cairo-Jerusalem trip, 179; career of, 300–*301;* at Christmas 1982: 219–221; at Christmas 1983: 287; dancing of, 234; Emaluth and, 285, 289, 292, 293; homework of, 267, 298; illness of, 222; insouciance of, 275; Marine casualties and, 265–66; MK's AUB presidential appointment and, 193, 196, 198; at MK's birthday, 262–63; at MK's burial, 19; MK's correspondence with, 239; MK's death and, 6–7, 10, 11, 13, 14, 16; at MK's memorial service, *18;* poison ivy and, 231; Proctor School and, 272; Shehadi and, 275; in Sierras, 240; SK and, 185, 243; summer occupations of, 168; U.S. Navy officers and, 250, 261; war buff enthusiasm of, 245–46, 247, 251; mentioned, 157, 227, 241, 295, 297

Kerr, Dorothy, 28, 30, 33, 230
Kerr, Doug, 28, 30, 33; in Ainab,
    131; MK's death and, 7; at
    MK's wedding, 104; vacation
    home of, 182
Kerr, Elsa, 26–27, 32, 33, 110,
    113, 121; at Ainab, 70, 71;
    American girls and, 58–59, 61;
    AZK's junior year and, 45–46,
    49, 65, 67; at Christmas 1955:
    75, 76; at Christmas 1982: 220;
    B. Dodge and, 28; D. Dodge
    and, 241–42; on MK's AUB in-
    auguration, 210–11; MK's
    engagement and, 99, 100; MK's
    fiftieth birthday and, 186; retire-
    ment of, 130–31, 264–65; Sixth
    Fleet and, 126; student curfews
    and, 53; SV's infancy and, 118,
    120, 127; Talhouk family and,
    83–84; widowhood of, 161,
    210; women's dorms and, 241,
    257; mentioned, 230, 239
Kerr, John, 131, 140–41, 240,
    257, 272, 301; Arafat and, 178;
    in Athens, 255; AZK's corre-
    spondence with, 190, 242–43;
    birth of, 134, 266; brush fire
    and, 172; in Cairo, 142, 159,
    180, 259, 267; Catholic Relief
    Services and, 17, 299; at
    Christmas 1982: 220–21; at
    Christmas 1983: 285, 288, 291;
    in England, 135; in Europe,
    150; household responsibilities
    of, 168, 175–76, 196; JDL at-
    tack and, 167; at MK's burial,
    19; MK's correspondence with,
    244–45; MK's death and, 7, 10,
    11, 13, 14; at MK's fiftieth
    birthday, 186; at MK's inaugura-
    tion, 211, 212, 213, 214–15; at
    MK's memorial service, 18;
    MK's presidential appointment
    and, 193; at MK's wedding an-
    niversary, 198; pet boa of, 157,

175–76; school years of, 143,
    144–45; in Sierras, 273; SK's
    birth and, 144; summer job of,
    241; at Swarthmore, 175, 185,
    191, 237, 238
Kerr, Malcolm:
—as AUB president, ii, xvi, 107,
    200–298; appointment of, 192–
    93; assassination of, 3–20, 161;
    candidacy of, 166, 179, 185,
    189–91; inauguration of, 18,
    210–18
—in Beirut: Arafat and, 178–79;
    AZK meets, 61–77; childhood
    of, 26, 28–35; courtship of, 86–
    100; family life of, 143–45;
    graduate studies in, 35; Jan.
    1982 visit of, 190; as teacher,
    108–35; as trustee, 169–70
—in Cairo, 140, 157–60, 164,
    168, 175–82, 259–60
—in California: brush fire and,
    172–73; family life of, 156; JDL
    attack on, 167; 1958 visit of,
    107; in Sierras, 240; wedding
    anniversary of, 198; wedding of,
    103–4
—in Cambridge (Mass.), 104–7
—in Deerfield, 33–34
—in Europe, 100, 150–51
—in France, 152–53
—in Jerusalem, 181, 188
—at Lake Tahoe, 34–35
—in Meadow Lakes, 220–21
—in New Hampshire, 272
—in New York, 196, 200, 230,
    272–73
—in Oxford, 139–40
—in Persian Gulf, 222–23
—in Princeton, 32, 34, 62
—in Switzerland, 144
—in Tunisia, 153–54
—in Tucson, 271
—at UCLA, 134, 140, 273; chair-
    manship at, 147; deanship at,
    155; directorships at, 166, 175;

memorial service for, 8, 299; resignation of, 193, 240; sabbatical of, 185
—in upper Egypt, 161
—in Washington, 102, 197
—writings of: *The Arab Cold War,* 141–42, 152–53; *The Elusive Peace in the Middle East,* 116–17; "Lebanese Views of the 1958 Crisis," 133; *Lebanon in the Last Years of Feudalism,* 133; *Rich and Poor States in the Middle East,* 161, 176
Kerr, Margot, 300
Kerr, Marion, 230; in Beit-el-Din, 35; childhood of, 28; at MK's fiftieth birthday, 186; at Wellesley, 33; in World War II, 30, 31
Kerr, Mary Ann, 182
Kerr, Stanley, 26–27, 33, 121, 211, 275, 291; at Ainab, 70, 71; Armenian jewelers and, 96–97; AZK entertained by, 65; death of, 161, 162, 210; B. Dodge and, 28; MK's engagement trip and, 100; Near East Relief and, 27, 58, 178, 204; retirement of, 130–31, 264–65; on Rue Abdul Aziz, 110; SV's infancy and, 118, 120, 127
Kerr, Stephen, 146, 168, 179, 185, 208, 243; basketball and, 246, 300; at Beirut Airport, 244–45; birth of, 143–44, 145, 266, 274; boyhood of, 155–56; brush fire and, 172; in Cairo, 159, 175, 178, 180; at Christmas 1982: 219, 220; college applications by, 230, 238; MK missed by, 222, 228; MK's AUB presidential appointment and, 196, 198; MK's correspondence with, 239; MK's death and, 7, 8, 10; at Palisades High School, 193, 221; at University

of Arizona, 240, 245, 271; mentioned, 157, 227, 241, 269, *301*
Kerr, Susie. *See* van de Ven, Susie (Kerr)
Keserwan, 246, 250, 297
Khaddam, Abdul Halim, 271
Khairallah, Shereen, 53
Khalaf, Nadim and Samir, 296
Khamis Mushayt, 168
Khan el Khalili bazaar (Cairo), 80
Khomeini Shiites, 88, 187, 232, 242
al-Khouri, Pierre, 297
Khuri, Ilyas, 295
Khuri, Zahi [Zaki?], 296, 298
Knio, Naziha (Hamza), 41–43, 44, 78; at St. Michel beach, *79;* teaching career of, 125; waterpainting of, 93; weekend house of, 99
Knesset, 167
Korf, Professor, 86
Krak des Chevaliers, 91–92
Kurani (housemother), 41
Kurani, David, 296
Kurani, Habib, 86
Kurdish women, 50

League of Nations, xiv
Lebanese Army, 204; on AUB campus, 234, 237, 272, 274, 275; Shiites vs., 250, 251, 272; U.S. aid to, 231; in West Beirut, 257. *See also* South Lebanon Army
Lebanese civil war (1958), 108, 111, 112
Lebanese civil war (1975—   ), xv–xvi, 209, 278; AUB status and, 190; in Baalbek, 88; in Beirut, 162; economic aspects of, 231; and extortion, 170, 296–97; Jan. 1977 truce in, 161; in Mieh Mieh, 91; model farm and, 124–25; U.S. and, 225, 233

Lebanese National Day, 273–74, 275, 283

"Lebanese Views of the 1958 Crisis" (Kerr), 133

Lebanon, xiv–xv; cultural life of, 59–60, 156–57; expatriates from, 41; foreign interference in, 187–89; Israeli border with, 91, 187, 224, 225, 284; Israeli demands upon, 223, 227; Israeli invasion of, xvi, 191, 194, 213–14, 231, 262; national elections in, 194; U.S. employees in, 167, 168; U.S.-Israeli treaty with, 233, 234; World War II era, 30, 32

Lebanon in the Last Years of Feudalism (Kerr), 133

Lebanon mountains, 73, 87–88, 98–99, 162

Levi Della Vida Conference (1979), xvii

Libya, 164, 165, 293

Litani River Valley, 213

Los Angeles Times, 269

Luxor, 77, 80, 161

Maadi (Cairo), 158, 176, 180–81, 299–300

McFarlane, Robert, 244, 261

Malcolm Kerr Scholars Program, 300

Malik, Charles, 217

Mandelbaum Gate (Jerusalem), 79

Maronites, 69, 70, 227, 229; AUB and, 179, 284; in Bisharri, 129–30; Druzes vs., 259; Israeli-U.S. support for, 231; Shiite Muslims and, 187

Maron of Antioch, 69

Marquand House (AUB), 9, 13, 14, 149; antique furniture for, 270; cook's family in, 251–52; inauguration guests in, 212–13; T. and M. Kennedy in, 270;

MK alone in, 201, 202–3, 221; 1978 reception at, 171; redecoration of, 4, 196, 248–49, 260–61, 286, 295; Southworths in, 242; World War II era, 33

Martyr's Square (Beirut), 41

Masefield, John, xvii

Massachusetts, 33, 104–7, 150, 157–58, 229–30

Mawlawi, Radwan, 205, 265

Mayflower Hotel (Beirut), 162

Medieval monastic traditions, 139–40

Meyer, A. J., 212

Middle East Airlines, 151

Middle East Centre (Oxford), xvi

Middle Eastern Center (Harvard), 106

Mieh Mieh, 89–90

Milk Bar (Beirut), 62, 64

Mishalani, Richard, 295, 296

Miss AUB contests, 93–94, 95, 237

Missionaries, 27, 54, 89, 124, 280

Miss Lebanon (1983), 287

Monroe, Elizabeth, 139

Morocco, 38–39, 154

Mosul, Iraq, 46, 47, 125

Mount Hermon, 73

Mount Lebanon, 247, 284

Mount Sanneen, 73, 134

Mount Sinai, 177

Moviegoing, 56, 65–67, 80, 91, 106, 128

Mruweh, Jamil, 280

Muhammad (housekeeper's son), 242

Muhammad (bodyguard), 207

Muhammad (cook), 203, 211, 212, 221, 242, 251

Muhammad (prophet), 39

Multinational peacekeeping force, 148, 272, 278

Muslim-Christian civil war. *See* Lebanese civil war (1975—   )

Muslim Lebanese, 47, 130, 170, 285, 296; in Baysoor, 74; in

Beirut, 268, 276; Gemayel election and, 194; political equilibrium and, 132, 156, 187; relative poverty of, 69, 146. *See also* Shiite Lebanese

Naaman, Lillian, 273
Nagorski, Chris, 118
Najeebe (housekeeper), 113–14, 145
Narcotics traffic, 145, 157, 232
Nasrawi, Tawfik, 295
Nasser, Gamal Abdel, 81, 141, 152, 160; Arab unity movement and, 95, 108, 132; Sadat and, 177; Six-Day War and, 148; Suez War and, 103
National Council on U.S.-Arab Relations, 300
National Democratic Party (Egypt), 177
NBA (National Basketball Association), 300
Near East Relief, 27, 28, 58, 178, 204
Near East School of Theology, 277
New Jersey (battleship), 260, 286
New York City, 161, 189, 191, 196, 219, 230
New York Philharmonic Orchestra, 88, 122
New York Times, 3, 186
Nickoley, Dean, 215, 217
Niebuhr, Reinhold, 106
Nile River, 80, 141, 300
Nixon-Kennedy presidential campaign, 131–32
Northrop Corporation, 171
Nseir, Elie, 296–97

Oberlin College, 168, 178
Occidental College, 39, 96, 106; AZK at, 35–36, 49, 81, 87,

102, 105; Khairallah at, 53; students of, 42–43, 46
Olson, Lute, 240, 271
Orpheus Choir, 285, 286
Ottoman Empire, 30, 73, 122, 190; Arab unity movement and, 95; AUB courses on, 85, 86; religious instruction and, 27, 54. *See also* Turkey
Oxford University, 34, 106; Middle East Centre, xvi; St. Antony's College, 134, 135, 139–40

Pacific Palisades home, 149–50, 190, 198, 241; brush fire near, 172–74; family reunions in, 8, 147, 155, 219, 300, 301; homesickness for, 159, 224; JDL attack on, 167, 169
Palestine, xiv, 31. *See also* Gaza Strip; West Bank
Palestine Liberation Organization. *See* PLO
Palestinian guerrillas, 147, 151, 187, 195
Palestinian prisoners, 278, 283
Palestinian question, 116, 132, 147, 167, 169; AUB and, 233; Camp David talks and, 168; Geneva talks and, 177; Reagan administration and, 188, 203; Six Day War and, 148
Palestinian refugees, 42, 94, 156, 180, 206, 231–32
Pan-Arabism, 95–96, 108, 122, 132, 141–42
Pearl Harbor attack, 24
Pedersen, Nelda, 213
Pedersen, Richard, 16–17, 213, 299
Penrose, Stephen, 17, 217
Persian Gulf, 83, 222–23
Phalangists. *See* Christian Phalangist Party
Phoenicians, 89, 153, 164
Pigeon Rock (Beirut), 92

PLO, 188, 203, 213, 224; exit of, 197, 198, 200, 202, 204–5, 208–9; factions of, 271; Gemayel election and, 194; Israeli cease-fire with, 189, 191, 194, 205, 206; Israeli siege of, 195, 197; West Beirut headquarters of, 187, 189. *See also* Palestinian guerrillas
Presbyterianism, 26, 27, 35, 54
Presbyterian junior year abroad program, 36–37
Princeton, N.J., 8, 32, 241, 299
Princeton Club (New York), 192
Princeton University, 34, 35, 62, 82
Prophet, The (Jibran), 98, 127
Protestantism, 28, 54, 217
Protestant missionaries, 27, 124
Provence, 151–52
Punic Ports (Tunis), 153
Pyramids, 80, *142,* 160

Queen Elizabeth (ship), 31–32

Ras Beirut, xiv, 115, 163, 195, 206; AUB dramas and, 284, 296; bomb explosions in, 226, 286, 290; cliffs of, 92, 93; intellectual freedom in, 145–46; PLO in, 187; war damage to, 201–2
Rassam, Amal, 93–94
Reagan, Ronald, 198, 203, 260, 278–79
Reagan administration, 188–89, 197
Reagan Plan, 203, 208
Red Cross (Beirut), 195
Red Sea, 31–32, 148, 180, 259, 300

Regier, Frank, 270
Regier family, 290
Regina Bar (Beirut), 61, 76–77
Religious fundamentalism, 177–78. *See also* Islamic fundamentalism
Residence permits, 235, 238
Reynolds, Al, 275
Rich and Poor States in the Middle East (Kerr), 161, 176
Rida, Rashid, 105
Riviera Hotel (Beirut), 207
Riyadh, 168
Roberts, David, 89
Rockefeller grants, 34, 35, 105, 134
Romans, 153. *See also* Greco-Roman ruins
Roosevelt, Theodore, 249, 261
Roosevelt Hotel (New York), 191
Rue . . . *See under* Beirut localities

Saba, Widad, 80
Sabra massacre. *See* Shateela-Sabra massacre
Sadat, Anwar, 177, 186, 189; at Camp David, 176; in Jerusalem, 160, 166–67, 168; 1973 Arab-Israeli War and, 160
Sadat, Jihan, 177
Sadr, Musa, 293
Sagan, Françoise, 106
al-Said, Nuri, 108
Said, Salwa, 195, 199, 297
Said-Shehadi family, 297
St. Antony's College (Oxford), 134, 135, 139–40
St. George Hotel (Beirut), 51, 81, 82–83
St. George's School (Jerusalem), 178, 179
St. Michel Beach (Beirut), 79, 119, 121, 232
Salam, Saeb, 204

Salem, Eli, 282–83
Salem family, 201, 202
SAM missiles, 272
Sanders, Jane (Zwicker), 48, 75, 87, 101, 104; in Beirut, 97–100; childhood of, 23–24, 26, 43; marriage of, 107; at Stanford, 102
Sanders, Tim, 104, 107
Santa Monica, 23–24, 25, 172
Santa Monica High School, 35–36
Santa Monica Presbyterian Church, 103
Sarkis, Elias, 170, 204
Saudi Arabia, 167, 168, 226
Scanlon, George, 267
Schanche, Don, 269
Shammas (housemother), 41
Shammas, Samia, 46–47, 78, 79, 93, 125
Sharaf, Abdul Hamid, 133–34
Sharon, Ariel, 204, 205, 206, 223, 227
Shateela-Sabra massacre, 206–7, 208
Shehadi, Rima, 248, 260, 261, 274–75, 286, 296
Shihab, Fuad, 108, 111
Shiite Iranians, 88, 187, 232, 242
Shiite Lebanese: Amiliya Technical School and, 238; Christmas celebrations and, 285; Iranian Shiites and, 187, 252; Lebanese Army vs., 251, 272; in southern Beirut, 232, 276, 278; Syrians and, 231; U.S. Marines vs., 250. *See also* Amal Party
Shimlan, 69, 74
Shouf mountains, 69–70, 249–50, 258, 270, 271, 283
Shultz, George, 219, 225
Sidon, 89, 209
Simaan, Joe, 207
Simonian, Ani, 277
Simonian, Vahe, 236, 237, 277, 279, 280–81

Simonian family, 233
Sinai Peninsula, 148, 160, 167, 180, 259
Six-Day War. *See* June War (1967)
Slade, Landry, 287
Smith, Vickie, 286
Smith family, 285–86, 287, 295
Smith's Grocery Store (Beirut), 285, 290
Smokers' Gate (AUB), 217
Snoubar pine nuts, 68, 70
Song of Solomon, 73
Souk el Gharb, 68–69, 99
Souk et-Tawili (Beirut), 51
Souk al-Franji (Beirut), 51
Southern California, 39, 167–168, 172–74
"Southern Suburbs." *See* Beirut localities
South Lebanon Army, 207
Southworth, Hamilton, 242
Soviet Union, 88, 103, 197–98
Spiegel, Major, 207–8
Stanford University, 102, 300
Storrs, Ronald, xiv
Student Cultural Club of the South, 283, 284, 293
Students, 117, 133, 263–64, 267–68, 271, 297–98; American, 58; Arab unity movement and, 95–96; campus organizations of, 284, 294–95; Christian, 96, 235, 274; at Christmas 1983: 290–91; moviegoing by, 65; Muslim, 75, 283; Palestinian question and, 116; political activism of, 267, 281, 291–92, 294–95; religious backgrounds of, 27, 298; women (*See* Women students)
Suez Canal, 179
Suez War, 103
Sunnis, 153–54, 186–87, 231, 232
Sutherland, Tom, 124–25, 238
Suzanne, Sister, 55, 56, 57

Swarthmore College, 175, 185, 191, 237, 238
Syria, 91–92, 224, 260, 263; Begin-Haig discussion of, 189; Egyptian-Iraqi union with, 140, 142; feudal Lebanon and, 156; under France, xiv; A. Gemayel-Khaddam talks and, 271; Iran and, 232; Israel and, 200, 262; Lebanese PLO factions and, 188; U.S. and, 225, 231; World War I era, 27
Syrian military forces, 203, 209, 224, 278; in Baalbek, 88; in Beirut, 169; in Beka'a Valley, 203, 272; in Eastern Lebanon, 281; Euphrates Valley Dam and, 249; in 1973 Arab-Israeli War, 160; shelling by, 234, 255, 256; in Six-Day War, 147
Syrian Protestant College. See American University of Beirut

Taiwan, 241, 281
Takiedeen, Diana, 65
Talhouk family, 84–85, 86
Tanios (chauffeur): at airport, 276, 287, 292; MK's burial and, 19; MK's inauguration and, 211–12; on shopping trip, 247, 248
Tel Aviv University, 181
Temple of Bacchus (Baalbek), 88, 122–23
Temple of Diana (Baalbek), 88
Temple of Jupiter (Baalbek), 88, 232
Thabet, Samir, 8, 9, 199, 229, 261
Toffet (Tunis), 153
Tripoli, 98, 127, 203, 271, 278
Tunisia, 153–54, 164
Tuqan, Suha, 296, 298
Turkey, 204; Armenians and, 58, 96, 97; AUB courses on, 62;

Baghdad Pact and, 95; veiling banned in, 122; World War I era, 27, 58, 178. See also Ottoman Empire
Twain, Mark, 249, 261
Tyre, 89, 90

United Nations, 33, 206, 261; Arab-Israeli conflict and, 117; military forces of, 148, 272, 278; PLO exit and, 197, 198; Refugee Welfare Agency, 232; Security Council, 116; Suez War and, 103
United States, 30–31, 65, 81, 190, 271, 273; aircraft of, 188–89, 270, 281; Arab-Israeli conflict and, 117; Baghdad Pact and, 95; citizens of, 82–83, 126, 132, 167–68, 171, 235, 238; Israeli invasion and, 195, 197, 206, 224–25; Israeli-Lebanese treaty with, 233, 234; ambassador to Lebanon, 118, 119; Lebanon policy of, 188–89, 203–4, 225–26, 231, 278; military forces of, xvi, 108, 110, 198; missionaries from, 89; 1973 Arab-Israeli War and, 160; Nixon-Kennedy campaign in, 131–32; students from, 58
—Central Intelligence Agency, 192
—Congress, 179, 198; House Foreign Relations Committee, 197
—Consul General, 32
—Embassy (Beirut), 201, 281; AUB and, 279; bombing of, 232–33, 234, 250, 261; British Embassy and, 256; Israeli invasion and, 195; Kennedy-Nixon debates and, 132
—Embassy (Tel Aviv), 91
—Marines, 208–9, 247, 281; AUB and, 279, 280, 286–87; bomb

attack on, 265–67; 1958 civil war and, 108–9, 110, 126–27, 133; PLO exit and, 198, 204–5; Shiites vs., 250
—National Security Council, 301
—Navy: Ainab and, 265; commanders of, 250, 261; guns of, 259–60; Sixth Fleet, 108–9, 126; World War II era, 30
—State Department, 93
Université St. Joseph, xiv, 52
University of Arizona, 10, 240, 245, 271, 300
University of California, Los Angeles, 139, 171, 181, 224; al-Ahram Center and, 168; AUC Study Abroad Program and, 175, 179; AZK at, 159; Hourani at, xvii; MK and (*See under* Kerr, Malcolm); Von Grunebaum Center for Near Eastern Studies, 160–61, 166, 168, 175
University of Southern California, 191, 210

van de Ven, Hans, 223, 233, 236, 281; AZK's correspondence with, 235–36, 242–43; at Cambridge University, 300; at Christmas 1982: 220, 221; engagement of, 227–28, 229; MK's correspondence with, 236–37, 244–245, 259–60; MK's death and, 7, 13, 14, *18,* 19; wedding of, 240, 241, 277
van de Ven, Susie (Kerr), 107, 111, 134–35, 166, 239, *301;* at AUB inauguration, 211, 212, *213, 214*–15; on AUB presidential appointment, 192–93; AUB students and, 117, 125; AZK's correspondence with, 190, 235–36, 242–43; baby clothes for, 248; baby outings of, 115; birth of, 6, 112–13, 266; in Cairo, 141, *142,* 157, 159–60, 178; at

Christmas 1982: 220, 221; engagement of, 227–28, 229; on European trip, 150; gifts for, 281; grandparents' care of, 118, 120, 127; at Harvard, 185, 186, 198, 237, 238, 300; honeymoon of, 241; household responsibilities of, 168, 175, 196; in Jerusalem, 178, 179, 180, 181; memorial sign by, *16, 19*–20; MK's correspondence with, 222–23, 236–37, 244–45, 259–60, 261; MK's death and, 7–8, 13, 14, 17; at MK's memorial service, *18;* in New York, 191, 200; 1977 Beirut visit of, 161–63; in rooftop apartment, 123; at St. Michel beach, 119; school years of, 143, 144–45; SK's birth and, *144;* wedding of, 240, 241, 277
Van Dyke Hall (AUB), 275
Vichy government, 30, 32
Von Grunebaum Center for Near Eastern Studies, 160–61, 166, 168, 175

Walter Reed Hospital, 27
Warren Junior High School, 105
Wazzan (prime minister), 204
West Bank, 147, 167, 203
West Beirut: car bomb explosion in, 281; Christian students in, 235; cliffs of, 92; Hariri reconstruction of, 248; Israeli occupation of, 205, 206; Israeli siege of, 195, 197; Lebanese Army in, 257; PLO headquarters in, 187, 189; Shiite conservatism in, 285; war damage in, 162
Wetmore, Olive, 101, 105
Wetmore, Ralph, 101, 105, 229–30

William's Fairy Saloon (Beirut),
   81–82
Women: careers of, 125; dress of,
   46, 50, 115; in Mieh Mieh, 90;
   moviegoing and, 66; veiling of,
   122; at William's Fairy Saloon,
   81–82
Women students, 42–43, 46, 78–
   79, 273; housing for, 41, 44,
   241, 257, 275; E. Kerr and,
   58–59, 61; Marines and, 266–
   67; sailors and, 126
World War I, 27, 52, 122, 190
World War II, 24–26, 30–31, 32,
   38, 42, 81

Yarzi, 170, 201
Yassin, Sayid, 161

Yemen, 298
Youtz, Bernice, 41

Zahle, 88, 122, 123
Zamalek (Cairo), 141
Zeinab (maid), 9, 15–16, 211,
   242, 260, 289
Zeidan, Nazieh, 279
Zeine, Ramsey, 291
Zeine, Zeine, 62, 64, 73, 217, 291
Zurayk, Constantine, 217
Zurayk, Huda, 5
Zwicker, Jane. See Sanders, Jane
   (Zwicker)
Zwicker, John and Susan, 23–26,
   101–2, 107, 196, 241, 262;
   AZK's junior year abroad and,
   37, 48; Pacific Palisades house
   and, 155, 172; wedding anniver-
   sary of, 180